Library of
Davidson College

POLISH BAROQUE AND ENLIGHTENMENT LITERATURE

AN ANTHOLOGY

POLISH BAROQUE AND ENLIGHTENMENT LITERATURE

AN ANTHOLOGY

MICHAEL J. MIKOŚ

Slavica Publishers, Inc.

Slavica publishes a wide variety of scholarly books and textbooks on the languages, peoples, literatures, cultures, history, etc. of the former USSR and Eastern Europe. For a complete catalog of books and journals from Slavica, with prices and ordering information, write to:

> Slavica Publishers, Inc.
> PO Box 14388
> Columbus, Ohio 43214

ISBN: 0-89357-266-7.

Copyright © 1996 by Michael J. Mikoś. All rights reserved.

All statements of fact or opinion are those of the authors and do not necessarily agree with those of the publisher, which takes no responsibility for them.

Printed in the United States of America.

TABLE OF CONTENTS

List of Illustrations   16
Foreword   20
Bibliography   21

I. BAROQUE

Introduction   38

Stanisław Żółkiewski
    Beginning and Progress of the Muscovy War   59

Piotr Kochanowski
    Gofred or Jerusalem Delivered
      Third Song
       1-6   66

Jan Żabczyc
    Angelic Symphonies
      Twentieth Symphony   70
      Thirty Fourth Symphony   72

Daniel Naborowski
    An Unexpected Response   74
    A Bad Wife   74
    Epitaph for Jan Kochanowski, Polish Poet   74
    The Brevity of Life   75
    On the Same   75
    Virtue is the Root of Everything   76
    To Ann   76
    Votum   77

Hieronim Morsztyn
    Non Licet Plus Efferre, Quam Intuleris   80
    Time   80
    Mors Ultima Linea Rerum   81

    Compendium
        A Man   81
        A Pleasant Counsel   82
        To Niemsta On His Third Marriage   82

Szymon Starowolski
    Sarmatian Warriors
        Stanisław Żółkiewski   83

    Lament of the Distressed Mother, the
        Polish Crown   86

Maciej K. Sarbiewski
    Odes
        I 19 Longing for the Heavenly
            Homeland   89
        II 3 To My Lute   91
        II 3 To My Lute   92
        II 19 From the Song of Songs   92
        II 26 To the Holy Virgin Mother   93
        II 26 To the Holy Virgin Mother   94
        III 3 To Cardinal Francesco
            Barberini   94

Samuel Twardowski
    Daphne Changed Into a Laurel Tree
        Zephyr I   96
        Zephyr II   97
        Zephyr III   97
        Zephyr IV   97
        Dawn 5, 6, 7, 8   98

    Fair Pasqualina   100

Table of Contents

	Lament I	101
	Epitaph for Sir Samuel Twardowski	102

Krzysztof Opaliński
    Satires
        *III. On Burdens and Oppression of
            Peasants in Poland*   104

Łukasz Opaliński
    *The New Poet
        Coffin--the Measure of Things*   110

Jan Andrzej Morsztyn
    Inconstancy   112
    The Fair Sex   113
    On His Young Lady   113
    To the Same Lady   113
    To a Young Lady   114
    Safe Treasure   114
    Inconstancy   114
    To a Lady   115
    A Clever Maiden   115
    Bee in Amber   115
    The Wonders of Love   115
    To a Corpse   116
    To a Butterfly   118

Wacław Potocki
    The Progress of the War of Chocim   119

    A Garden of Trifles
        The World--A Prison   125
        What Man Cannot Conceal   125
        What Time Finds, Time Ruins   125
        On My Poems   126
        Shaved or Shorn   126
        Wise Answers   126

	Man's Life	127
	Let the Drunk World Sleep	127
	What the Eyes Cannot See, the Heart Does Not Regret	128

Jan Sobieski

            Letters to Marysieńka
                June 9, 1665   130
                September 13, 1683   132

Zbigniew Morsztyn

            To a Virtuous Lady   136
            Song of Captivity   136

            Epitaphs
                For Captain Paweł Morsztyn   142
                For Both Parents   142

            Emblems
                Emblem 8   143
                Emblem 39   143
                Emblem 41   144
                Emblem 47   145

Wespazjan Kochowski

            A Monument to the Brave Soldiers   147
            A Curse on the Sons of the Crown   149

            Polish Epigrams
                Gold Scepters   151
                Old-fashioned Manners   152
                Requirements for Good Cheer   152
                Pares ab Adam   152

            Polish Psalmody
                Psalm XXII   154
                Psalm XXIV   155

Table of Contents

Stanisław H. Lubomirski
    Somnus
        Primus — 158
        Secundus — 158
        Tertius — 159
        Quartus — 159
        Quintus — 159

    Sonnet on the Great Suffering of Jesus Christ — 160

    The Poems of Lent
        Coepit lavare discipulorum pedes — 161

    Tobias Delivered
        Sarah's Prayer — 161
        The River Tiger — 162
        A Quiet Moment Comes After a Storm — 162

Jan Chryzostom Pasek
    Memoirs
        1659 — 164
        1680 — 166

Anonymous
    On Proud Masters — 170
    On Youth and Love — 170
    The Siege of the Bright Mountain of Częstochowa — 170
    Fame — 173
    Time Destroys Everything — 173
    Running to the Stable — 173

II. ENLIGHTENMENT

Introduction	175
Chronological Table	197

Stanisław Konarski
On the Effective Method of Deliberating — 199

Elżbieta Drużbacka
On Proud Narcissus — 206

Wacław Rzewuski
On the Equality of Earthly Happiness — 209
A Grove — 210

Franciszek Bohomolec
A Drinking Song — 212
The Monitor, 16, 1765 — 215

Jędrzej Kitowicz
Diaries or Polish History
  On the Polish King — 216

Description of Customs During the Reign of August III
  About the Education of Children — 223
  On Public Schools — 223

Adam Naruszewicz
To the Stream — 227
To a Sad Friend — 229
Voice of the Dead — 230
Balloon — 231

Satires
    IV. The Corrupt Age   233
    VI. A Gaunt Man of Letters   236

Ignacy Krasicki

Monachomachia or the War of the Monks   240

Diverse Poems
    4. Sacred Love of Our Cherished Homeland   244
    19. Gravestone of a Peasant   244

Fables and Parables
    Preface to *Fables*   244

Part I
    8. The Rat and the Cat   246
    18. Son and Father   246
    20. The Mouse and the Cat   246
    21. Birds in a Cage   246
    23. The Oak and the Pumpkin   247

Part II
    5. The Animals and the Bear   247
    6. The Stream and the Fountains   247
    9. The Bear and the Fox   247
    15. The Marriage   248
    17. Two Dogs   248
    18. A Friend   248

Part III
    1. The Elephant and the Bee   248
    4. The Child and the Father   249
    6. The Bigot   249
    13. The Stream and the River   249
    16. The Master and the Dog   249
    20. The Eagle and the Owl   249
    21. The Inkstand and the Pen   250

23. The Nightingale and the Goldfinch	250
26. The Wagon Driver and the Butterfly	250

Part IV
3. The Lamb and the Wolves	250
4. The Turtle and the Mouse	251
7. The Penitent Wolf	251
26. The Wise Man and the Fool	251
28. The Stubborn Oxen	251

New Fables

Part I
15. Children and Frogs	252

Part II
12. The Heron, the Fish, and the Cray-fish	252
13. The Peasant and the Calf	253

Part III
15. The Torch and the Candle	253

Part IV
1. The Crow and the Fox	254

Satires
6. Drunkenness	254
8. The Fashionable Wife	257

The Monitor, 37, 1776	262
Mister Pantler	265

Stanisław Trembecki
To Madame Kossowska When Dancing	268

Table of Contents

Epithalamion for Dorant and Clymene	271
To Miss Tekla	272
In the Album of Marcjanna K.	273
A Deer Looking at Himself	273

Konstancja Benisławska

Calling on All Creatures to Praise God	275
Midday Prayer	276

Franciszek Karpiński

To Justina. Longing in Spring	280
Recollection of Past Love	280
The Lament of a Sarmatian at the Tomb of Zygmunt August	282
Mazurka	284
Morning Song	285
Night Song	285
Song on the Birth of Our Lord	286

Franciszek Kniaźnin

To the Stars	288
The Looms	290
To Whiskers	291
Two Linden Trees	291
To Love	292
To God	293
On Eliza	294

Kajetan Węgierski

A Complaint of a Canon Against a Smith	295
Every Man to His Taste	296
A Philosopher	296
A Letter to Rhymesters	297

Anonymous
    A Brave Pole on the Field of Mars   300

Józef Wybicki
    If One Could in a Few Days   302
    The Song of the Polish Legions in
        Italy   302

Wojciech Bogusławski
    A Supposed Miracle or Cracovians
    and Mountaineers
        A Wedding Song   305
        A Song of Bardos   307

Franciszek Zabłocki
    On a Decree Authorizing an Army
        of One Hundred Thousand   308
    To the Assembled Estates   310
    The Fop Suitor   311

Hugo Kołłątaj
    To Stanisław Małachowski
        Ninth Letter   319

    To the Illustrious Deputation   323
    Political Law of the Polish Nation   329

Stanisław Staszic
    Remarks on the Life of Jan Zamoyski
        Education   334

    Warnings for Poland
        To the Lords   336
        Peasants' Lands or an
            Industrious Peasant   339

    Testament   341

Table of Contents

Jakub Jasiński
    My Song   342
    To the Nation   343

Julian Niemcewicz
    Yearnings in Solitude   346
    The Return of the Deputy   346
    Historical Songs
        Bolesław the Wrymouth   353
        Funeral of Prince Józef Poniatowski   355

    Diaries
        Travel from Petersburg to Sweden   359

Cyprian Godebski
    A Poem to the Polish Legions   364
    Initials on the Sycamore Tree   366

Alojzy Feliński
    Hymn on the Anniversary of the Proclamation of the Kingdom of Poland   367
    Barbara Radziwiłł   368

Kazimierz Brodziński
    To Hanna   376
    A Shepherdess's Song   377
    The Raszyn Field   377
    To the Muse   379

Kajetan Koźmian
    To the Dancing Cracow   380
    To Sophie Przewłocka Copying "Czarniecki"   381

LIST OF ILLUSTRATIONS

BAROQUE

I. King Władysław IV by an unknown artist of the Rubens School (Photograph by Bożena Seredyńska, courtesy of Muzeum Pałac in Wilanów), p. 39.

II. Meeting of the armies of King Charles X of Sweden and George Rakocsi of Transylvania in Poland, 1657. Engraving by Erik Dahlbergh in Samuel Pufendorf's *Histoire du Regne de Charles Gustave,* Nürnberg, 1697 (Photograph by Alan Magayne-Roshak, author's collection), p. 42.

III. Sash from Słuck, XVIII c. (Photograph by Jan Kościesza-Jaworski, courtesy of Instytut Sztuki PAN in Warsaw), p. 46.

IV. The Column of Zygmunt III (1644) and the Royal Castle in Warsaw (Photograph by Henryk Poddębski in 1924, courtesy of Instytut Sztuki PAN in Warsaw), p. 54.

V. Title page of *Gofred or Jerusalem Delivered,* Cracow 1618 (Photograph by Krystyna Dąbrowska, courtesy of Biblioteka Uniwersytecka in Warsaw), p. 67.

VI. Wilanów Palace (Photograph by Bożena Seredyńska, courtesy of Muzeum Pałac in Wilanów), p. 71.

VII. Krasiński Palace in Warsaw, 1676-1689 (Photograph by Jerzy Langda, courtesy of Instytut Sztuki PAN in Warsaw), p. 79.

VIII. The Church of the Nuns of the Holy Sacrament in Warsaw (Photograph by Witalis Wolny, courtesy of Instytut Sztuki PAN in Warsaw), p. 87.

IX. Title page of Maciej Sarbiewski's *Lyricorum Libri IV,* designed by Rubens, Antwerp, 1632 (Courtesy of Instytut Sztuki PAN in Warsaw), p. 90.

List of Illustrations

X. Branicki Palace in Białystok, 1697 (Courtesy of Instytut Sztuki PAN in Warsaw), p. 99.

XI. Barbara Lubomirska, coffin portrait, second half of the 17th century (Photograph by Bożena Seredyńska, courtesy of Muzeum Pałac w Wilanowie), p. 109.

XII. *Autumn* (1684-1686) by Jerzy Eleuter Siemiginowski, Wilanów Palace (Photograph by Wojciech Holnicki, courtesy of Muzeum Pałac in Wilanów), p. 117.

XIII. Armour and pennons of Polish hussars (Photograph by Stanisław Michta, courtesy of Państwowe Zbiory Sztuki na Wawelu), p. 124.

XIV. Interior of a Turkish tent captured at Vienna (Photograph by Adam Wierzba, courtesy of Państwowe Zbiory Sztuki na Wawelu), p. 131.

XV. Detail of the siege of Cracow, 1655. Engraving by Erik Dahlbergh in Samuel Pufendor's *Histoire du Regne de Charles Gustave*, Nürnberg, 1697 (photograph by Alan Magayne-Roshak, author's collection), p. 140.

XVI. King Jan Sobieski and his family, after 1693 (Photograph by Bożena Seredyńska, courtesy of Muzeum Pałac in Wilanów), p. 153.

ENLIGHTENMENT

XVII. King Stanisław August Poniatowski, coronation portrait by Marcello Baciarelli (Courtesy of Muzeum Narodowe in Warsaw), p. 176.

XVIII. Tadeusz Kościuszko, portrait by F. John after Józef Grassi, ca. 1792 (Photograph by Stefan Deptuszewski, courtesy of Instytut Sztuki PAN in Warsaw), p. 178.

XIX. Old Audience Room in the Royal Castle of Warsaw (Photograph by Henryk Poddębski, courtesy of Instytut Sztuki PAN in Warsaw), p. 184.

XX. "The General View of Warsaw from Praga" by Bernardo Bellotto (Canaletto), 1770 (Photograph by Jerzy Langda, courtesy of Instytut Sztuki PAN in Warsaw), p. 185.

XXI. The Temple of Sibyl in Puławy, 1798-1809 (Photograph by Ewa Kozłowska-Tomczyk, courtesy of Instytut Sztuki PAN in Warsaw), p. 188.

XXII. Stanisław Konarski, portrait from the Wilanów Gallery (Courtesy of Instytut Sztuki PAN in Warsaw), p. 200.

XXIII. *Monitor,* I, 1763 (Photograph by Kazimiera Pilaszek, courtesy of Biblioteka Narodowa in Warsaw), p. 213.

XXIV. Bird's eye view of the Łazienki Royal Palace and Theatre in Warsaw (Photograph by Wojskowa Agencja Fotograficzna, courtesy of Łazienki Królewskie in Warsaw), p. 219.

XXV. The Church of the Nuns of the Visitation in Warsaw, 1755-1761 (Photograph by Piotr Koziński, courtesy of Instytut Sztuki PAN in Warsaw), p. 228

XXVI. Ignacy Krasicki, portrait by Per Krafft (Courtesy of Łazienki Królewskie in Warsaw), p. 239.

XXVII. Title page of Jan Krasicki's *Fables and Parables,* Warsaw, 1779 (Photograph by Kazimiera Pilaszek, courtesy of Biblioteka Narodowa in Warsaw), p. 245.

XXVIII. Ball Room in the Łazienki Royal Palace in Warsaw (Courtesy of Łazienki Królewskie in Warsaw), p. 269.

XXIX. Franciszek Karpiński, portrait by the unknown painter (Photograph by Krystyna Dąbrowska, courtesy of Biblioteka Uniwersytecka in Warsaw), p. 279.

List of Illustrations

XXX. Franciszek Dionizy Kniaźnin, lithograph portrait by Leśniewski (Photograph by Kazimiera Pilaszek, courtesy of Biblioteka Narodowa in Warsaw), p. 289.

XXXI. Franciszek Zabłocki, engraved portrait by Polkowski (Photograph by Kazimiera Pilaszek, courtesy of Biblioteka Narodowa in Warsaw), p. 309.

XXXII. Stanisław Małachowski, portrait by Marcello Baciarelli (Photograph by Jan Kościesza-Jaworski, courtesy of Instytut Sztuki PAN in Warsaw), p. 320.

XXXIII. The Senators' Hall in the Royal Castle of Warsaw during the proclamation of the Third of May Constitution, 1791. Etching by J. Łęski after the drawing by Jan Norblin. (Courtesy of Instytut Sztuki PAN in Warsaw), p. 333.

XXXIV. Prince Józef Poniatowski, portrait by Józef Grassi (Photograph by Jan Kościesza-Jaworski, courtesy of Instytut Sztuki PAN in Warsaw), p. 356.

FOREWORD

This is the third volume of my anthology of Polish literature in English. The first volume, entitled *Medieval Literature of Poland. An Anthology*, was published by Garland in New York and London in 1992, while the second one, *Polish Renaissance Literature. An Anthology*, published by Slavica, appeared in 1995. Like the preceding volumes, this book is addressed primarily to college students and general readers.

This collection of English texts is devoted to Polish poetry and prose in the age of the Baroque and the Enlightenment. In an attempt to be comprehensive, I included over two hundred selections from the works of major poets and prose writers, more than two thirds of them rendered into English for the first time. The main purpose of my translation method, described in some detail in the Foreword to *Polish Renaissance Literature*, was to create lucid texts which would be faithful to the spirit and letter of the originals.

James Shey and James Liddy read the manuscript with a critical eye. Stefan Nieznanowski, Zygmunt Kubiak, Ewa Thompson, Samuel Fiszman, and Halina Filipowicz offered their support and suggestions at various stages of this project. The anonymous readers made many valuable comments, while John W. Bowden got the text ready for publication. To all of them I express my thanks. The preparation of this volume was made possible in part by a grant from the Graduate School of the University of Wisconsin-Milwaukee and by a grant from the National Endowment for the Humanities.

University of Wisconsin-Milwaukee

M.J.M.
December 1995

SELECT BIBLIOGRAPHY

ENGLISH ANTHOLOGIES AND TRANSLATIONS

Bloch, Alfred. *The Real Poland: An Anthology of National Self-perception.* New York: Continuum Publishing Co., 1982.

Bowring, John. *Wybór Poezyi Polskiey. Specimens of the Polish Poets; With Notes and Observations on the Literature of Poland.* London: Baldwin, Craddock and Joy, and Rowland Hunter, 1828.

Carpenter, Bogdana. *Monumenta Polonica. The First Four Centuries of Polish Poetry.* Ann Arbor: Michigan Slavic Publications, 1989.

Kapolka, Gerard T. "Krasicki's Fables." *The Polish Review,* XXXIII, 3, 1987, 271-279.

Kirkconnell, Watson. *A Golden Treasury of Polish Lyrics.* Winnipeg: The Polish Press Ltd., 1936.

Krasicki, Jan. *The Adventures of Mr. Nicholas Wisdom.* Translated by Thomas H. Hoisington. Evanston, Il.: Northwestern University Press, 1992.

Niemcewicz, Julian Ursyn. *Under Their Vine and Fig Tree. Travels through America in 1797-1799, 1805 with some further account of life in New Jersey.* Translated and Edited with an Introduction and Notes by Metchie J. E. Budka. Elizabeth, New Jersey: The Grassman Publishing Company, Inc., Vol. XIV in the Collections of The New Jersey Historical Society at Newark, 1965.

Olszer, Krystyna E. (ed.) *For Your Freedom and Ours: Polish Progressive Spirit from the 14th Century to the Present.* 2nd Enlarged Edition. New York: Frederick Ungar Publishing Company, 1981.

Pasek, Jan Chryzostom. *Memoirs of the Polish Baroque.* Ed. and translated by Catherine S. Leach. Berkeley: University of California Press, 1976.

Pasek, Jan Chryzostom. *The Memoirs of Jan Chryzostom z Gosławic Pasek.* Translated, with an Introduction and Commentaries by Maria A.J. Święcicka. New York: The Kosciuszko Foundation; Warsaw: Polish State Publishers, 1978.

Peterkiewicz, Jerzy and Burns Singer. *Five Centuries of Polish Poetry 1450-1970.* 2nd ed. Westport: Greenwood Press, 1979.

Potocki, Jan. *The Saragossa Manuscript: A Collection of Weird Tales.* Edited by Roger Caillois. Translated by Elizabeth Abbott. New York: Orion Press, 1960.

Potocki, Jan. *The New Decameron. Further Tales from the Saragossa Manuscript.* Translated by Elizabeth Abbott. New York: Orion Press, 1967.

Potocki, Jan. *The Manuscript Found in Saragossa.* Translated by Ian Maclean. New York: Viking Penguin, 1995.

Sarbiewski, Maciej Kazimierz. *The Odes of Casimire.* Translated by G. Hils. With an Introduction by Maren-Sophie Roestvig. Los Angeles: William Andrews Clark Memorial Library, University of California, 1953. (The Augustan Reprint Society)

Sarbiewski, Maciej Kazimierz. *E rebus humanis excessus and other poems.* In *An Anthology of Neo-Latin Poetry.* Edited and translated by Fred J. Nichols. New Haven and London: Yale: University Press, 1979, 592-611.

Segel, Harold B. *The Baroque Poem.* New York: Dutton, 1974.

Soboleski, Paul. *Poets and Poetry of Poland. A Collection of Polish Verse.* 3rd ed. Milwaukee: The Paul Soboleski Society, 1929.

Strzetelski, Jerzy. *An Introduction to Polish Literature. An Anthology.* Kraków: Uniwersytet Jagielloński, 1977.

Żółkiewski, Stanisław. *Expedition to Moscow. A Memoir.* Translated by M.W. Stephen. Introduction and Notes by Jędrzej Giertych. Preface by Sir Robert Bruce Lockhart. London: Polonica Publications, 1959.

POLISH ANTHOLOGIES

Adamczewski, Stanisław. *Bajka polska wieku Oświecenia w wyborze.* Warszawa: Spółdzielnia Wydawnicza Książka, 1947.

Badowski, Alicja and Tomasz Przedpełski. *Oświecenie.* Warszawa: PWN, 1993.

Baumfeld, Gustaw B. *Klejnoty poezji staropolskiej: Nowa antologia.* Warszawa: Towarzystwo Wydawnicze, 1919.

Bełza, Władysław. *Antologia polska. Wybór najcelniejszych utworów ze stu poetów polskich.* 4th ed. Lwów: H. Altenberg, 1906.

Borowy, Wacław. *Od Kochanowskiego do Staffa. Antologia liryki polskiej.* 4th ed. Warszawa: PIW, 1981.

Brückner, Aleksander. *Sielanka polska XVII wieku.* Kraków: Krakowska Spółka Wydawnicza, Biblioteka Narodowa I 48, 1922.

Budzyk, Kazimierz, Hanna Budzykowa and Juljan Lewański. *Literatura mieszczańska w Polsce od końca XVI do końca XVII wieku.* 2 vols. Warszawa: PIW, 1954.

Bukowski, Kazimierz. *Biblia a literatura polska. Antologia.* Warszawa: WSiP, 1984.

Chrościelewski, Tadeusz et al. *Księgi humoru polskiego.* Vol. I. *Od Reja do Niemcewicza.* Ed. by Stanisław Czernik et al. Łódź: Wydawnictwo Łódzkie, 1958-68.

Chrzanowski, Ignacy. *Wybór staropolskich bajek ezopowych od Biernata Lubelczyka do Mickiewicza.* Kraków: Biblioteka Pisarzów Polskich 55, 1910.

Delaperrière, Maria and Franciszek Ziejka. *Panorama de la litterature polonaise des origines à 1822.* Warszawa: PWN, 1991.

Duralska-Macheta, Teresa. *O edukacji dawnych Polaków. Materiały z XVI-XVII wieku.* Warszawa: Nasza Księgarnia, 1982.

Folkierski, Władysław. *Sonet polski. Wybór tekstów.* Kraków: Biblioteka Narodowa, 1925.

Goliński, Zbigniew. *Abyśmy o ojczyźnie naszej radzili. Antologia publicystyki doby stanisławowskiej.* Warszawa: PIW, 1984.

Gruchała, Janusz and Stanisław Grzeszczuk. *Staropolska poezja ziemiańska.* Warszawa: PIW, 1988.

Grydzewski, Mieczysław. *Wiersze polskie wybrane.* 2nd ed. London: Orbis, 1948.

Grzeszczuk, Stanisław and Anna Niewolak-Krzywda. *Literatura polska do końca XVIII wieku.* 3rd ed. Rzeszów: Wydawnictwo Uczelniane WSP, 1982.

Grzeszczuk, Stanisław and Anna Niewolak-Krzywda. *Literatura polska. Średniowiecze-Renesans-Barok. Wybór tekstów.* 2 vols. 5th ed. Rzeszów: Wydawnictwo Uczelniane WSP, 1990.

Grzeszczuk, Stanisław. *Antologia literatury sowizdrzalskiej XVI-XVII wieku.* 2nd ed. Wrocław: Ossolineum, 1985.

Grzeszczuk, Stanisław. *Staropolskie frywolności plebejskie.*
    Białystok: KAW, 1989.

Hertz, Benedykt. *Antologia bajki polskiej.* Warszawa: PIW,
    1958.

Jackl, Jerzy. *Wokół "Doświadczyńskiego". Antologia romansu i
    powieści.* Warszawa: PIW, 1969.

Kaleta, Roman. *Anegdoty i sensacje obyczajowe wieku
    Oświecenia w Polsce. Dokumenty. Wspomnienia.
    Facecje.* Warszawa: Czytelnik, 1958.

Kamieńska, Anna. *Od Czarnolasu. Najpiękniejsze wiersze
    polskie.* Warszawa: Iskry, 1971.

Kapuścik, Janusz and Wojciech Podgórski. *Poeci żołnierzom
    1410-1945. Antologia wierszy i pieśni żołnierskich.*
    Warszawa: MON, 1970.

Kolbuszewski, Jacek. *Najpiękniejsze epitafia polskie.*
    Warszawa: SiT, 1989.

Kostkiewiczowa, Teresa and Zbigniew Goliński. *Oświeceni o
    literaturze. Wypowiedzi pisarzy polskich 1740-1800.*
    2 vols. Warszawa: PIW, 1993, 1995.

Kostkiewiczowa, Teresa and Zbigniew Goliński. *Świat
    poprawiać--zuchwałe rzemiosło. Antologia poezji polskiego
    Oświecenia.* Warszawa: PIW, 1981.

Kott, Jan. *Poezja polskiego Oświecenia. Antologia.* 2nd ed.
    Warszawa: Czytelnik, 1956.

Kott, Jan and Stanisław Lorentz. *Warszawa wieku Oświecenia.
    Antologia poezji i prozy.* 2nd ed. Warszawa: PIW, 1956.

Koźmiński, Karol. *Poezja legionów (1796-1807; 1914-1918)*
    Warszawa: Główna Księgarnia Wojskowa, 1936.

Kridl, Manfred. *An Anthology of Polish Literature.* New York:
    Columbia University Press, 1957.

Krzyżanowski, Julian and Kazimiera Żukowska-Bilip. *Dawna facecja polska XVI-XVIII w.* Warszawa: PIW, 1960.

Lemański, Jan. *Satyra polska. Antologia.* Warszawa: M. Orgelbrand, 1914.

Lewański, Julian. *Dramaty staropolskie. Antologia.* 6 vols. Warszawa: PIW, 1959-1963.

Libera, Zdzisław. *Poezja polska XVIII wieku.* 2nd ed. Warszawa: Czytelnik, 1983.

Libera, Zdzisław. *Poezja polska 1800-1830.* Warszawa: Czytelnik, 1984.

Maciejewski, Janusz. *Literatura barska. (Antologia).* 2nd ed. Wrocław: Ossolineum, 1976.

Malewska, Hanna. *Listy staropolskie z epoki Wazów.* Warszawa: PIW, 1977.

Marcinkiewicz, Jan. *Historia w poezji. Antologia polskiej poezji historycznej i patriotycznej.* Warszawa: Nasza Księgarnia, 1965.

Marx, Jan. *Staropolska poezja erotyczna.* Warszawa: WAiF, 1989.

Merwin, Bertold. *Polskie listy miłosne od XV do XIX wieku.* Lwów: Wydawnictwo Polskie, 1922.

Michalski, Waldemar. *Pod Twoją obronę... Matka Boska w poezji polskiej.* Lublin: Wydawnictwo Kurii Biskupiej, 1986.

Miłaszewska, Wanda, Jan Rembiński and Stanisław Miłaszewski. *Chór wieków. Antologia poetycka.* Poznań: Księgarnia św. Wojciecha, 1936.

Mitzner, Zbigniew (Szeląg, Jan). *Wybór satyr z literatury polskiej XV-XX w.* Warszawa: LSW, 1953.

Montusiewicz, Ryszard, Tadeusz Piersiak and Wojciech Wydra. *W kręgu dawnej poezji.* Warszawa: PAX, 1983.

Mrowcewicz, Krzysztof. *Wysoki umysł w dolnych rzeczach zawikłany. Antologia polskiej poezji metafizycznej epoki baroku od Mikołaja Sępa Szarzyńskiego do Stanisława Herakliusza Lubomirskiego.* Warszawa: IBL, 1993.

Nadolski, Bronisław. *Wybór mów staropolskich.* Wrocław: Ossolineum, Biblioteka Narodowa I 175, 1961.

Nowak, Jerzy R. *Myśli o Polsce i Polakach.* Katowice: Wydawnictwo Unia, 1994.

Okoń, Jan. *Dramaty eucharystyczne Jezuitów XVII wieku.* Warszawa: PAX, 1992.

Okoń, Jan. *Staropolskie pastorałki dramatyczne. Antologia.* Wrocław: Ossolineum, 1989.

Opacki Ireneusz and Zbigniew Nowak. *Oświecenie i Romantyzm. Teksty do ćwiczeń z historii literatury polskiej (dla studentów II r. filologii polskiej.)* Katowice: Uniwersytet Śląski, 1979.

Prosnak, Jan. *Siedem wieków pieśni polskiej. Śpiewnik dla młodzieży z komentarzem historycznym.* 2nd ed. Warszawa: WSiP, 1986.

Ratajczak, Dobrochna. *Polska tragedia neoklasycystyczna.* Wrocław: Ossolineum, 1988.

Rożej, Stefan J. *Bogiem sławiena Maryja. Antologia twórczości poetyckiej o Matce Boskiej Jasnogórskiej.* Rzym: Abilgraf, 1981.

Siomkajło, Alina. *Mała muza: od Reja do Leca. Antologia epigramatyki polskiej.* Warszawa: PIW, 1986.

Skwarczyński, Zdzisław. *Bajka polska wieku Oświecenia w wyborze.* Warszawa: Książka i Wiedza, 1951.

Sokołowska, Jadwiga and Kazimiera Żukowska. *Poeci polskiego baroku.* 2 vols. Warszawa: PIW, 1965.

Sokołowska, Jadwiga. *I w odmianach czasu smak jest. Antologia poezji polskiego baroku.* Warszawa: PIW, 1991.

Sokołowska, Jadwiga. *Antologia polskiej poezji barokowej.* Warszawa: PIW, 1988.

Taszycki, Witold. *Obrońcy języka polskiego. Wiek XV-XVIII.* Wrocław: Ossolineum, Biblioteka Narodowa I 146, 1953.

Taszycki, Witold. *Wybór tekstów staropolskich XVI-XVIII w.* 3rd ed. Warszawa: PWN, 1969.

Tuwim, Julian. *Cztery wieki fraszki polskiej.* Warszawa: Czytelnik, 1957.

Tuwim, Julian. *Polski słownik pijacki i antologia bachiczna.* Warszawa: Czytelnik, 1959.

Vinzenz, Andrzej. *Helikon sarmacki, wątki i tematy polskiej poezji barokowej.* Notes by Marian Malicki. Wrocław: Ossolineum, Biblioteka Narodowa I 259, 1989.

Witkowska, Alina. *Polski romans sentymentalny.* Wrocław: Ossolineum, 1971.

Woźnowski, Wacław. *Antologia bajki polskiej.* 2nd ed. Wrocław: Ossolineum, 1983.

Woźnowski, Wacław. *Antologia literatury polskiego Oświecenia.* Kraków: Instytut Filologii Polskiej, Uniwersytet Jagielloński, 1979.

Wójcicki, Kazimierz W. *Biblioteka starożytna pisarzy polskich.* Vol. 6. 2nd ed. Warszawa: S. Orgelbrand, 1843-1854.

Zieliński, Andrzej. *Poezja powstania listopadowego.* Wrocław: Ossolineum, 1971.

Zieliński, Andrzej. *Ulotna poezja patriotyczna wojen napoleońskich (1805-1814)*. Wrocław: Ossolineum, 1977.

Żukowska, Kazimiera. *Poeci polscy od średniowiecza do baroku*. Warszawa: PIW, 1977.

Żurakowski, Bogusław. *Antologia bajki polskiej.* 2 vols. Kraków: Wydawnictwo Literackie, 1986.

GENERAL SURVEYS AND CRITICAL STUDIES

Aleksandrowska Elżbieta et al. *Bibliografia literatury polskiej "Nowy Korbut." Oświecenie.* Vol. 4-6. Warszawa: PIW, 1966-1972.

Bardach, Artur and Stanisław Herbst. *Kultura polska w źródłach i opracowaniach.* Warszawa: LSW, 1961.

Bartkiewicz, Magdalena. *Polski ubiór do 1864 roku.* Wrocław: Ossolineum, 1979.

Błoński, Jan and Mieczysław Klimowicz. *Helikon sarmacki: wątki i tematy polskiej poezji barokowej.* Kraków: Ossolineum, 1988.

Bochnak, Adam and Kazimierz Buczkowski. *Decorative Arts in Poland.* Warsaw: Arkady, 1972.

Bogucka, Maria. *Dawna Polska. Narodziny, rozwój, upadek.* Warszawa: Wiedza Powszechna, 1985.

Bogucka, Maria. *Dzieje kultury polskiej do 1918 roku.* Wrocław: Ossolineum, 1991.

Brückner, Aleksander. *Dzieje kultury polskiej.* Vol. III. Warszawa: Książka i Wiedza, 1958.

Budzyk, Kazimierz. *Szkice i materiały do dziejów literatury staropolskiej*. Warszawa: PIW, 1955.

Chrościcki, Juliusz and Andrzej Rottermund. *Atlas of Warsaw Architecture*. Warsaw: Arkady, 1978.

Chrzanowski, Ignacy. *Historia literatury niepodległej Polski. (965-1795) (z wypisami)*. 13th ed. Warszawa: PWN, 1983.

Cobban, Alfred (ed.). *The Eighteenth Century. Europe in the Age of the Enlightenment*. New York: McGraw-Hill, 1969.

Cydzik, Jacek and Wojciech Fijałkowski. *Wilanów*. Warszawa: Arkady, 1975.

Czubiński, Antoni and Jerzy Topolski. *Historia Polski*. Wrocław: Ossolineum, 1988.

Davies, Norman. *God's Playground. A History of Poland*. 2 vols. New York: Columbia Unversity Press, 1982.

Delaperrière, Maria (ed.). *Le Baroque en Pologne et en Europe*. Paris: Inalco, 1990.

Dobrowolski, Tadeusz. *Sztuka polska od czasów najdawniejszych do ostatnich*. Kraków: Wydawnictwo Literackie, 1974.

Dobrowolski Tadeusz and Władysław Tatarkiewicz (eds.). *Historia sztuki polskiej w zarysie*. Vol. II. Kraków: Wydawnictwo Literackie, 1962.

Dobrzycki, Stanislas. *History of Polish Literature*. In: *Polish Encyclopaedia*. Vol. I. Geneva: Committee for the Polish Encyclopaedic Publication, 1926.

Dziechcińska, Hanna (ed.). *Literary Studies in Poland*. Vol. III. *Renaissance. Baroque*. Wrocław: Ossolineum, 1979.

Fijałkowski, Wojciech. *Wilanów*. Warszawa: Arkady, 1983.

Grochulska, Barbara. *Małe państwo wielkich nadziei.* Warszawa: KAW, 1987.

Grodzicki Stanisław and Eligiusz Kozłowski. *Polska zniewolona 1795-1806.* Warszawa: KAW, 1987.

Guerquin, Bohdan. *Zamki w Polsce.* Warszawa: Arkady, 1974.

Halecki, Oscar. *A History of Poland.* New York: David McKay Company, 1976.

Hernas, Czesław. *Barok.* Warszawa: PWN, 1980.

Ichnatowicz, Ireneusz et al. *Społeczeństwo polskie od X do XX wieku.* 2nd ed. Warszawa: Książka i Wiedza, 1988.

Iłowiecki, Maciej. *Dzieje nauki polskiej.* Warszawa: Interpress, 1981.

Jabłoński, Krzysztof and Włodzimierz Piwkowski. *Nieborów. Arkadia.* Warszawa: Sport i Turystyka, 1988.

Jaroszewski, Tadeusz. *Księga Pałaców Warszawy.* Warszawa: Interpress, 1985.

Karpowicz, Mariusz. *Barok w Polsce.* Warszawa: Arkady, 1988.

Karpowicz, Mariusz. *Jerzy Eleuter Siemiginowski, malarz polskiego baroku.* Wrocław: Ossolineum, 1974.

Kębłowski, Janusz. *Dzieje sztuki polskiej.* Warszawa: Arkady, 1987.

Kieniewicz, Stefan et al. *History of Poland.* 2nd ed. Warsaw: PWN, 1979.

Klemensiewicz, Zenon. *Historia języka polskiego.* Warszawa: PWN, 1981.

Klimaszewski, Bolesław (ed.). *An Outline History of Polish Culture.* Warsaw: Interpress, 1984.

Klimowicz, Mieczysław. *Oświecenie.* 4th ed. Warszawa: PWN, 1980.

Klimowicz, Mieczysław. *Literatura Oświecenia.* Warszawa: PWN, 1990.

Kłoczowski, Jerzy et al. *Chrześcijaństwo w Polsce.* Lublin: Wydawnictwo Towarzystwa Naukowego KUL, 1980.

Korolko, Mirosław. *Klejnot swobodnego sumienia. Polemika wokół Konfederacji Warszawskiej w latach 1573-1658.* Warszawa: PAX, 1974.

Kostkiewiczowa, Teresa. *Klasycyzm. Sentymentalizm. Rokoko. Szkice o prądach literackich polskiego Oświecenia.* Warszawa: PWN, 1979.

Kostkiewiczowa, Teresa and Zbigniew Goliński (eds.). *Pisarze polskiego oświecenia.* 2 vols. Warszawa: PWN, 1992, 1994.

Kostkiewicz, Teresa (ed.). *Słownik literatury polskiego oświecenia.* 2nd ed. Wrocław: Ossolineum, 1991.

Kot, Stanisław. *Uroki wsi i życia ziemiańskiego w poezji staropolskiej.* Warszawa: Osobne odbicie z *Księgi pamiątkowej na 75-lecie "Gazety Rolniczej,"* 1937.

Kozakiewiczowa, Helena. *Renesans i manieryzm w Polsce.* Warszawa: Auriga, 1974.

Kridl, Manfred. *A Survey of Polish Literature and Culture.* New York: Columbia University Press, 1957.

Krzyżanowski, Julian et al. (eds.) *Literatura polska. Przewodnik encyklopedyczny.* 2 vols. Warszawa: PWN, 1984.

Krzyżanowski, Julian. *A History of Polish Literature.* Warsaw: PWN, 1978.

Mikoś, Michael J. *Early Maps of Poland (1508-1772) in the American Geographical Society Collection.* Milwaukee: The American Geographical Society Collection, 1982.

Mikoś, Michael J. "Monarchs and Magnates: Maps of Poland in the Sixteenth and Eighteenth Centuries." In: *Monarchs, Ministers and Maps. The Emergence of Cartography as a Tool of Government in Early Modern Europe.* Ed. by David Buisseret. Chicago and London: University of Chicago Press, 1992.

Miłosz, Czesław. *The History of Polish Literature.* 2nd ed. Berkeley: University of California Press, 1983.

Morawińska, Agnieszka. *Polish Painting 15th to 20th Centuries.* Warsaw: Auriga, 1984.

Morfill, W.R. *The Story of Poland.* London: T. Fisher Unwin, 1893.

Mrozowska, Kamilla. *By Polaków zrobić obywatelami.* Kraków: KAW, 1993.

Nadolski, Andrzej. *Polska broń. Broń biała.* Wrocław: Ossolineum, 1974.

Nelson, Lowry, Jr. *Baroque Lyric Poetry.* New Haven and London: Yale University Press, 1961.

New Constitution of the Government of Poland. The facsimile of the 2nd edition of the original English translation published in London in 1791. Washington, D.C.: The Embassy of the Republic of Poland, 1991.

Nieznanowski, Stefan. *Studia i wizerunki. O poezji staropolskiej i jej badaczach.* Warszawa: PAX, 1989.

Nowak-Dłużewski, Juliusz. *Okolicznościowa poezja polityczna w Polsce: Zygmunt III.* Warszawa: PAX, 1971; *Dwaj młodsi Wazowie.* Warszawa: PAX, 1972; *Dwaj królowie rodacy.* Ed. by Stefan Nieznanowski. Warszawa: PAX, 1980.

Krzyżanowski, Julian. *Tradycje literackie polszczyzny. Od Galla do Staffa.* Ed. by Maria Bokszczanin. Warszawa: PWN, 1992.

Kuchowicz, Zbigniew. *Człowiek polskiego baroku.* Łódź: Wydawnictwo Łódzkie, 1992.

Kunert, Ilse (ed.). *Studien zur polnischen Literatur-, Sprach- und Kulturgeschichte im 18. Jahrhundert: Vorträge der 3. deutsch-polnischen Polonistenkonferenz, Tübingen, April 1991.* Köln: Böhlau Verlag, 1993.

Kuraszkiewicz, Władysław. *Polski język literacki. Studia nad historią i strukturą.* Warszawa-Poznań: PWN, 1986.

Libera, Zdzisław. *Oświecenie.* Warszawa: Biblioteka Polonistyki, 1974.

Libera, Zdzisław. *Wiek Oświecony.* Warszawa: PIW, 1986.

Libera, Zdzisław. *Rozważania o wieku telerancji, rozumu i gustu.* Warszawa: PIW, 1994.

Libera, Zdzisław, Jadwiga Pietrusiewiczowa and Jadwiga Rytel. *Literatura polska. Od średniowiecza do oświecenia.* Warszawa: PWN, 1988.

Lorentz, Stanisław et al. *Stare Miasto i Zamek Królewski w Warszawie.* Warszawa: Arkady, 1971.

Łoziński, Jerzy and Adam Miłobędzki. *Guide to Architecture in Poland.* Warsaw: Polonia Publishing House, 1967.

Michałowska, Teresa with Barbara Otwinowska and Elżbieta Sarnowska-Temeriusz (eds.). *Słownik literatury staropolskiej. (Średniowiecze. Renesans. Barok).* Wrocław: Ossolineum, 1990.

Mikocka-Rachubowa, Katarzyna. "Barok i rokoko w Polsce." In: *Sztuka świata.* Vol. 7. Ed. by Jose Pijoan et al. Warszawa: Arkady, 1994, 359-377.

Nowicka-Jeżowa, Alina. *Sarmaci i śmierć. O staropolskiej poezji żałobnej.* Warszawa: PWN, 1992.

Ochlewski, Tadeusz (ed.). *Dzieje muzyki polskiej w zarysie.* 2nd ed. Warszawa: Interpress, 1983.

Olszewski, Henryk. *O skutecznym rad sposobie.* Kraków: KAW, 1991.

Pelc, Janusz. *Barok--epoka przeciwieństw.* Warszawa: Czytelnik, 1993.

Piszczkowski, Mieczysław. *Obrońcy chłopów w literaturze polskiej.* Kraków: M. Kot, 1948.

Platt, Dobrosława. *Kazania pogrzebowe z przełomu XVI i XVII wieku.* Wrocław: Ossolineum, 1992.

Polski Słownik Bibliograficzny. Kraków: Polska Akademia Umiejętności, 1935-.

Prejs, Marek. *Poezja późnego baroku. Główne kierunki przemian.* Warszawa: PWN, 1989.

Reddaway, W.F. et al (eds.). *The Cambridge History of Poland. From Augustus II to Piłsudski (1697-1935).* Cambridge: University Press, 1941.

Rose, William J. "Stanisław Konarski, Preceptor of Poland." *The Slavonic Review*, IV, 10, 1925, 23-41.

Rose, William J. "Stanisław Staszic, 1755-1826." *The Slavonic Review*, 33, 1954-55, 291-303.

Rożek, Michał. *Blaski i cienie baroku.* Kraków: KAW, 1992.

Saintsbury, George. *A History of English Prosody. From the Twelfth Century to the Present Day.* 3 vols. New York: Russell and Russell, 1961.

Sajkowski, Alojzy. *Barok.* 2nd ed. Warszawa: WSiP, 1987.

Sowiński, Janusz. *Polskie drukarstwo.* Wrocław: Ossolineum, 1988.

Starnawski, Jerzy. *W świecie barokowym.* Łódź: Uniwersytet Łódzki, 1992.

Suchodolski, Bogdan. *A History of Polish Culture.* Translated by E.J. Czerwiński. Warsaw: Interpress. 1986.

Szwejkowska, Helena. *Książka drukowana XV-XVIII wieku. Zarys historyczny.* 5th ed. Wrocław-Warszawa: PWN, 1987.

Szypowscy, Maria and Andrzej. *Warszawski Zamek Królewski.* Warszawa: Sport i Turystyka, 1989.

Tatarkiewicz, Władysław. *Łazienki Warszawskie.* Warszawa: Arkady, 1968.

Tazbir, Janusz. *A State Without Stakes: Polish Religious Toleration in the Sixteenth and Seventeenth Centuries.* New York: Kosciuszko Foundation, 1973.

Tazbir, Janusz. *Kultura polskiego baroku.* Warszawa: Omnipress, 1986.

Trzeciak, Przemysław. "Renesans i manieryzm w Polsce." In: *Sztuka świata.* Vol. 6. Ed. by Jose Pijoan et al. Warszawa: Arkady, 1991, 329-353.

Wallis, Mieczysław. *Canaletto malarz Warszawy.* Warszawa: Auriga, 1961.

Wimmer, Jan. *Wiedeń 1683. Dzieje kampanii i bitwy.* Warszawa: MON, 1983.

Warnke, Frank J. *European Metaphysical Poetry.* New Haven and London: Yale University Press, 1961.

Wójcik, Zbigniew. *Liberum veto.* Kraków: KAW, 1992.

Wójcik, Zbigniew. *Wojny kozackie w dawnej Polsce.* Kraków: KAW, 1989.

Zachwatowicz, Jan. *Architektura polska.* Warszawa: Arkady, 1966.

Zahorski, Andrzej. *Naczelnik w sukmanie.* Kraków: KAW, 1990.

Zahorski, Andrzej (ed.). *Warszawa w wieku Oświecenia.* Wrocław: Ossolineum, 1986.

Zamoyski, Adam. *The Polish Way. A Thousand-Year History of the Poles and Their Culture.* New York: Franklin Watts, 1988.

I. BAROQUE

INTRODUCTION

HISTORICAL BACKGROUND

The reign of Władysław IV Vasa (1632-1648) brought the Commonwealth of Poland and Lithuania a period of relative calm and prosperity. As a result of a peace treaty signed with Muscovy in Polanowo in 1634, with Sweden in Stumsdorf in 1635, and with Turkey in 1634 and 1635, the territory of the Commonwealth extended to almost 390,000 square miles, with a population of more than ten million people. The King was able to reorganize the army, which grew to about thirty thousand men, modernize the artillery, strengthen fortifications, build new Baltic ports, and enlarge a commercial fleet. Exports kept growing until the middle of the century, reaching an average of 140,000 metric tons of grain annually, while trade in livestock brought additional profits.

But signs of the internal weakening of the state, already visible at the end of the sixteenth century, were proliferating. The role of the central administration, which had no officers in the provinces, was diminishing. The powerful magnates gained influence over the landless gentry and, using their services, reduced the effectiveness of the Sejm, while gaining control over the Senate and local dietines, most importantly in matters of taxation. The huge estates became for all practical purposes independent fiefdoms, in which great noblemen maintained strong armies, employed impoverished clients, and exercised a firm control over their subjects.

The lot of the peasants, who constituted almost 70% of the population, was steadily getting worse. The Polish economy, which was mainly based on industrial agriculture, relied mostly on exports of foodstuffs and raw materials, while its imports consisted of finished products and colonial goods. With a gradual but steady fall in prices of grain in Western Europe, the landowners were increasing the exploitation of the peasants. They demanded more serf labor, instituted various monopolies, and required payments in kind. In many regions of the country,

Introduction

I. King Władysław IV

peasants were obliged to work four days a week on the lord's estate. They responded by slower work. At the same time, unable to cultivate their own land efficiently, they limited themselves to subsistence farming. With overall productivity declining, many peasants became impoverished, not a few lost their land. Dissatisfied and unable to find redress in courts, they frequently resorted to desertion and at times to armed uprisings.

Nowhere was the situation more inflamed than in the eastern territories of the Commonwealth, especially in the Ukraine. The vast and fertile plains were the home of the Cossacks, free soldiers who established their own units and armies for the defense of the local population against the Tartars and Turks. They also engaged in audacious raids south of the border, penetrating at times as far as Crimea and even the outskirts of Constantinople. The Commonwealth enlisted some Cossack units and used them to defend its borders. Those Cossacks who were not registered in the service of Poland and who persisted in their adventurous exploits, thus exposing the country to retaliatory attacks launched by the Ottoman Empire, were being forced to disband and to join the local population in serf labor. The majority of Cossacks refused to be relegated to serfdom. Since most of them were of Ruthenian origin, they raised the banner of the Orthodox faith in order to find support among the masses of peasants and to rally them against the local magnates, who owned close to 80% of houses and land in the major areas of the Ukraine. Inevitably, they ran into conflict with Polish authorities. Beginning in the 1580's, sporadic Cossack rebellions and uprisings erupted throughout the Ukraine and Byelorussia, followed by hard-fought battles, and bloody reprisals.

In 1648, the grandiose plans of King Władysław IV of liberating the Balkans from the Turkish yoke failed for lack of support in the Sejm and among his foreign allies. The Cossacks, whose participation in an anti-Turkish campaign was sought after and who were promised new privileges, felt betrayed. After reaching an alliance with the Crimean Tartars, they rose in rebellion under the leadership of Bohdan Chmielnicki. When they defeated the Polish army at Żółte Wody and Korsuń in the spring of 1648, most of the local population took up arms, and large regions of the Ukraine were engulfed in fire and drenched with blood.

In June 1651, the Polish army led by Prince Jeremi Wiśniowiecki defeated the combined forces of Cossacks and

Tartars at Beresteczko. Unable to fight against Poland on his own, Chmielnicki turned for help to Tsar Alexis. The treaty of Perejasław in January 1654, which stipulated the incorporation of the Ukraine into Russia in return for military assistance, was followed in the spring of that year by the Russian invasion of Poland. When the war was finally over and the truce signed in Andruszów in 1667, Poland lost vast territories of the Ukraine, nearly the whole region falling under the sway of Russia.

The situation of Poland deteriorated rapidly in July 1655 when the army of Charles Gustavus of Sweden crossed the borders of Great Poland and Lithuania. Aided by treacherous magnates, among them Krzysztof Opaliński, the Voivode of Great Poland, and Janusz Radziwiłł, the Grand Hetman of Lithuania, who surrendered their whole provinces to the enemy, the Swedish army quickly overran the country, taking Warsaw in September and Cracow in October. The Swedes, who plundered and burned down churches, castles, and towns in their path, were followed by the invading forces of Frederick William, the Elector of Brandenburg, and George Rakocsi, Prince of Transylvania, eager to have a hand in the partition of the Commonwealth.

King Jan Kazimierz (1648-1668), who succeeded his brother, was forced to seek refuge in Silesia, from where he issued calls for resistance. Appalled by the rapacity of the invaders, Polish peasants, then burghers and noblemen, took arms in various parts of the country, engaging the enemy in partisan warfare. The heroic forty days' defense of the monastery of Częstochowa, the shrine of the venerated Black Madonna, was one of the turning points of the war. Before long the whole nation rose against the invaders. The King returned in January 1656, rallying his forces, which were led brilliantly by Stefan Czarniecki. In 1656, threatened with defeat, Charles Gustavus and the major units of his army beat a retreat. In the peace treaty signed with the Swedes in Oliwa in 1660, Poland regained its territories.

The Cossack rebellion and Swedish invasion brought enormous devastation to the whole country. The size of the Commonwealth was reduced by more than twenty five percent, mostly in the east, its population dropped from ten to six million. The richest regions of the Republic lay in ruins. The crops in many areas were razed, the countryside was ravished by famine and plague. Large fields of arable land lay waste, the quantity of

II. Meeting of the armies of King Charles X of Sweden and George Rakocsi of Transylvania in Poland, 1657

livestock was reduced, crop yields fell significantly. Grain production in 1657 decreased by more than fifty percent compared to the pre-1655 level. About twenty percent of towns and villages were destroyed. The urban population declined by close to seventy per cent. Major cities of Warsaw, Cracow, Poznań, Lublin, and Wilno lay in ruins, only Gdańsk and Lwów survived intact. Revenues of the treasury shrank drastically, causing devaluation, while useless currency was flooding the market, bringing chaos.

As big as these losses were, the political system of the Commonwealth suffered even more. In 1652, the debates of the Sejm were broken by a single deputy, a client of Janusz Radziwiłł. From that time on, by exercising the rule of the *liberum veto* (free dissent), which originated to protect the rights of the minority, hired deputies were able to paralyze parliamentary procedures, on occasions using it even before the debates of the Sejm began. When King Jan Kazimierz presented a program of parliamentary and electoral reforms (1661-62), powerful nobles led by Marshal Jerzy Lubomirski and supported by Vienna and Berlin defeated the bills. Sentenced to banishment and disgrace for high treason by the Sejm Tribunal, Lubomirski attacked the royal forces at the head of the rebellious army. After two years of a fratricidal war that devastated the country, Lubomirski defeated the royal troops at Mątwy (1667). Even though he won the battle, Lubomirski asked pardon of the King and retired in Austrian Silesia. The King, his authority destroyed and his reforms thwarted, abdicated after his wife's death in 1668 and went to France, where he died four years later.

The new king, Michał Korybut Wiśniowiecki (1669-1673), Prince Jeremi's son, showed himself incapable of managing Poland's internal and international affairs. When in 1672 the Turkish forces of Sultan Mohammed IV invaded Podolia and captured the fortress of Kamieniec Podolski, Poland surrendered at Buczacz the whole province and the southern part of the Kiev region, agreeing in addition to pay a yearly tribute. The ignominy of the treaty was erased by Hetman Jan Sobieski, who in 1673 led the Polish army to a splendid victory over the Ottoman forces at Chocim and was rewarded with the royal crown.

King Jan III Sobieski (1674-1696) was a shrewd politician and a brilliant military commander. He reformed the army and after a series of victorious campaigns secured a temporary peace treaty with Turkey in 1676. But the danger of Turkish invasion did not recede. In 1683 Poland concluded an alliance with Austria and when in July of that year a Turkish army of over one hundred thousand men lay siege to Vienna, Sobieski rapidly led Polish forces of twenty six thousand men to relieve the capital city.

On September 12, 1683, Sobieski as Commander-in-Chief of the combined allied forces of seventy four thousand men, led his army to a splendid victory over the Grand Vizier's forces. The furious charge of the winged Hussars, the heavy cavalry strike force that swooped down from the heights of the Schafberg straight towards the Vizier's white tent, broke the resistance of the enemies. The Ottoman army was in flight and the King of Poland triumphantly entered the walls of Vienna, hailed as the savior of Christian Europe.

Yet this great victory proved to be no panacea for the political and economic crisis that gripped the country. Exhausted by constant warfare that had devastated its territory since 1648, Poland was in no position to take part in new military expeditions, launched by the Holy League against the Turks. The King, who was personally involved in unsuccessful military campaigns in Moldavia, was unable to stem the spreading anarchy or to carry through any constitutional reforms. Ailing and disillusioned, he withdrew to his residence in Wilanów, and when he died in 1696, the once proud Commonwealth of Poland and Lithuania entered its final period of existence.

CULTURAL BACKGROUND

The Baroque style, which flourished in Poland from the end of the sixteenth century to the middle of the eighteenth century, was primarily designed to delight the spectator with splendors of art. Unlike the Renaissance artist who attempted to recreate the beauty and harmony of nature, the baroque artist strived above all to present his own vision of the world, born of imagination and fantasy. This vision was often disharmonious and unsettled, reflecting the turbulent times of seventeenth century Europe. Grand in its dimensions, it was also exuberant and dramatic, though at times tinged with affectation and with religious exaltation.

Introduction

Polish Baroque coexisted with Sarmatism, a cultural trend which gained popularity among the gentry in reaction to foreign influences and invasions. The Sarmatians claimed that they descended from an ancient tribe of warriors who inhabited the environs of the Black Sea and who later settled in the valleys of the Vistula and the Dnieper. Since most of them belonged to the landed gentry, they praised the idyllic existence and republican virtues of the country squire. They spoke of the unique attributes of the Polish character, particularly of its religious dedication and military prowess, as demonstrated in the defense of the country against foreign encroachments. They advocated the golden freedom of the gentry, lauded their political system and institutions, and opposed the absolute power of the monarchy. Many of them felt superior to other nations and believed in a historical mission of the Polish people.

In material culture, Sarmatism produced an original fusion of Western and Eastern styles. Oriental influence was especially evident in arms, dress, and decoration. The Polish cavalry rode Arab horses and adopted many Eastern weapons, most notably the saber with a curved blade and richly decorated handle modelled on a Persian scimitar, as well as the dagger, luxurious sheaths, helmets, and saddles. During military campaigns, many mounted men shaved their heads in the Tartar fashion.

The Polish nobleman wore a long coat lined with cloth of gold, a silk sash belt, and soft leather knee-boots of Eastern origin. His manor was decorated with Persian rugs, Turkish kilims, tapestries, and silk embroideries studded with jewels. If oriental products were too expensive, he turned to the Koniecpolski manufactory in Brody, which produced attractive samite fabrics and original rugs or to Armenian craftsmen, who wove fine sash belts in Stanisławów, and whose art was imitated in Olesko and Słuck. In everyday life he enjoyed color, opulence, and festivity. He observed with pomp religious holidays, ceremonies, and rituals, such as the day of the patron saint, weddings, and funerals.

A major source of patronage of the arts was the Church. The sacral Baroque architecture in its first phase was mainly associated with the Jesuit Order. The Jesuits, who were brought to Poland in 1564, spearheaded the victorious movement of the Counter Reformation. They established churches and colleges in many major cities, competing successfully with the best Protestant schools in Toruń, Gdańsk, and Elbląg or with Comenius's school of the Bohemian Brothers in Leszno. Their

III. Sash from Słuck, XVIII c.

churches in Nieśwież (1582-1593), founded by Mikołaj Krzysztof Radziwiłł, in Lublin, and in Poznań, were modelled on the famous church of Il Gesu in Rome (1568-1584). The most representative church of that provenance, Saint Peter and Saint Paul's in Cracow, was founded by King Zygmunt III, prominent patron of the arts. Its interior and decorative stone facade were designed by Giovanni Baptista Trevano, the royal architect.

Numerous other churches and chapels were built by foreign and local artists under the patronage of pious magnates and burghers. Particularly impressive were the churches of Wilno. The Chapel of Saint Casimir next to the Wilno Cathedral founded by King Władysław IV and the Church of Saint Teresa, both designed by Constantino Tencalla, as well as Saint Peter and Saint Paul's, famed for its harmonious synthesis of architecture and sculpture, were splendid examples of local Baroque, characterized by fluent lines, light proportions, and graceful decorations. The Camaldolese Church at Bielany near Cracow, with a broad stone facade flanked by two towers and stuccoed interiors decorated with paintings by Tommaso Dolabella, founded by Crown Marshal Mikołaj Wolski and built by Andrea Spezza, formed the centerpiece of a monastic complex which included about twenty hermit houses. In many shrines the faithful could pray at the Stations of the Cross, of which the Calvary at Zebrzydów, founded by Mikołaj Zebrzydowski and built between 1603 and 1609, is best known. Forty two small churches and chapels of different styles were added to the original Bernardine Monastery and Church to accommodate pilgrims who have been coming to the site ever since.

The royal patronage was emanating from Warsaw, the new capital of the Commonwealth. The King's residence at the Castle was reconstructed under the supervision of Trevano and architects Giacomo Rotondo and Matteo Castelli between 1596 and 1619. Three new wings, each three storeys high, two small towers, and a decorative clock tower with a beautifully shaped dome were added to house the royal court and Sejm halls. The interiors, displaying coffered ceilings with polychrome beams, multi-colored marbles from Flanders, and oak floors, were richly decorated with paintings by the royal painter Tommaso Dolabella, arrases from the Low Countries, and Oriental carpets. A permanent opera and an orchestra performed in the Castle, and during the reign of Władysław IV a theatre hall was built in the south wing, where plays of Shakespeare were staged. The

Vasas owned splendid collections of art, including paintings by Rubens, his disciple Pieter Claes van Soutman, and Rembrandt, of sculpture, gold, and amber.

In the square outside the Castle, a column of red marble with a statue of King Zygmunt, designed by Constantino Tencalla, sculpted by Clemente Molli, and cast by Daniel Tym, was erected in 1644. A suburban palace for King Zygmunt was built by Trevano in a beautiful garden in Ujazdów between 1619 and 1625. A square building with four towers and a loggia looking down towards the Vistula, the palace of Ujazdów served as a model for magnates eager to imitate the court architecture, for example, in Voivode Denhoff's residence in Kruszyna (1630), which had only two towers, and Lubomirski's castle in Łańcut (1629-1641), designed by an Italian architect Matteo Trapola.

The most representative and sumptuous royal Baroque residence was erected for King Jan Sobieski in Wilanów near Warsaw. Built in stages between 1677 and 1696 by Agostino Locci and several groups of artists, painters, and decorators, the palace grew to resemble a Roman villa, surrounded by the Italian-French gardens laid out with fountains, grottos, and courtyards. The exterior was embellished with medallions, allegorical figures, busts of the Roman consuls and emperors, and statues of ancient deities, while the symmetrically arranged interior was lavishly decorated with plafonds, fresco paintings, and fabrics made of damask, silk, and satin.

The magnates throughout Poland competed with the kings. The monumental castle Krzyżtopór in Ujazd, built for Krzysztof Ossoliński by the Italian architect Lorenzo Senes in the style *palazzo in fortezza* between 1627 and 1644, had several courtyards surrounded by massive star-shaped fortifications. Inside, the palace had 365 windows, fifty two rooms, twelve grand halls, and four towers, to represent the days, weeks, months, and seasons of the year. Captured, looted, and destroyed by the Swedes between 1655 and 1657, it has never been restored.

The castle in Wiśnicz, originally the seat of the Kmita family, was rebuilt between 1615 and 1621 for Stanisław Lubomirski, the Voivode of Cracow. The work was carried out under the supervision of Matteo Trapola, who designed new bastion fortifications, an arcaded courtyard with a loggia, a tower, and a chapel. He also designed on a nearby hill the fortified church and monastery of the Carmelites. The Bishops' Palace in Kielce, with elaborately painted ceilings, and the summer residence of Grand

Introduction

Hetman Stanisław Koniecpolski in Podhorce, an original design of two eminent military architects, Andrea dell'Aqua, an artillery theoretician, and Guilleaume Levasseur de Beauplan, who was also a prominent cartographer, were other magnificent buildings attesting to the wealth and taste of aristocratic patrons.

The new style of Baroque architecture was most evident in the capital city of Warsaw. The Dutch architect Tylman of Gameren designed the palace of the Krasiński family. Adorned with sculptures by Andrzej Schlueter from Gdańsk and frescoes by Michelangelo Palloni, the palace became recognized as the most splendid Warsaw residence in the mature Baroque style. Tylman of Gameren built a small palace and a commercial building for Queen Maria Sobieska, and to commemorate the King's victory at Vienna the Church of the Nuns of the Holy Sacrament, a symbolical structure in the form of a Greek cross joined to an octagon. He also designed Saint Anne's Church in Cracow, known for its simple exterior and lavish stuccoed interiors by Baltasare Fontana, and the Branicki Palace in Białystok, with curved colonnades and spacious courtyards.

Sculptures that profusely decorated churches, castles, and palaces were made out of stucco, stone or black marble from Dębnik near Cracow. Particularly popular was stucco, a flexible material allowing the artist to quickly fashion allegorical forms and elaborate patterns of vegetation. The art of stucco sculpture was propagated by Giovanni Falconi who decorated the Cracow churches of Saint Anne and of Saint Peter and Saint Paul with dynamic human figures, expressive statues of angels, and luxuriant garlands of fruits and flowers. Italian artists Pietro Perti and Giovanni Galli adorned many churches of Wilno and Lwów with thousands of majestic figures of saints draped in refined costumes and with lavish floral decorations. Schlueter, who worked for King Jan Sobieski in Wilanów, became known for the ubiquitous *putti* and for classical stone figures and reliefs which graced the facade of the Krasiński Palace in Warsaw. Sebastian Sala, who perfected the art of funeral sculpture, used marble for his distinct sepulchers and busts of magnates and bishops in churches and cathedrals of Sieraków, Rzeszów, Gniezno, and Cracow. The most consummate examples of the art of casting were the silver coffins of Saint Adalbert in Gniezno Cathedral and of Saint Stanisław in Cracow Cathedral, both made by Peter van der Rennen from Gdańsk, and the bronze door in the cathedral of Cracow, by Michał Weinhold.

Closely related to sarcophagal sculptures were Sarmatian coffin portraits. These realistic pictures of men and women, children and old people, magnates and nobles, were painted on tin or wood and usually attached to the coffins to honor the deceased. Some of these mostly hexagonal or octagonal portraits, of which about one thousand have been preserved, were hung on the church walls, while others, painted on silk fabrics, were kept at home.

The art of portraiture was extremely popular. Baroque painters recorded a veritable gallery of the nobles who sat for them, displaying their wealth and prominence. Herman Han and Bartłomiej Strobel, who were influenced by Dutch and Flemish art, painted portraits of abbots, burghers, and magnates in Pomerania and in other parts of Poland. Adolf Boy and Daniel Schultz from Gdańsk painted kings, queens, and prominent magnates, for example King Jan Kazimierz and Prince Bogusław Radziwiłł. Some of these paintings were engraved and printed in large numbers by Wilhelm Hondius, an eminent graphic artist and cartographer who settled in Gdańsk in 1636, and by Jeremiasz Falck, a portraitist and engraver.

The generous patronage of Jan Sobieski, whose intention was to establish an academy of painting in Wilanów, attracted eminent artists. Michelangelo Palloni executed narrative mythological frescoes, such as *The History of Amor and Psyche*, and religious pictures in the galleries of the palace, while Martino Altomonte painted battle canvases, among them *The Rescue of Vienna*, and religious scenes. Jerzy Eleuter Siemiginowski, a court painter of Jan Sobieski, who drew the King and his family in classical Roman poses, was the author of colorful frescoes, most notably of four plafonds representing the seasons, some filled with dramatic scenes, others with peaceful landscapes. Jan Reisner composed allegorical scenes, for example in his *Dawn*, while other painters glorified heroic deeds of the victorious King.

Warsaw also became the musical center of Poland. Many Italian composers, to mention only Luca Marenzio and Annibale Stabile, were brought to the court of King Zygmunt to write music for the royal orchestra, which was directed by Asprilio Pacelli and Marco Scacchi, later by Bartłomiej Pękiel and Jacek Różycki. Adam Jarzębski, a poet and violinist, wrote for the royal musicians *Canzoni e Concerti*, original compositions for three and four voices. Marcin Mielczewski, who was a member of King Władysław's orchestra, composed instrumental *Canzoni* and church concerts, e.g., *Triumphalis dies* and *Deus in nomine tuo*, the most representative types of Polish Baroque music. Bartłomiej Pękiel, considered by many the most outstanding composer of the period, was the author of two monumental masses, *Audite mortales*, an oratorio on the Last Judgment, and *Missa pulcherrima*, a mass *a capella*.

Musical life flourished in cathedrals, collegiate churches, and monasteries, of which the orchestra of the chapel at the Wawel Cathedral, conducted by Grzegorz Gorczycki, and of the Primate in Łowicz were best known. Choirs were founded at churches and schools, music was played during religious and secular ceremonies. Many noblemen supported their own companies of musicians. Stanisław Lubomirski had his own opera theatre in Wiśnicz, while Krzysztof Radziwiłł and Janusz Tyszkiewicz maintained their music ensembles in Wilno, in a characteristic display of the noblemen's interest in the arts.

LITERARY BACKGROUND

The natural simplicity of Renaissance literature and its balance between content and form were gradually abandoned in the seventeenth century. Inspired by the visual arts and literary models from Italy, contemporary writers dispensed with the rigors of structure, introduced a variety of styles, and freely combined various genres. They often used elaborate language and fashioned sophisticated poetic figures, taking delight in complex metaphors, contrasts, and enumerations. Some poets, overly concerned with the refined form of expression, paid less attention to the intellectual content of their works.

The language which they had at their disposal was the mature vernacular. Latin was still used by poets, for example, by Maciej Sarbiewski, and prose writers, such as Starowolski and Kochowski, especially in historical works. Many writers indulged in 'macaronism,' a popular fashion which gradually turned into a mannerism, as they used Latin words and phrases to embellish the pages of their Polish texts, especially in memoirs and treatises. Yet even though Latin was taught at schools and understood by many educated people, the role of the native tongue, strengthened by the Reformation, became dominant.

Middle Polish was a refined instrument in the poet's hand. Not unlike English, which combined the speech of the Anglo-Saxons with diverse outside influences, mostly in the form of lexical borrowings, Polish kept adding to its Slavic core a variety of foreign loans. It absorbed many Latin words, for example, *klasa* 'class'; *dedykacyja*, 'dedication'; *frukt* 'fruit'; French *kadet* 'cadet'; *dama* 'dame'; *biżuteria* 'jewelry'; and Italian *aria, balet,* and *opera*. In constant contact with the Ruthenian and Ukrainian languages, which it enriched with many words, Polish borrowed from them, e.g., *bohater* 'hero'; *druh* 'friend'; and *sioło* 'village'. Military engagements with Tartary and Turkey brought other borrowings, to mention only *karabela* 'curved sword'; *kindżał* 'double-edged dagger'; and *kulbaka* 'saddle'.

In morphology, instead of three types of noun declensions, a distinction was established between the plural virile nouns (e.g., *ci synowie* 'these sons'), and the remaining nouns (e.g., *te dziewczyny*, 'these girls', *te koty* 'these cats', *te domy* 'these houses'). The dual form of the nouns and the old conditional forms of the verb gradually disappeared. At the beginning of the eighteenth century, the lexical, morphological, and syntactic structure of Middle Polish took a form which was not much different from the Polish of today.

The breakdown of a uniform philosophy, caused by the Reformation and the Counter Reformation, brought about a conflict between the values of this world and those of the spiritual one. Baroque poets coped with a dramatic distinction between the visible and invisible world, attempting to determine man's choice and course in life. The themes of impermanence of our existence, of death, corrupt body, and sin were intermingled with the themes of splendors of the world and its pleasures, mostly of love, both profane and sacred, and presented in a series of ingenious contradictions.

Intense religious polemics continued to provide a creative impulse to Baroque poets and prose writers. Many of them, following Sęp Szarzyński and Sebastian Grabowiecki, grappled with profound religious questions. The conflict between antiquity and the spirit of Christianity became the main topic of Maciej Sarbiewski's Latin poetry. His interpretations and paraphrases of Horace's *Odes*, which brought him international popularity as a "Christian Horace," dealt with the divine presence manifested in the beauty of nature and with human yearnings for union with God. Sarbiewski extolled the happiness of monastic life, while in his patriotic songs he glorified his native Mazovia and his country.

Religious and patriotic themes were also dominant in the poems of Wespazjan Kochowski, who considered himself above all a propagator of faith. A soldier, poet, and historian who could write in a down to earth language as well as in an elaborate style, Kochowski felt that his role was to record historical events, inspire, and teach. His major work, *A Polish Psalmody*, written in melodious biblical prose, dealt with the central question posed by metaphysical poetry, namely the meaning of human existence. Some of the psalms propagated Sarmatian beliefs about the unique role of the Polish nation.

Recurrent themes of man's constant struggle on this earth and of the redeeming power of pious love found expression in Zbigniew Morsztyn's cycle of *Emblems,* modelled on Latin, Spanish, and French paraphrases of the *Song of Songs.* A prevailing motif of these devotional poems was a love dialogue between the Bride and the Bridegroom. Biblical inspiration permeated the lyrical poetry of Stanisław Lubomirski, author of the *Poems of Lent,* who made verse adaptations of Ecclesiastes, and who paraphrased in twelve songs the books of Tobias, presenting the story of a young Tobias as a historical romance.

Many seventeenth century poets and prose writers followed in the footsteps of medieval annalists and chroniclers, showing a lively interest in history. The artistic stimulus was provided by Piotr Kochanowski's translation of Tasso's *Jerusalem Delivered*, which for many years served as a model and best representation of the epic poem in Polish literature. This story of Christian heroism during the first crusade (1096-1099) found a receptive audience in Poland, engaged in the protracted war with Turkey. The glorious military deeds of the Polish soldiers were faithfully recorded and extolled in poetry and prose.

It was the diary of Jakub Sobieski, a leading participant in the war against Turkey and father of King Jan Sobieski, which Wacław Potocki used in his *War of Chocim* to recreate the historical background, describe the progress of events, and recount the victory of the Polish army under Hetman Jan Chodkiewicz in the battle of 1621. Writing "for the immortal glory of the Polish nation," Potocki contrasted in his epic narrative heroic scenes from the battle of Chocim with satirical descriptions of his

IV. The Column of Zygmunt III (1644) and the Royal Castle in Warsaw

effeminate contemporaries, moralizing about the harmful influence of the noblemen of privilege on the state of the republic.

The wars with Muscovy and Sweden found a perceptive chronicler in Samuel Twardowski, who wrote also about his journey to Turkey. His long narrative *The Civil War with the Cossacks and Tartars, Muscovy, Afterwards With Sweden and Hungary* combined vivid scenes based on eye-witness accounts with numerous facts and documents pertaining specially to the embattled south-eastern regions of Poland during the Chmielnicki uprising. Kochowski's four volumes of Latin *Annales Poloniae*, dedicated to King Jan Sobieski, covered the same events during the reigns of King Jan Kazimierz and King Michał Wiśniowiecki. Szymon Starowolski described in *The Perfect Knight* the ideal Christian soldier who selflessly serves his country, defends the faith, and strives for moral uprightness, while in his *Sarmatian Warriors* he portrayed brave kings and military commanders from Poland's past. Hetman Stanisław Żółkiewski, one of the valiant generals described by Starowolski, was the author of the memoirs entitled *Beginning and Progress of the Muscovy War*, a succinct description of his campaigns and diplomatic activity. In his voluminous correspondence to his wife, Jan Sobieski recounted major events and political developments from the period between 1665 and 1683.

Military activities of the average nobleman also became a subject of literary interest. Participants of war campaigns transformed their experiences and reminiscences into poems or recorded them in diaries and memoirs. Zbigniew Morsztyn, who fought in the Cossack and Swedish wars and was imprisoned by the Swedes, wrote a plaintive *Song of Captivity*, as well as the epitaph for Paweł Morsztyn, killed in the 1652 battle at Batoh. The same battle, in which the Polish troops were defeated by Tartars and Cossacks, inspired Kochowski to commemorate his fallen comrades in a moving poem *A Monument to the Brave Soldiers*. All these works strengthened the Sarmatian spirit of patriotism, piety, and heroism.

The most vivid and revealing description of the soldier's lot, indeed of the common nobleman's life in that period, was compiled by Jan Pasek in his *Memoirs*. A lively self-portrait of a garrulous and headstrong man showed Pasek with sword in hand during a victorious campaign under the famous commander Stefan Czarniecki against the Swedish troops in Denmark, then enjoying domestic life, then as a participant in rowdy activities at social functions and public assemblies.

Political life was treated frequently, although not profoundly, in literature. A spirit of reform, carried over from the sixteenth century, found expression in a series of treatises by Starowolski, who criticized in *Reform of Polish Customs* the shortcomings of public life and sounded the tone of patriotic alarm in his poetic homily *Lament of the Distressed Mother, the Polish Crown*. Łukasz Opaliński called in *A Conversation Between a Parson and a Country-squire* for drastic changes of the government, most urgently for the strengthening of the royal power and for regulation of the workings of the Sejm. His brother Krzysztof Opaliński, author of a collection of fifty vituperative *Satires,* mixed indignant judgments of society with keen observations and warnings concerning Poland's political and economic future.

The different types of seventeenth century literature were displayed in a variety of genres and styles. Next to the popular epic poem, the romance, mostly of French origin, became fashionable at the Court and among the aristocracy. Twardowski's *Daphne Changed Into a Laurel Tree*, its theme taken from mythology, and *Fair Pasqualina*, a poem of adventure paraphrased from the Spanish, as well as Lubomirski's comedy *Ermida or The Shepherdess Princess*, were the best known adaptations. The drama, which in its classical variety was practiced in the Jesuit and Protestant school theatres, was staged mostly in the form of comic interludes, as for example, the amusing story of *Peasant Into King* by Piotr Baryka, and during liturgical celebrations, most often showing Christ's birth and death.

The growth of poetic forms was best manifested in the development of the epigram, which was modelled on Kochanowski's *Trifles*. These short occasional poems, descriptive or satirical, melancholy or humorous, written by erudite poets and rhymesters, provide a valuable source of information about public events and local incidents, about people of various ranks and their daily affairs. Some of these trifles were mere anecdotes, others, in the fashion of popular coffin portraits, took the form of epitaphs extolling virtues of the deceased. Potocki's two anthologies, *Moralia* and *A Garden of Trifles*, varied in style and tone, contained thousands of spontaneous poems revealing with vividness and realism the country life and customs of the gentry. Similar vignettes were drawn by Kochowski, the author of *Polish*

Epigrams, and by Hieronim Morsztyn in his *Compendium*. Equally popular were the collections of poetry and diaries kept by many noblemen in their homes. These private anthologies, called *Silva rerum,* contained memoirs, documents, and poetic texts, preserved by the families and read for pleasure. Even more common were the texts of medieval tradition circulated by vagrants and itinerant actors. These satires and parodies mocked the moral norms and served to entertain the lower classes.

It was, however, the court poems of Jan Andrzej Morsztyn that exemplified best the poetic art of the mature Baroque. A translator of Giambattista Marino's poems praising worldly pleasures and Corneille's *Le Cid*, Morsztyn excelled as a poet of love and moral subtleties, to a great degree because of his virtuosity of language and masterly technique. His intricate verses, filled with color and light, were embellished with flowery ornamentations and elaborate metaphors.

Morsztyn often employed a conceit--a figure of speech which establishes a striking parallel between two apparently dissimilar things or situations. In the sonnet *To a Corpse*, a dramatic monologue addressed to the dead, a complaining lover compares and contrasts death and love. He describes physical facts and inner turmoil. The dead is immune to any sensations, while the narrator suffers profound spiritual and psychological pain. The bold conceit serves to exaggerate the misfortunes, suggesting that it is better to be dead than to suffer from the pangs of unrequited love.

Another sonnet, *The Wonders of Love* is a story of a gradual dependence on deceptive emotions, which are inflamed by increasingly stronger passions. The narrator becomes unable to satisfy his desires, as he finds himself emotionally starved. But it is when he turns to his beloved and begins to sing her beauty, as he does in the lines *To the Same Lady*, that the poet composes with flair the intricate verses of Baroque court poetry:

Your eyes are not eyes, but suns that shine bright,
    In whose glow all reason must lose its light;
Your lips are not lips, but rosy coral,
    Which capture every sense by their color;
5   Your breasts are not breasts, but a pure design
    From heaven, which our will in chains confine;
Thus the eyes, breasts, lips blind, bind, and confine
    Reason, sense, will with glow, color, design.

STANISŁAW ŻÓŁKIEWSKI (1547-1620)

Stanisław Żółkiewski, an ancestor to King Jan Sobieski, was born into a magnate family near Lwów. He attended schools in Lwów, was well read, and spoke foreign languages. He was secretary to King Batory and took part in many military operations, both in Poland and on its eastern borders. In 1610, in the battle of Klushino, Żółkiewski defeated the Muscovite army. He entered Moscow, which for more than two years remained in the hands of the Polish garrison. In 1612 and in 1617, Żółkiewski commanded military campaigns in Rumania and in the Ukraine. In 1618 he became Chancellor of the Crown. In 1620, at Cecora, in a battle against a Turkish army, Żółkiewski was surrounded by the overwhelming forces of the enemy and killed. His heroic death gave rise to a veritable legend about the Christian knight slain by the pagans in defense of the Holy Faith.

Żółkiewski's left behind letters and *Testament*. His anonymous memoir entitled *Beginning and Progress of the Muscovy War*, written in the third person, is a concise account of a major event in the history of Poland and Muscovy.

Beginning and Progress of the Muscovy War
During the Reign of His Grace King Zygmunt III
Under the Command of Sir Stanisław Żółkiewski,
Voivode of Kiev and Field Hetman of the Crown[1]
(selection)

When, as already has been mentioned, the Hetman learned from the captives as well as from the Frenchmen that the enemy army was approaching, he summoned all the knights to council. There he presented the reports that the enemy army was only four miles away from Klushino, and asked whether it would be better to leave part of our army besieging the fort, break through, and meet the enemy on the field or to wait for him where we were.

As usual, opinions varied. For some, looking at the small size of our army, with not much to divide, believed that if we divided further our small force we could be easily defeated by the enemy; that after the departure of our army, those in the fort seeing that our camp *praesidium*[2] was weak, could attack us. There were, however, not a few who suggested that the camp should be fortified as well as possible and the army should meet the enemy on the field; for if allowed to come close, they would be able to press us hard from field-works without giving battle, as they had done at Aleksandrova Sloboda, at Troitsa, at Dimitrov, to deprive us of food, and to defeat us easily without resorting to arms.

The Hetman, not declaring for either side, took time for further reflection. He ordered, however, that they should be ready for the command to set off. For although he had already decided to meet the enemy on the field, he put off revealing it as much as he could, lest some traitor (and he most particularly watched out for the Muscovites, who were quite numerous in the camp) noticed and informed Prince Shuyski's army and Voluyev.[3] It was only one hour before the army set out, when without sounding of trumpets or beating of drums he sent out ordinances that the army should move off in the order which had been sent out to the colonels in writing; for from the beating of the drums Voluyev would have quickly understood that we were setting out.

Out of all those who were *in conspectu*[4] of the fort, nobody moved, taking care not to reveal the plan to the enemy. The Hetman left Jakób Bobowski, the cavalry captain, seven hundred horse, what there was of the royal infantry, and two regiments of Cossacks, committing to his command the camp and the siege of the fort. Two hours before the sunset, the Hetman himself set out to battle with his army *silenti agmine*.[5] At this time the nights are very short. We covered during the whole night those four miles of woods. The road was not good. We came upon the enemy army, however, still before dawn. Because of the smallness of our forces, the enemy took us lightly and expected even less that we would be bold enough to challenge such a great power; indeed, they hoped we would flee, not waiting at Tsarovo. In the evening, Pontus[6] boasted at a banquet given by Prince Dimitri Shuyski (he was getting money, for on that day they were paid three hundred and fifty thousand zloties), recalling: "When I was taken prisoner at Volmar with Charles's army, the Hetman gave me a lynx fur. Now I have a sable fur for him, which I will offer him," as he was hoping to capture the Hetman.

As they were taking us lightly, they were not on their guard. We came upon them asleep. If our whole army closed in, we would have roused them unclothed, but we could not have gotten out from those woods fast enough. The Hetman took with him two cannons, but they blocked the way so that the army could not move ahead. There was another obstacle which prevented us from attacking them at once. Across the whole field leading to the enemy camp there were hedges, and between those hedges lay two villages. It was therefore necessary to wait for the arrival of the army and to break the hedges. The Hetman, fearing that the enemy might have put some of his many musketeers in the villages, which were located in the middle of the field so that they could punish us from behind the hedges, ordered the villages to be set on fire. It was only then that the enemy realized what was happening. However, the Muscovites and foreign soldiers, not knowing the reason for this delay, ascribed it to the magnanimity of the Hetman, who capable of striking at them while they were asleep did not want to do it but gave them a warning that it was time to prepare themselves. Yet if not for the reasons mentioned above, they would probably not have experienced that delay.

Meanwhile, before our other forces came up, Zborowski's regiment, which was in the vanguard, stood in battle order on the right wing. Next came the regiment of Struś, Starost of Chmielnik, which stood on the left wing. The regiment of Kaznowski and Ludwik Wajher, commanded by Samuel Dunikowski, stood in flank and reserve positions of the right wing; the regiment of the Hetman, commanded by Prince Janusz Porycki, on the left wing, also in flank and reserve positions. In broken formation *propter omnes casus*[7] stood some troops, as if in the middle. The Hetman himself kept watch here and there. There were also some four hundred Cossacks *levis armaturae*.[8] They were called the Pohrebiszczans, as they came from Pohrebiszcze, the property of the princes of Zbaraż, forming the majority of the group; they were commanded by Piaskowski. The Hetman ordered them to stand by the woods, as it were on the flank of the left wing. Those two cannons and the Hetman's infantry regiment had not yet arrived.

When the army stood in battle order, the Hetman rode from troop to troop, heartened his men, pointing out that *necessi-*

tas in loco, spes in virtute, salus in victoria,⁹ and ordered them to beat the drums and sound the trumpets for battle.

The enemy had also stood in battle order. The foreign Swedish force which claimed the count and payment for ten thousand horsemen and foot soldiers, but most probably amounted to over eight thousand, stood on the right; the Moscow army, which as Prince Dimitri Shuyski himself said was more than forty thousand horse and foot soldiers strong, took the left.

As already mentioned, the hedge between us was long. There were, however, gaps in it so that when we attacked, we had to move through them. That hedge was a big obstacle to us, for Pontus put there his infantry which inflicted losses on our men as they were moving forward and back through the gaps. The battle lasted a long time because both our men and their troops, particularly the foreigners, fought hard. Our men, who came against Muscovite troops, had the easier task, because the latter did not withstand the charge, began to flee, our men pursuing them. At this time, the cannons arrived with some infantry and helped a lot in the battle. For the gunners shot from the cannons at the German infantrymen standing by the hedge and our infantrymen, though not numerous but experienced and tried in many battles, sprang to the attack and at once several Germans fell down, hit by the cannons or muskets. The Germans shot back, killing two or three of the Hetman's men. But seeing that our men were coming at them with determination, the Germans began to escape from the hedge to the woods, not far away. The French and English cavalrymen, taking courage, clashed with our troops in the field. But when all these German foot soldiers who stood by the hedge in our way were gone, our cavalry troops gathered together and charged at the foreign cavalry with pikes, those who still had them, with sabers, and rapiers. *Destituti praesidio*¹⁰ of the Muscovites and of that infantry, they were unable to resist and began to flee towards their camp. But our troops rode after them there as well, and hitting and slashing, chased them through their own camp. At that point Pontus and Horn¹¹ escaped. There still remained three thousand or more of the foreigners. They stood on the edge of the woods. The Hetman began to think what stratagem to use. But the foreigners had no leaders and saw that the Muscovites escaped, even though some of them still remained in the palisaded village near Prince Dimitri's camp, the Prince himself being there. Wishing to save their lives they sent to the Hetman asking for negotiations. The Hetman also seeing the difficulties, as it would not be easy to push them away from the woods, consented. It was decided that they would surrender voluntarily. Most of them promised *addicere stipendiis*[12] of His Majesty, and all pledged and confirmed through the chief captains, later in writing, that they would never serve in the Muscovite army against His Majesty. The Hetman also promised to preserve them in health and property and to obtain from His Majesty a safe conduct to their homeland for those who did not wish to serve.

Interim[13] when these negotiations were going on, Prince Andrei Galitzin and Prince Danilo Mezecki,[14] who had fled from the battlefield to the woods, hastened back with three hundred horse in a roundabout way so that our men could not stop them to that palisaded village, in which, as already mentioned, Prince Dimitri himself still remained. Both Pontus and Horn also returned with them. And indeed Pontus would have gladly broken the agreement, but the soldiers firmly supported it. Prince Dimitri and Prince Galitzin, seeing (because it was *in conspectu*[15]) that the foreigners were negotiating with the Hetman, began to escape swiftly through the back of the village and across the camp, which was beyond the village, towards the woods. They spread around in full view the most valuable things: cups, silver goblets, robes, sable furs. Our men rushed to pursue them, but few continued the chase. They fell on the spoils in the camp, for the Muscovites had done this to detract our men from giving chase. When we advanced against the enemy, we had only cannons and the carriage of the Hetman himself; coming back, the carts and coaches almost outnumbered us. The Muscovite coaches stood harnessed and our men had only to load them with spoils and drive off. Many of them, however, were bogged down in the awful forest and our cavalry could barely pass by them. The Hetman, fearing that in his absence the camp might be in some danger from Voluyev, made haste and returned there on the same day.

Prince Dimitri, although he was pursued by few, fled headlong. In the swamp, he lost his horse and his boots. He rode back barefoot on a wretched peasant nag to a monastery near Mozhaysk. There he got a horse and boots, and without delay rode on to Moscow. He told the people of Mozhaysk, who had come to him, to beg compassion and mercy of the victor since they had no means of defending themselves. So they sent to the Hetman in their own name and in the name of several other castles--Borisov, Verega, and Ruza--offering their allegiance.

This battle took place on July fourth. Close to twelve hundred foreigners perished, most Muscovites were killed while pursued in various places. Our men were not without losses, either. Captain Lanckoroński lost his life, so did more than one hundred of his comrades, not counting pages and stagecoach horses. Excluding those who recovered, more than four hundred men were killed.

Notes

1. The Field Hetman of the Crown was the second highest rank, after the Grand Hetman of the Crown, in the armed forces of the Kingdom of Poland.
2. *praesidium*--'defense, garrison.'
3. Prince Shuyski-Skopin, military leader, was a cousin of Tsar Vasili Shuyski. Grigor Voluyev, Muscovite military leader, surrendered to Żółkiewski after the battle of Klushino.
4. *in conspectu*--'in sight of.'
5. *silenti agmine*--'in a silent march.'
6. Jacob Pontus de la Gardie, son of a French nobleman who entered the service of King Charles of Sweden, fought in the Swedish-Polish war in Livonia. He was captured at Volmar in 1601 and spent four years in Polish captivity. He commanded later the Swedish army sent to Russia to fight against Poland.
7. *propter omnes casus*--'against all eventualities.'
8. *levis armaturae*--'lightly armed.'
9. 'necessity of battle dictated by position, hope in valour, salvation in victory.' (Tacitus, *Annales*, 2, 20)
10. *destituti praesidio*--'deprived of the protection.'
11. Evert Karlsson Horn, Swedish general, second in command to Jacob Pontus de la Gardie in his Russian campaign.
12. *addicere stipendiis*--'join the army.'
13. *interim*--'at that time.'
14. Andrei Galitzin and Danilo Mezecki were Muscovite statesmen and military leaders.
15. *in conspectu*--'in sight.'

Stanisław Żółkiewski

Text: Żółkiewski, Stanisław. *Początek i progres wojny moskiewskiej*. Ed. by Wacław Sobieski. Kraków: Krakowska Spółka Wydawnicza, Biblioteka Narodowa I 12, 1925, 38-44.

PIOTR KOCHANOWSKI (1566-1620)

Piotr Kochanowski, nephew of Jan Kochanowski, spent his youth at the courts of magnates. In 1583, a year after his father's death, he entered the University in Königsberg, where he studied until 1586. From 1588 to 1594 Kochanowski studied in Padua, and later spent long periods of time in Rome, Naples, and Abano. In 1602, Kochanowski became a royal secretary, carrying out various official duties until 1607. In 1615 he settled in Cracow, where he worked on his translations of Ariosto's *Orlando Furioso* and Tasso's *Jerusalem Delivered*, supported by Jan Tęczyński, his patron and later the Voivode of Cracow.

Published in 1618, eighteen years after a controversial English translation by Edward Fairfax, Kochanowski's *Jerusalem Delivered* was quickly recognized as a masterpiece of Polish epic poetry.

Torquatto Tasso
Gofred or Jerusalem Delivered
Translated by Piotr Kochanowski
(selections)

Third Song

1

    A soft breeze blowing at the break of day
    Was a sign to all that Dawn just arose,
    She would meanwhile her golden locks array
    In a garland embellished with a rose.
5   All knights eagerly their armors display
    As they get ready, when a big horn blows;
    Clamorous drums resound time and again
    And troops are ordered to start their campaign.

2

    The prudent hetman knows how to command,
10 He puts gentle rein on their eagerness:
    Easier rash Vistula to keep in hand,

GOFFRED
ABO
IERVZALEM
WYZWOLONA
TORQVATA TASSA.

Przekładánia
PIOTRA KOCHANOWSKIEGO
Sekretarzá Ie° K. M.

Cum Gratia & Priuilegio S. R. M.

W KRAKOWIE,
W Drukárni Fránćiszká Cezárego /
Roku Páńskiego / 1618.

V. Title page of *Gofred or Jerusalem Delivered*

When it gathers its waters in excess,
Easier to down the wind, its force make bland,
When it strips Carpathians of high forests.
15   He lines them up as they move on their way,
He forms the units and makes his survey.

3

They ride so fast that they had a feeling
As if wings were attached to their shoulders;
The sun by then close to the noon would cling,
20   The hottest moment of the day's progress,
When the holy city appeared therein,
Not farther off than a mile to traverse.
All the knights burst out into joyful cries,
On longed for Jerusalem cast their eyes.

4

25   So would seasoned sailors usually do,
Who for long days through the waves of the shoals,
Under stars unknown here and there sailed through,
Into the shifting turns of violent squalls--
When at the end, poor souls, would clearly view
30   The beloved homeland and the longed for halls,
And one to the other shows the shore's lanes,
Not feeling any more their earlier pains.

5

As joy and hope of future happiness
Was growing up steadily in their hearts,
35   Repentance full of sacred humbleness
Entered then among other devout parts.
No doubt that it was brought by forgiveness
Of the Holy Spirit to their hard hearts:
The eyes filled with tears do not dare to look
40   At the place where Christ mortal wounds partook.

6

    Muffled sighs and words that were suspended,
    Tears and sobbing only were heard in the air,
    Those people whose hearts are deeply troubled
    Will often do it--and soon shed despair.
45 Such noise is made by a forest disturbed
    By slow winds or when a calm sea lays bare
    With dispatch brine waves pushed back furthermost
    Either from a shoal rock or from a coast.

Text: Kochanowski, Piotr, Torquato Tasso. *Gofred abo Jeruzalem wyzwolona*. Ed. by Stanisław Grzeszczuk. Notes by Roman Pollak. Warszawa: PIW, 1968, 115-117.

JAN ŻABCZYC (d. after 1629)

Little is known about Żabczyc, whose works were published anonymously and ascribed to other poets. He was born to a burgher's family, served at court, and settled in Cracow. He was the author of a compendium of proverbs and aphorisms, entitled *The Court Ethics* (1615) and *The Eternal Calendar.* His *Angelic Symphonies* (1630), a collection of popular Christmas carols, combine religious poetry with simple songs. They contain many realistic details from the life of Polish peasants celebrating the miracle of the Nativity.

Angelic Symphonies

Twentieth Symphony

"Why, why, why, why do you lie poor,
My Savior?" "Are you not yet of this sure
That I descended from heaven hither,
Seeing that you must be saved instanter?"

5   "Why, why, Lord, do you lie undressed?"
"Then why don't you run to clothe me in haste;
When you look at me, the Lord who is bare,
To suffer want willingly now prepare."

"Why, why do you lie in the barn?"
10   "So I could take a lost sheep on my arm,
Bring the miserable soul to my flock,
Ugly sins at once uproot with their stock."

"Why, why are you in the manger?"
"So that you could soon be led to Father
15   From this vale of tears and misery,
And enjoyed with me a golden century,

Became too a prince in heaven,
An heir in my beloved Father's Garden,
Sinners, why do you fail to follow suit,
20   If you want to join God in your pursuit?"

VI. Wilanów Palace

"We will follow You willingly,
We give promise to serve You faithfully,
Only set us free from our privation,
When this poor world nears its expiration."

Thirty Fourth Symphony

Why is Herod killing the innocents
And trying to end Christ's life in torments?
Because he liked the *sceptrum* and the crown,
He did not want them to be handed down.

5   A new king in the land he could not bear,
When he found out that He was born somewhere,
For the other kings were leading the way
To offer Him gifts and wishing Him say

That on His Father's throne He would sit down,
10   The son of David in the golden crown,
And that the scepter of the Jewish land
Would remain eternally in His hand.

Herod asked them to pay him a visit,
The three monarchs with their extensive suite,
15   He wished to greet them in Jerusalem,
When they were coming back from Bethlehem.

The enraged Herod is killing infants,
In vain poor mothers burst into laments,
Yet this evil king failed in all he strived,
20   He killed the infants, but Jesus survived.

For the angel told Joseph in his dream
To hurry to Egypt with the Virgin,
So as to escape the cruel warrant,
There Jesus waited for his last moment.

25   So the old man faithful to his Maker,
To protect Messiah the Redeemer
Of mankind, took Him to the far-off land,
In which he did not know a single man.

Text: Sokołowska Jadwiga and Kazimiera Żukowska. *Poeci polskiego baroku.* Vol. 1. Warszawa: PIW, 1965, 128-129, 137-138.

DANIEL NABOROWSKI (1573-1640)

Daniel Naborowski was born and educated in Cracow. He continued his studies in Wittemberg (1590-1593) and in Basle, where he studied medicine from 1593 to 1595. He also studied law in Orleans, worked in Strasbourg, and learned military engineering from Galileo in Padua. After returning from abroad in 1602, he served as secretary and physician at the court of Janusz Radziwiłł, a powerful magnate. As a diplomatic envoy of Radziwiłł, he travelled abroad frequently. After Radziwiłł's death, Naborowski continued his diplomatic career at the court of Krzysztof Radziwiłł. At the end of his life, he obtained the position of city judge in Wilno, where he died.

Naborowski's poems remained unpublished for a long time; the first full edition of his poetry appeared in 1961. A translator from many foreign languages, Naborowski wrote letters, trifles, epitaphs, and laments, praising in the last years of his life the charms of country life (*Votum*).

An Unexpected Response

"Cuckolded husbands ought to be drowned"--said a man,
His wife: "Time to learn to swim, my dear, you began."

A Bad Wife

Awful may be a storm at sea,
Awful floodwaters, flowing free,
Awful are the wild fire breezes,
Awful are the plague diseases,
5   Cureless poverty is painful,
But a bad wife is most dreadful.

Epitaph for Jan Kochanowski, Polish Poet

Here rests the one who rests, but do not pass judgment
By his grave, guest, but by his virtues' monument.

He is Phoebus's high priest,[1] whose poems profound,
Attest that no one equal to him has been found.

Notes

1. Phoebus (Apollo) was the god of poetry.

The Brevity of Life

An hour after hour inconceivably goes by:
A forebear lived, then you, now an heir came to life.
In brief: you won't be next day, what you are today,
And since you lived, they'll call you he who passed away;
5   Sound, shade, smoke, wind, flash, word[1]--that's what life is known for.
The sun which once passed by will not rise ever more,
Like a wheel with no brake fleeting time runs away,
Many who yearn for old age were thrown off astray.[2]
Just now when you are thinking, poor soul, you die out;
10 Between death and birth our life hardly marks about
A fourth of an instant; for many another
The cradle became a grave, a tomb their mother.

Notes

1. 'Word'--Naborowski speaks literally here about 'voice and point', i.e. vowels and consonants. The whole set phrase was used to show the quickly passing time.

2. Many people who plan to live long fall off the wheel of Fortune.

On the Same

   A day chases a day and later remains there,
From where eternal time no return will confer.
No day and hour comes about without harm to man,
Who also passes away with each day that ran.
5   Our life--food for an hour that will briefly sojourn;
Who dropped from the register will never return;

He will rest in deep sleep in the eternal night.
Keep it always in mind, o you man full of pride:
He lives twice, who while still alive prepares to die;
10   He dies twice, who believes that death he can defy.

Virtue Is the Root of Everything

Everything on earth is trifle, trifle throughout!
'Tis naught, your palace was at great cost laid about;
'Tis naught, lavish dishes are set on your table;
'Tis naught, gold, silver are piled under your gable;
5   'Tis naught, your wife is fair and of noble descent;
'Tis naught, by your side many grandchildren attend;
'Tis naught, your villages and large hamlets abound;
'Tis naught, that crowds of servants follow you around;
'Tis naught, that no one is just as intelligent;
10   'Tis naught, that everybody finds you most pleasant;
'Tis naught, that happiness stays always at your door;
'Tis naught, you become an abbot or a prior;
'Tis naught, though the crown of pope, emperor you wear;
'Tis naught, Fortune raised you o'er Great and Little Bear;
15   'Tis naught, if you rule a thousand years in good grace,
For all these things will pass and rate no worthy place.
Only virtue and glory, which from virtue flows,
Endures eternally and eternally glows.
He who lives by it is content, though he has naught,
20   Who dies without it has nothing from the whole lot.

To Ann

With time everything passes, with time years go by,
With time states come to naught, with time this world will die.
With time the wit slows down and mind starts to dither,
With time good looks, beauty, grace begin to wither.
5   With time meadows in blossom lose their loveliness,
With time the verdant trees turn out to be leafless.
With time squabbles subside, with time bloody struggles,
With time sorrow, too, and with time heartfelt troubles.
With time night gives way to day and day yields to night,
10 Everything in the world pays homage to time's might.

My true affection to you, o Ann, my dearest,
In contempt of time, will never come to a rest.

Votum[1]

Dear little huts[2] and the Wilia wading places,
You are now for me like magnificent cities,
When after my labors, after my frequent quests,
I have a chance to repose in your dense forests.
5   There, my dear thresholds will see, if God shall evoke,
Those riding boots, spurs, as well as the hanging cloak,
And what a traveller used on the pilgrimage.
Let no one call me more to go on long voyage,
Even if he gave me Indian treasures replete,
10 Even if he offered to me the Spanish fleet.
By God, how blind to reach four corners of the earth?
In toil, labor, and hardships to squander one's years,
Not to fear drudgery or piercing frostiness,
Nor of the violent sea great precariousness.
15 Happy who makes his living from a piece of land,
Three times happy he who with little is content.
From his meager household, though he is penniless,
He won't even turn away a dog, they attest,
He isn't deceived by the hope of unsure favor,
20 Nor does he, wretched man, spend his years in failure.
He is not terrified, his conscience free from slur,
Delighting more his Creator than his master,
He wasn't felled suddenly by a bloody weapon,
Nor overcome by an unexpected maelstrom,
25 But he departs from this world blessing his children,
And his wife closes down his eyes with her own hand.
His burial place is covered with a green barrow,
He rests forever in the underworld shadow.
O happy barrows; happy also these shadows
30 Which after we die, give to us so much repose.
If I still kept wandering widely everywhere,
And was taken by death on the road unaware,
Who would bury me then? Who for me, departed,
Would cry in foreign land by my grave ill-fated?
35 I bid you now farewell, Tatras, Alps, high and steep,

I bid you farewell forever, o mighty deep,
I bid you farewell vain but jealous offices,
Together with them, you courtly hypocrisies.
Let me sit in the shadow of the green oak grove,
40 Delighting in the tasks to the Muses we owe.
I will be learning of heavenly wisdom there,
Praise the Lord and Jesus forever everywhere,
What makes me pleasing to Him, and what redeems me,
How to tell the truth from an obscene falsity.
45 I have now brought to a close, o God, my order,
Permit me to live and die in my own corner.
My peaceful corner, I offer myself to you,
In you let me, old man of no use, find rest too,
You, until God wills it, provide me with good health,
50 You cover my dead body with a piece of earth.

Notes

1. *votum*-'promise', 'pledge'; here it means the poetic program.
2. Naborowski refers to his manor house Kiernów on the River Wilia.

Text: Naborowski, Daniel. *Poezje*. Ed. by Jan Dürr-Durski. Warszawa: PIW, 1961, 46, 59, 69, 158, 158-159, 166-167, 180-181, 185-186.

VII. Krasiński Palace in Warsaw, 1676-1689

HIERONIM MORSZTYN (ca. 1581-1623)

Not much is known about the life of Hieronim Morsztyn. Born in an Arian family and orphaned early, he was brought up by his uncle Samuel Łaski, royal secretary, and educated at the Jesuit college in Braniewo. He was also associated with the magnates' courts in Lublin and Wilno.

Morsztyn's major works are *Worldly Pleasure* (1606), *Matrimonial Appetisers* (1650), and *Compendium*, a collection of over three hundred poems, written between 1606 and 1613, but never published. In his trifles and songs, Morsztyn praised the beauty of the world, contrasting it with the burden of sin and with eternal bliss.

Non Licet Plus Efferre, Quam Intuleris[1]

Man comes to this world naked, in pain and in sin
His own mother bears him, for the woman's chagrin
He comes to this world with tears, he goes out with tears.
Brings nothing in or takes out when he disappears.
5   Want, trouble, sickness, winter and summer complaints,
These are of human life in the world the full gains.

Notes

1. 'You may take away no more than you brought in.' (Seneca, *Epistle*, 102, 25. In: *Seneca as Lucillum epistulae morales*. With an English Translation by Richard M. Gummere. 3 vols. Cambridge: Harvard University Library, The Loeb Classical Library, 1962.)

Time

All matters by time have been spanned,
I am living, death close at hand.
One in the boat, the other gone,
One is dead, the other is born.

5   A thrifty father's each owned thing
Through hands of generous offspring

Appears in the house of strangers;
One hoarded, the other squanders.

In no time will one have to die,
10   If death happens to be nearby.
And who in this world is able
This twisted knot to untangle?

All things have their limitations,
Whatever all the world's nations
15   May as their own possessions name,
Every thing the years will reclaim.

Mors Ultima Linea Rerum[1]

A clod of earth my castle, my room a sawed board,
My vault one foot deep, this is my underground ward,
A hard rock--a pillow, a rotten rag--outfit,
A worm is a servant--that's the whole world's profit.

Notes

    1. 'Death is the line that marks the end of all.' (Horace, *Epistles*, 1, 16, 79. In: *Satires, Epistles and Ars Poetica*. With an English Translation by H. Rushton Fairclough. Cambridge: Harvard University Press, The Loeb Classical Library, 1966).

Compendium

A Man

He is not a man who strives for a soldier's pay,
    Nor who stains his hands with blood a fool to repay.
Not he who has ample courage and great power,
    Nor he for whom life is not worth living longer.
5   Not he who tears ropes and breaks an iron horseshoe
        In his hands, not the one who can twist and wrench too

A steel nail or can stop a mill wheel in its gate
    Or who can break up with his forehead an oak plate.
Not the one who breaks with his head somebody's door,
10   Nor he who gulps down several gallons or more.
Not the one who manages with luck his duels,
    Nor in whose heart no fear of enemy dwells.
Not he whose arm is stronger or can withstand blows,
    Not he who can endure considerable woes.
15 But the one who bore bravely Fortune's punishment
    Or disappointments and who never underwent
Any change at all in good days or in distress,
    Him I call a man and thank for his manliness.

A Pleasant Counsel

Safer to lie with a girl 'neath a green tree crown,
    Playing a graceful lute, under an eiderdown,
Than to carry a sharp pointed spear and a shield
    Or have a heavy visor press your brow afield.

To Niemsta on His Third Marriage[1]

You get married a third time--she must be fearless,
    If she has ventured to become your third mistress.
Don't think of the fourth though you found a good market,
    Because both girls and women will be quite upset.
5 And with good reason, since the one who would wed you
    The fourth time, would be then saying to life adieu.
So spare the third, I advise, for if you lose her,
    You'll pay for this loss with idleness forever.

Notes

1. The poet refers probably to Jerzy Niemsta, judge from Zator and deputy to the Sejm in 1629.

Text: Sokołowska, Jadwiga. *I w odmianach czasu smak jest. Antologia polskiej poezji epoki baroku.* Warszawa: PIW, 1990, 152, 153, 154, 167, 168, 168-169.

SZYMON STAROWOLSKI (c. 1588-1656)

Starowolski was born into an impoverished family of a West Lithuanian boyar. At the age of seventeen, he entered the court of Jan Zamoyski in Zamość, a leading center of Renaissance Poland. He travelled in the service of the Ostrogski family to Germany, France, and Holland. From 1612 to 1619, Starowolski studied and taught at the Cracow Academy, and then in the Cistercian monastery in Wąchock. From 1619 to 1621, he was a secretary to Jan Karol Chodkiewicz, Grand Hetman of Lithuania. Connected with many other courts of powerful magnates, Starowolski travelled abroad repeatedly. In 1639 he became a priest and worked as a cantor, canon, and preacher in Tarnów and Cracow.

Starowolski wrote in Latin and in Polish. He left behind over seventy works in the fields of historiography, law, geography, and music. He wrote biographies of distinguished Polish writers, e.g., *Scriptorum Polonicorum Hekatontas*, of bishops, and soldiers. In his Latin works, addressed to foreign readers, he defended the good name of Poland, while in his Polish treatises he called for a thorough reform of the Commonwealth.

Sarmatian Warriors (1631)

CXXVI. Stanisław Żółkiewski

When I enter upon the subject of describing the glorious deeds of Stanisław Żółkiewski, I will appear like the person who wants to light a torch next to the sun. He is already seen quite clearly in the light of fame and glory of his deeds held in high esteem by all and the name of this man will never be forgotten as long as outstanding people and great virtues are treated with respect. First, he was a commander of a cavalry unit, then of a wing, then of a regiment, and finally the Field Hetman of the Crown. Together with Jan Zamoyski[1] he took part in all the battles in Muscovy and Livonia, in Podolia and Silesia, as well as in Wallachia. He was a man of ancient customs, in the prime of life, solemn in speech, famous for the brave deeds of his ancestors. At all stages of his military career he observed the ancient customs and thanks to that he reached its very pinnacle, as he received at the end of his life from Zygmunt III, the most illustrious King of Poland who rules us graciously, the ranks of Grand Hetman of the Crown and Grand Chancellor of the Crown. For in only one battle on the fields of Klushino he conquered the northern territories of Muscovy, which were not reached by the Roman legions. In that battle he put to the sword thousands of Russians, took prisoner thousands of Germans, Frenchmen, Englishmen, Scots, and representatives of other nations, brought from foreign lands. Yet together with the commandant, Swedish companion, builder of bridges,[2] he preserved his army intact. That is why he was able to bring later to King Zygmunt in Warsaw the Grand Tsar of Moscow himself, together with his brothers, nearly the whole senate, and the patriarch. He forced the whole state of Muscovy to swear obedience and fealty to Władysław, the King's son, when he took in his possession Moscow, the very capital. True enough that later inexperienced people and those who easily pass judgment considered him to be an unwarlike man, as he delayed the campaign against the Turks. It seemed to them that he was postponing the battle out of laziness and slowness.[3] And yet after some time, even after his death, everyone had to admit that no one was more decisive in action and a more prudent commander than he. For he always preserved peace among the quarreling princes in the camp and according to a Spartan custom he did not consider how many enemies he had, but where they were. He took lightly gossip concerning himself, as he was aware that according to Velleius[4] people praise what is safe. He was not fearful or treacherous, but with foresight he avoided a military risk, which at other times he did not hesitate to take. Wishing to fulfill his last task, he kept back without respite the Tatar and Turkish forces at Cecora in Wallachia for eight days and nights with only few units of cavalry. Against this great power, he was defending Gaspar Gracjan,[5] who together with the whole province became a vassal of the Polish King. Before Żółkiewski suffered there a great defeat at the barbarians' hands and his army panicked, he did his best to make sure that the army preserved its good name in retreat and it did not forget about military strategy. In this fashion he marched in tight formation in the direction of Poland and was approaching the River Dniester. Then on account of quarrels and discords the discipline, which was still maintained after defeats, disintegrated and all soldiers left the camp during the second watch with great hue and cry and then, not knowing the way and without an order, everyone was trying to advance to the head of the group and reach the Dniester as fast as possible. Such behavior brought about an obvious outcome. The barbarians, who through their scouts found out about this situation, arrived unexpectedly with great haste and in spite of our soldiers' resistance either put them to the sword or took them prisoner. Nearly all those who together with the Hetman put up a fierce resistance perished with him in a bloody battle. The enemy carried the Hetman's head around the camp, impaled on a spear for derision, bringing us great shame and--who would not know about it?--carried it in the streets of Constantinople after their triumphal return. I cannot say whether this defeat brought upon us more shame or more ruin; one thing is sure, however, namely that the enemy won victory because of our discord. The headless body was brought back to Poland; friends, relatives, and his wife buried it; afterwards they bought out the head for gold and brought it to the widow. Let us place a short epitaph on the coffin of the man who so meritoriously served his fatherland and the whole of Christianity:

Passer by, if you love the fatherland, deplore the fate of a great man! Here rests Stanisław Żółkiewski, Chancellor and Grand Hetman of the Crown, senator tested in all virtues and particularly famous for his military art and effective counsel.

He gained experience in various wars under the eyes of Mikołaj Mielecki[6] and Jan Zamoyski, famous masters of military art and, so to say, pupils of Mars himself. It should be mentioned that besides his many other valiant deeds he nearly brought down within several months the Duchy of Muscovy, so powerful for many centuries. He brought triumphantly to King Zygmunt Tsar Ivan Shuyski himself, with brothers Dimitri and Vasili, and the patriarch. After several years, however, the favorable fate turned away from him; even though he made a triumphant march through Constantinople after his death, he left for his descendants quite an eloquent example of instability and changeability of human condition. When in hatred they charged him with procrastination, he set out with a few regiments for Wallachia to support Gaspar Gracjan. He was surrounded there by countless forces of barbarians and after the battle that lasted eight days he was struck, not without impunity, by the Turkish

A steel nail or can stop a mill wheel in its gate
    Or who can break up with his forehead an oak plate.
Not the one who breaks with his head somebody's door,
10   Nor he who gulps down several gallons or more.
Not the one who manages with luck his duels,
    Nor in whose heart no fear of enemy dwells.
Not he whose arm is stronger or can withstand blows,
    Not he who can endure considerable woes.
15 But the one who bore bravely Fortune's punishment
    Or disappointments and who never underwent
Any change at all in good days or in distress,
    Him I call a man and thank for his manliness.

A Pleasant Counsel

Safer to lie with a girl 'neath a green tree crown,
    Playing a graceful lute, under an eiderdown,
Than to carry a sharp pointed spear and a shield
    Or have a heavy visor press your brow afield.

To Niemsta on His Third Marriage[1]

You get married a third time--she must be fearless,
    If she has ventured to become your third mistress.
Don't think of the fourth though you found a good market,
    Because both girls and women will be quite upset.
5 And with good reason, since the one who would wed you
    The fourth time, would be then saying to life adieu.
So spare the third, I advise, for if you lose her,
    You'll pay for this loss with idleness forever.

Notes

1. The poet refers probably to Jerzy Niemsta, judge from Zator and deputy to the Sejm in 1629.

Text: Sokołowska, Jadwiga. *I w odmianach czasu smak jest. Antologia polskiej poezji epoki baroku.* Warszawa: PIW, 1990, 152, 153, 154, 167, 168, 168-169.

after defeats, disintegrated and all soldiers left the camp during the second watch with great hue and cry and then, not knowing the way and without an order, everyone was trying to advance to the head of the group and reach the Dniester as fast as possible. Such behavior brought about an obvious outcome. The barbarians, who through their scouts found out about this situation, arrived unexpectedly with great haste and in spite of our soldiers' resistance either put them to the sword or took them prisoner. Nearly all those who together with the Hetman put up a fierce resistance perished with him in a bloody battle. The enemy carried the Hetman's head around the camp, impaled on a spear for derision, bringing us great shame and--who would not know about it?--carried it in the streets of Constantinople after their triumphal return. I cannot say whether this defeat brought upon us more shame or more ruin; one thing is sure, however, namely that the enemy won victory because of our discord. The headless body was brought back to Poland; friends, relatives, and his wife buried it; afterwards they bought out the head for gold and brought it to the widow. Let us place a short epitaph on the coffin of the man who so meritoriously served his fatherland and the whole of Christianity:

Passer by, if you love the fatherland, deplore the fate of a great man! Here rests Stanisław Żółkiewski, Chancellor and Grand Hetman of the Crown, senator tested in all virtues and particularly famous for his military art and effective counsel.

He gained experience in various wars under the eyes of Mikołaj Mielecki[6] and Jan Zamoyski, famous masters of military art and, so to say, pupils of Mars himself. It should be mentioned that besides his many other valiant deeds he nearly brought down within several months the Duchy of Muscovy, so powerful for many centuries. He brought triumphantly to King Zygmunt Tsar Ivan Shuyski himself, with brothers Dimitri and Vasili, and the patriarch. After several years, however, the favorable fate turned away from him; even though he made a triumphant march through Constantinople after his death, he left for his descendants quite an eloquent example of instability and changeability of human condition. When in hatred they charged him with procrastination, he set out with a few regiments for Wallachia to support Gaspar Gracjan. He was surrounded there by countless forces of barbarians and after the battle that lasted eight days he was struck, not without impunity, by the Turkish

O, how much longer, o, how much longer,
I have to wander through this vale?
Open up, grave! Open up, silent grave!
I'll lie down without fear at last:
15   I will toss down chains of a carnal slave,
I will cast off dust of my dust.
I will get free of my body's burden,
Get free of pain, depravity,
My spirit will fly away to heaven,
20   Soaring to its native city.

Text: Bukowski, Kazimierz. *Biblia a literatura polska. Antologia.* Warszawa: WSiP, 1984, 256. Translated into Polish by Władysław Syrokomla.

II 3 To My Lute

Daughter of an old sonorous beech tree,
Take a rest from sounds of your company,
And until fair weather will allow for
    Hang up on my poplar.

5   Along your sound-board and through every string,
Zephyr will touch you, gently caressing,
It will more perfectly each tune rehearse
    Than we with our fingers.

And I in a moment, resting my head,
10   Will drink from the nearby spring or instead
Enchanted by its soothing run and sweep,
    Ashore will fall asleep.

What now? The sky gets darker and the clouds
Foreshadow thick torrents of water shrouds.
15   Let us rise! For so fair days in this world
    With rain will quickly swirl.

Text: Sarbiewski, Maciej Kazimierz. *Poezje wybrane.* Ed. by Jakub Lichański. Warszawa: Ludowa Spółdzielnia Wydawnicza, 1986, 21. Translated into Polish by Jan Andrzej Morsztyn.

II 3 To My Lute

Child of boxwood plant, my sonorous lute,
Hang quietly on a slender poplar,
    When the sky smiles in a sunny salute
        And a light breeze plays in the leaves afar:

5   Let the muffled whispers of mild Eurus[1]
Rock you to and fro, when they gently soar,
    While I soothe my mind in utter stillness,
        Resting at ease on the grass of the shore.

Alas! Waves of enormous clouds cover
10   The sky azure! The stormy rains come close!
    Let us rise! Joys that gracefully glimmer,
        Are swiftly disturbed by ominous woes!

Notes

1. Eurus was the east wind.

II 19 From the Song of Songs
My beloved is like a roe or like a young hart

You shun me, o Christ, like a fearful roe,
Which is carried off by the hurricane
Or by the Northern wind's unforeseen flow
Towards a distant plain.

5   Whether early frost throws into a fright
The trembling leaves or when Jove faraway
Sets with his thunders the mountains[1] alight,
She keeps running away.

But I won't stop to seek you everywhere,
10   "Return, o Savior!", I will cry loudly,
When you again suffer a sudden scare,
I'll cry: "Return to me!"

sword, for our greater sorrow, yet for his greater happiness. It also put an end to so many toils of the man who wanted and desired so much. It took place in the year of Our Lord 1620.

Notes

1. Jan Zamoyski (1542-1605), Grand Chancellor and Grand Hetman of the Crown, was chancellor to three kings.
2. Starowolski refers here most likely to Edward Hornstajn.
3. In 1617 Żółkiewski signed a treaty with the Turks.
4. Velleius Paterculus (ca. 20 B.C.-30 A.D.) was a Roman historian and officer. The above quote is from his *History of Rome* (2, 115).
5. It was during Żółkiewski's campaign to aid Gracjan of Moldavia that he was defeated and killed at Cecora in 1620.
6. Mikołaj Mielecki (d. 1585) was the Grand Hetman of the Crown who fought under King Batory against Muscovy.

Lament of the Distressed Mother, the Polish Crown (1655)

> *Regina Poloniae, tu nos ab hoste protege et hora mortis suscipe.*[1]

Lament of the Dying Poland

Vocem meam audi secundum misericordiam tuam, Domine et secundum iudicium tuum vivifica me.[2]

A miserable mother, I leave this world without providing my children with the last will; I am dying in pains and worries, having not blessed my wicked sons. I am approaching the end of my life assigned in heaven, not having around any descendant who would close with a kind hand my eyes that become fixed at death; who after my soul leaves the body would carry me like a mother to the grave, crying mournfully, and moved by human piety, would toss a clump of earth into my grave; or who out of gratefulness for once bringing forth so many virtuous sons, erected over me a mound, as they did over Queen Wanda or over

VIII. The Church of the Nuns of the Holy Sacrament in Warsaw

King Krakus,[3] in the eternal memory for the future ages, and who would write after having built a worthy pyramid or a marble column:

> Here lies Poland, lost by the wrath of wicked men,
> The golden freedom is buried next to her, then
> Sacred Catholic faith was laid in the same pit,
> The old virtue of our ancestors went with it.
> 5 Pretense and unrestraint, excessive wantonness,
> Pride, disobedience, and repulsive greediness
> Of people of all estates, obscene heresies,
> And also soldiers' unbearable abuses--
> Ruined the distressed homeland in a violent manner,
> 10 This viperous issue--she quoth--killed their own mother.
> You that are passing by this way, my dear reader,
> If you love virtue, please, this grave don't pass over
> Without most sincere tears, without a bitter sigh,
> But from the depth of your heart my downfall decry.

Notes

1. 'Queen of Poland, protect us from the enemy and receive us in the hour of death.'

2. 'In your steadfast love hear my voice;
O Lord, in your justice preserve my life.' (Psalm 119, 149)

All biblical references in this volume are to *The New Oxford Annotated Bible. New Revised Standard Version.* Ed. by Bruce Metzger and Roland Murphy. New York: Oxford University Press, 1989.

3. King Krakus (or Krak) and Queen Wanda were the legendary rulers of Poland.

Text: Starowolski, Szymon. *Wybór z pism.* Ed. by Ignacy Lewandowski. Wrocław: Ossolineum, Biblioteka Narodowa I 272, 1991, 79-83, 317-318.

MACIEJ KAZIMIERZ SARBIEWSKI (1595-1640)

Sarbiewski was born in Sarbiew in Mazovia. He was educated in the Jesuit Colleges in Pułtusk, Wilno, and Braniewo, and then taught in the Jesuit Colleges in Kroże and Połock. From 1620 to 1622 he studied theology at the Wilno Academy and from 1623 to 1624 in the Collegium Germanicum in Rome, where he took holy orders. Sarbiewski found patronage at the court of Pope Urban VIII, to whom he dedicated several poems and from whom he received many honors for his literary achievements. After returning to Poland, Sarbiewski taught in Połock (1626-1627) and then in the Wilno Academy. In 1635 he was named court preacher to Władysław IV. He died in Warsaw.

Sarbiewski's Latin *Lyricorum Libri*, published in Kroże, Wilno, Cologne, and Antwerp, one edition dedicated to Pope Urban VIII and illustrated by Rubens, gained great popularity in Europe. In his poems, Sarbiewski combined humanistic themes with motifs from the Bible and dealt with religious as well as political topics. Numerous translations and paraphrases of his poems appeared in Germany, France, and England, influencing some poets, among them Henry Vaughan and Abraham Cowley.

Many Polish poets, beginning with his contemporaries, translated Sarbiewski's *Lyrics* into the vernacular. Several of these translations, some of them of the same poem, are given here in English.

Odes

I 19 Longing for the Heavenly Homeland

The heavenly homeland delights my eyes,
Rich setting of the firmament,
The youthful radiance of the moonrise,
A sparkling light of stars' ascent.
5   Light next to light is flickering gaily,
Balanced in the circle of dance,
Lamp next to lamp is standing faithfully,
Guarding the heavenly entrance.
My eyes fixed on the heavens in wonder
10   Travel like guests over the trail,

IX. Title page of Maciej Sarbiewski's *Lyricorum Libri IV*, 1632

O, how much longer, o, how much longer,
I have to wander through this vale?
Open up, grave! Open up, silent grave!
I'll lie down without fear at last:
15   I will toss down chains of a carnal slave,
I will cast off dust of my dust.
I will get free of my body's burden,
Get free of pain, depravity,
My spirit will fly away to heaven,
20   Soaring to its native city.

Text: Bukowski, Kazimierz. *Biblia a literatura polska. Antologia*. Warszawa: WSiP, 1984, 256. Translated into Polish by Władysław Syrokomla.

II 3 To My Lute

Daughter of an old sonorous beech tree,
Take a rest from sounds of your company,
And until fair weather will allow for
    Hang up on my poplar.

5   Along your sound-board and through every string,
Zephyr will touch you, gently caressing,
It will more perfectly each tune rehearse
    Than we with our fingers.

And I in a moment, resting my head,
10 Will drink from the nearby spring or instead
Enchanted by its soothing run and sweep,
    Ashore will fall asleep.

What now? The sky gets darker and the clouds
Foreshadow thick torrents of water shrouds.
15 Let us rise! For so fair days in this world
    With rain will quickly swirl.

Text: Sarbiewski, Maciej Kazimierz. *Poezje wybrane*. Ed. by Jakub Lichański. Warszawa: Ludowa Spółdzielnia Wydawnicza, 1986, 21. Translated into Polish by Jan Andrzej Morsztyn.

II 3 To My Lute

Child of boxwood plant, my sonorous lute,
Hang quietly on a slender poplar,
    When the sky smiles in a sunny salute
        And a light breeze plays in the leaves afar:

5   Let the muffled whispers of mild Eurus[1]
Rock you to and fro, when they gently soar,
    While I soothe my mind in utter stillness,
        Resting at ease on the grass of the shore.

Alas! Waves of enormous clouds cover
10   The sky azure! The stormy rains come close!
    Let us rise! Joys that gracefully glimmer,
        Are swiftly disturbed by ominous woes!

Notes

1. Eurus was the east wind.

II 19 From the Song of Songs
My beloved is like a roe or like a young hart

You shun me, o Christ, like a fearful roe,
Which is carried off by the hurricane
Or by the Northern wind's unforeseen flow
Towards a distant plain.

5   Whether early frost throws into a fright
The trembling leaves or when Jove faraway
Sets with his thunders the mountains[1] alight,
She keeps running away.

But I won't stop to seek you everywhere,
10   "Return, o Savior!", I will cry loudly,
When you again suffer a sudden scare,
I'll cry: "Return to me!"

>   Whether you are concealed by the green tops
>   Of Libanus[2] or by rosy meadows
> 15 Of Bethulia[3] or Salem's fields of crops[4]
>   Or Capernaum furrows;[5]
>
>   Abandon at last this incessant flight,
>   For you won't escape, always watchful sky
>   Will detect your face, and in the dark night
> 20 The moon's gold horns will spy.[6]
>
>   The deserted shore is crying for you,
>   And the Western wind sighs in open space,
>   To you from the sky, when the still night drew,
>   The stars' watch sends its rays.

Notes

1. The mountain chain of Ceraunia is in northern Greece. Its rocky promontory was extremely dangerous for sailors.
2. Libanus, a mountain chain in Syria.
3. Bethulia, a place in Galilee, home of the biblical Judith.
4. Salem, an ancient name of Jerusalem.
5. Capernaum, a city in ancient Palestine on the Sea of Galilee.
6. The goddess of birth, moon, and hunt was Cynthia (Diana), often represented with horns of the crescent on her head.

Text: Sarbiewski, Maciej Kazimierz. *Liryki.* Ed. by Mirosław Korolko with Jan Okoń. Warszawa: PAX, 1980, 103, 157. Translated into Polish by Tadeusz Karyłowski.

II 26 To the Holy Virgin Mother

>   O, Mary, Queen of the golden heaven,
>   Leave far behind the sun's azure region,
>   Descend from the blue of the radiant lane,
>   With the Poles remain.
> 5   Let the Most Holy Child come with you now,

The crown of bright stars on his sacred brow.
The angels too, their golden quills gleaming,
Peace and well-being.

Text: Bukowski, *Biblia a literatura polska*, 199. Translated into Polish by Julian Ejsmond.

II 26 *To the Holy Virgin Mother*
When Poland was afflicted by storms, famine, and war

O, Mary, Queen of the golden heaven,
Towards the vales of Mazovia, Bug region,[1]
In a cloud chariot burning rainbow bright
    Descend in snow light!

5   Let the golden Child appear with You
And the host of winged beings float down too,
With Health, Peace, and in field flowers bounty
    The Horn of Plenty.

Notes

1. Mazovia is the central region of Poland. The River Bug in central Poland flows into the Vistula.

III 3 *To Cardinal Francesco Barberini*[1]
Compassion is a great attribute of princes

Happy who knows no fear before the storm's anger,
When the earth trembles--and firmly holds the scepter;
He does not demand, and yet uses the goods here,
Does not grasp, but owns. You, holding power not dear,
5   Never purchase applause among plain commoners,
Nobles don't die because of your bloody slaughters,
You are praised by people's just love. The rest doesn't count!
This one source will give you the limitless goods' fount.

Notes

1. Cardinal Barberini was a nephew of Maffeo Barberini, from 1623 Pope Urban VIII. Sarbiewski wrote panegyrical poems to these patrons of arts.

Text: Sarbiewski, *Liryki,* 181, 195. Translated into Polish by Tadeusz Karyłowski.
Latin texts: Sarbiewski, Maciej Kazimierz. *Liryki*. Ed. by Mirosław Korolko with Jan Okoń. Translated into Polish by Tadeusz Karyłowski. Warszawa: PAX, 1980, 74, 102, 156, 180, 194.

SAMUEL TWARDOWSKI (c. 1600-1661)

Samuel Twardowski was born in Lutynia (Great Poland) in the family of an impoverished nobleman. He attended the Jesuit College in Kalisz and spent many years at various magnates' courts. He fought at Chocim and took part in a diplomatic mission to Turkey. These experiences and his interest in history found expression in *The Important Mission of His Grace Duke Krzysztof Zbaraski* (1633), *Władysław IV, King of Poland and Sweden* (1649), and *The Civil War With the Cossacks and Tartars, Muscovy, Afterwards With Sweden and Hungary* (1681). Twardowski was also the author of pastoral romances, adapted from mythology (*Daphne Changed Into a Laurel Tree*, 1638) and from Spanish verse narratives (*Fair Pasqualina*, 1655), which showed his poetic skill and artistic sensitivity.

Daphne Changed Into a Laurel Tree[1]
(selections)

Prologue

Four Zephyrs, south winds, greet Dawn[2]

1
Zephyr I

Drift away, o night, drift away deep night!
Dawn has scattered mists and dreadful shadows,
She rose from her bed in gold robes bedight,
Just before the rays that the sun bestows.
5   So whatever moves in water, in air,
All the creatures lift your voices in song,
Dawn has arisen, darkness passed somewhere,
Disturbing clouds in the sky are now gone.

2
Zephyr II

     Let us sing, the day harnesses swift steeds![3]
10   We are bowing our heads to you, gracious
     Lucifer.[4] Your fair temples Venus guilds,
     When she returns to her native Paphos.[5]
     For you the Muses sing on Helicon,[6]
     Before they can come up to Apollo,
15   So you as well celebrate him in song,
     Who live in the air, in the sea below!

3
Zephyr III

     Entering in the morn a splendid bed,
     You let your rosy ray pierce the window,
     Where upon the breast of his beloved,
20   A lover perished in the afterglow.
     You are enwrapping transparent fountains,
     And stirring lightly the silvery foam,
     Until full of life and new confidence,
     Naiades[7] move their gills in their water home.

4
Zephyr IV

25   In heavy toil you endow thirsty grain
     With pearly dew and the cooling weather,
     You tune birds' voices, sweeter than sugar cane,
     When they are perched on branches together,
     So that they twitter and with sorrow coo,
30   When golden-haired Phoebus rises to go.
     If they are singing, you sing for him too,
     Who live in the air, in the sea below.

5
Dawn

Why don't I sing for my own benefit
Nor join in your most accomplished chorus?
35   Jove has chosen me the sky to befit,
He gave me reins of swift-footed horses,
At my most joyous hour of the morning
The plants will bloom in the verdant garden,
Even the tulips in their beauty's spring,
40   Without my fresh, cool dewdrops are stricken.

6

Look at the rose, how for my appearance
In graceful light at purple break of day,
It opens its leaves with heavy pearls dense,
And how it will young lovers' heads array.
45   Soon it will wither, just before your eyes,
When the midday fire comes to cause its grief,
Pluck it, pluck it now! For later it dries,
When it stands too long and is bare of leaf.

7

For me meadows bloom with pretty flowers,
50   From where wreaths by beautiful hands woven,
Among the tables decked in May bowers[8]
Are shared as gifts by young men and women.
When I, gay Hesperus,[9] make my way in,
The tired reapers sing gently for me,
55   The flocks are playing, shepherds are laughing,
And tender zephyrs from all sides blow free.

8

I sing, while Phoebus with his golden mane
Blows from his nostrils flames that are immense,

X. Branicki Palace in Białystok, 1697

Depart, o stars, before the swift whip's reign
60 Of Phaeton[10] will drive you from the heavens!
So we, who face too his persistent blows,
As we have finished the songs we began,
Give him a scepter. His pride overflows.
Let him rule the world, its whole wide stretched span.

Notes

1. Daphne was a nymph transformed into a laurel tree and thus enabled to escape the pursuing Apollo.
2. Zephyr was a soft warm breeze.
3. Helios, god of the sun, drove a golden chariot.
4. Lucifer was another name for the dawn or morning star.
5. Venus was born of the seafoam in Paphos on Cyprus.
6. The Boetian mountain Helicon was supposed by the ancient Greeks to be the residence of Apollo (Phoebus), the god of sunlight, prophecy, poetry and music, and of the Muses.
7. Naiades were the nymphs believed by the Greeks and Romans to live and give life and perpetuity to lakes, rivers, springs, and fountains.
8. Another reading: 'decked in May clusters.'
9. Hesperus or Venus was the evening light. Hesperus is identified with Dawn here. The meaning of the line is: 'When I turn into the evening light.'
10. Phaeton, son of Helios, attempted to drive the chariot of the sun, setting the earth on fire. Phaeton also was the name of one of Dawn's horses.

Fair Pasqualina
(selection)

Also with this beauty and rare white complexion
    The heavens granted her such sweet disposition
That wherever she went, wherever turned her eyes,
    It appeared that she reigned alone under the skies
5 And was pure delight. For if she went anywhere,
    In her footsteps roses and violets blossomed there;
When she burst out laughing, as if a large window

>   Opened on charming rose gardens that on the moon
>   grow,
>   She would place her tongue so that between her sweet lips,
> 10   She was showing her teeth clearer than crystal tips
>   And so she kept them behind those well enclosed lists
>   Like one who either from too much laughter desists,
>   Or isn't as talkative as Thais[1] in her chatter,
>   But what she wanted to say she would first ponder,
> 15   With her poise bringing all lots of satisfaction,
>   Yet setting aside desire and deep affection
>   To those people who loved her. So if the ancients
>   Counted three graces they praised without reticence,
>   Then solely from her eyes thousands were set ablaze
> 20   And when she wished they changed again in many
>   ways
>   Into different shapes and figures. Just like Phoebe,[2]
>   When she arranges her long tresses leisurely,
>   She alone takes a leading role, while far away
>   Other lights of heavenly torches have to stay.

Notes

1. Thais was a famous Greek courtesan who lived in the fourth century B.C.
2. Phoebe, 'the bright one,' was a Titaness, identified later as a moon goddess.

TO MARIANNA TWARDOWSKA
MY DELIGHTFUL CHILD, ONLY DAUGHTER,
WRITTEN BY HER FATHER

Lament I

>   And so my beloved girl, who in course of time
>   Would inherit in this world all best things of mine,
>   You went away from me! I'm a hapless father,
>   Who barely had time to delight in his daughter,
> 5   Now I mourn her, as only her name will linger.
>   The same when fragrant Eurus[1] blows and I
>   slumber,

    I'm dreaming of golden apples and in anguish
        Reach out to grasp; in vain, what's left is a mere wish!
    Likewise I'll be able only to dream of you,
10   And wherever I go, your graceful shade pursue.

Notes

1. Eurus was the east wind, blowing in the morning.

EPITAPH FOR SIR SAMUEL TWARDOWSKI, POLISH POET,
written by himself in 1661

    Father Nicholas from Skrzypna, from Ponętów mother,
        Born to the good woman second month of the year.
    The first years of my life I spent in Kalisz school,[1]
        Also on the field of Mars I let the sword rule,
5   At Chocim[2] and elsewhere. After that I travelled
        With Zbaraski to Turkey,[3] from which I gathered
    First fruits of Minerva.[4] Precious time of the days
        That was left, I spent going to many a place
    For assemblies, sejms, missions, appearing at court.
10   And yet, steadfast, I never found a better port
    Struggling with my Fortune that never wanted to
        Make me a well-off man. So I took a wife who
    Came from the old Gaj house, and many sons siring,
        Sometimes also on scented Parnassus[5] strolling,
15   I wrote many a poem, which in future years
        Will attest that my life in this world wasn't useless.
    Finally I died and now rest in this grave here,
        Finding better rations in the heavenly sphere.

Notes

1. Twardowski was educated in the Jesuit school in Kalisz.
2. In 1621, Twardowski fought against Turkish forces at Chocim.
3. As a courtier of prince Krzysztof Zbaraski, Twardowski was a member of the diplomatic delegation to Turkey, from where he returned in 1623.
4. Minerva was the Roman goddess of crafts and arts.

5. Parnassus was the mountain in central Greece, the sacred dwelling place of Apollo and the Muses.

Texts: Twardowski, Samuel. *Dafnis w drzewo bobkowe przemieniela się*. Ed. by Roman Pollak and Stefan Saski. Wrocław: Ossolineum, Biblioteka Pisarzów Polskich, B 6, 1955, 49-51.
Twardowski, Samuel. *Nadobna Paskwalina*. 2nd ed. Ed. by Jan Okoń. Wrocław: Ossolineum, Biblioteka Narodowa I 87, 1980, 18-19.
Sokołowska, *I w odmianach czasu smak jest*, 308-309, 310.

KRZYSZTOF OPALIŃSKI (1609-1655)

Krzysztof Opaliński was born into an aristocratic family in Sieraków in Great Poland. From 1620 to 1625, Krzysztof and his brother Łukasz, attended the well-known *gymnasium* in Poznań, founded by Bishop Lubrański, and then studied in Louvain (1626-1629), Orleans (1629), and Padua (1630). After their return to Poland, Krzysztof Opaliński became involved in political activities and in 1637 became, like his father, the Voivode of Poznań. In cooperation with Comenius, he organized an excellent school in Sieraków. He was also a patron of writers and a bibliophile. Dissatisfied with the policies of King Jan Kazimierz, he surrendered the whole province to the invading army of the Swedes at Ujście in 1655.

Opaliński's *Satires*, published in Leszno in 1650, were his major work. Modelled on Juvenal's satires, they were written in unrhymed syllabic verse, giving vent to the author's indignation with numerous evils of public life in Poland.

Satires

Satire III

On Burdens and Oppression of Peasants in Poland

    I believe God punishes Poland for nothing
    But for the cruel oppression of her subjects
    Which is worse than serfdom. It's as if the peasant
    Were not your fellow man or a human being.
5   The heart often trembles, flesh shivers, when one thinks
    Of this serfdom that's harder than the pagan one.
    For God's sake, Poles, are you truly out of your minds!
    All the goods, welfare, nourishment, all the crops
    Are provided by your subjects. Their hands feed you,
10 So why do you treat them in such a cruel way?
    The camel, they say, can't bear loads beyond his strength
    And when they load him so that he feels it's too much,
    He will immediately lie down right in that place
    And will not want to stand up. It's opposite here;
15 Beyond natural and divine laws a peasant

Must bear what his lord puts on his shoulders even
If he were to die. Preachers scold, confessors scold,
They threaten with hell; no avail, bishops themselves
Do the same through their stewards and through their prelates--
20 If not even more. So a needy nobleman
Has an excuse when he sees that his betters sin.
Firstly, about the burdens in labor alone:
Where they had in the past twenty peasants or more,
They have now eight or ten and yet they tell those ten
25 To do the same what twenty were doing before.
Where before one person would come out of a house,
Later two men, then three, and even four were called,
Where before they worked for two or three days a week,
Often they do not have any free time at all.
30 Where beer retail was free, mostly in church estates,
Now this too is over, and they make you drink beer,
With which they should poison devils themselves in hell.[1]
You say: But I have children, various expenses.
The devil will take all of it--both crops and you
35 And children, for such a harvest is not lasting.
I do not mention that you are fleecing peasants.
Servants or hands will say: There is a rich peasant,
He has cattle, sheep, quite a lot of other goods,
This will be quite useful in the kitchen. Barley
40 Crop was good, wheat too--useful to make beer for guests.
This poor soul has collected a pretty penny,
It will come in handy for expenses. They stir
Against a poor wretch. It's not hard to find a cause.
They fine him one, two hundred, they'll nearly tear out
45 His soul. And why so? Because he is the richest.
They'll say about another: He has enough land,
And good land, it will do for a manorial farm,
Take it from him; throw off all from their land,
To set a farm there. --That will happen in one week.
50 The poor souls cry: father, mother, children, and all,
Sending their bloody complaints only to heaven
And demanding reprisal, which is not tardy,
If not in this world, then in the other it comes,
When they repay lavishly evil for evil.
55 And yet we do not care, as we don't want to care
What will happen to us after death. Nor do we

Pay attention to hell or keep it in our minds.
But someone may ask: Have you yet disclosed it all?
One hundred mouths, one hundred tongues--still not enough--
60 To express justly all abuses of peasants.
I still know of some more I want to talk about.
When the spring arrives, and it does not rain in May,
Witches are the cause. One ox died, then the second,
Or one of the new livestock, they blame the witches.
65 So they take and torture an innocent woman,
Until she denounces fifteen. The torturer
Pulls and burns her, till she talks and names all that are
In the village; it's strange the woman won't name
The lord and lady, who should be burned for torture
70 And execution of their own guiltless people.
Even though the village hasn't more than thirty souls,
They'll burn fifteen of them. What--by God--is the cause?
The master is not well and cannot recover,
Pines away and his children die at home at times--
75 As if both consumption and death weren't natural
And sent down from God Himself! I will not mention
Those who sit in judgment in such a court: mindless
Peasantry, assessors, and also those people
Who have something against the innocent peasants.
80 And is it something new to torment people
For still other reasons? An official will have
A peasant hanged without the lord's knowledge. For what?
Maybe he stole or killed? Is there any witness?
No postponement is long enough to save one's head.
85 Wait and first carry on an investigation.
"And what's this for? He is a peasant and subject."
The subject isn't a man? " Er... no, leave me alone,
I know what I'm doing." Another will brand them,
Will beat them cruelly, will let them rot in jail,
90 He will even beat with rods, like children at school,
Gray-haired and good old men--without any reason.
They will use a pretext they don't drink in the inn,
Though the beer is bad, quite sour, and tastes awful.
I'll say, hard to keep silent, when I travelled once
95 Through certain hamlets, I ordered beer from the inn.
They carried it out. Then I asked: "So is your beer
Always like that? " They said: "It's a hundred times worse,
And yet we must drink it, because the lord will give

The innkeeper a number of barrels a week,
100 For which the innkeeper must promptly pay him back,
Whether we drink or not. The innkeeper makes up
For his loss from us, but first he figures out well,
How many gallons each peasant should be getting.
If he won't come to the inn, they'll bring his share home.
105 You drink, though it's bad, and if you do not want it,
Pour it out to the hogs, but pay the innkeeper."
It is the same with barley, flour, salt, and herrings,
Which are imposed again and again upon the peasants.
O cruel oppression, not seen anywhere else!
110 To weigh down the peasant with such heavy burden,
As he has to give constantly from his poor soil
To ruler, to Republic, to lord, to soldier,
To officials, to scribes, to clerics, to lord's men,
To haiduks[2] and to Cossacks, his wife and children.
115 They just fleece him in town and inn, at court and church,
They nearly skin him, and still will keep going on!
The bailiffs alone, my God, what they are doing
And how frequently they rebuke the poor wretches.
And why? For the lord said so, he should be obeyed.
120 And these oppressions in the bygone times had caused,
After cruel Ryksa with her son Casimir[3]
Were driven out of the country, that all the serfs
Rose up in rebellion against their own masters.
So they had to run away and hide in forests
125 And other wild places--with them also bishops,
As well as many castellans and governors,
When peasants were searching for them, to claim justice.
Also the weary load of the Pawluks, Muchas,
Nalewajkos[4]-- the rebellious leaders--who brought
130 On the homeland bloody war and cruel shame too,
Close upon an ultimate collapse, when God sent
This *flagellum*,[5] through the rebellion of peasants,
Punishing first the hetmans with defeat and jail,
Then the homeland with ugly and desperate retreat,
135 Finally with a shameful and abusive peace,[6]
For it is said '*per quae quis peccat, per eadem Punitur.*'[7] Oh, how we have indeed suffered this!
I close as I began; God punishes Poland

Most for her subjects, indeed, he'll keep punishing
140 If you, Pole, will not ever come to your senses.

Notes

1. Peasants were forbidden to brew beer and produce alcohol. The noblemen, to increase their income, allowed peasants to drink in the inns only the beer provided by their own breweries. Cf. lines 92-106.
2. Haiduks were Hungarian mercenary foot soldiers who were eventually elevated to noble rank. In many European countries, including Poland, haiduks were male attendants or servants dressed in livery resembling the costume of Hungarian haiduks.
3. Opaliński alludes to the peasant rebellion of 1037, which followed the expulsion of Ryksa, wife of Mieszko II, and her son Casimir, future ruler of Poland (1039-1058).
4. Pawluk was the leader of the Cossack rebellion of 1637. Mucha led the peasant rebellion in the fifteenth century. Semen Nalewajko was the Cossack leader who fought against the Turks and then in 1596 rebelled against Poland. His forces were defeated and he was beheaded in Warsaw in 1597.
5. *flagellum*--'whip.'
6. Opaliński refers to the defeats suffered by Poland at Korsuń (1648), Piławce (1648), and to the peace treaty of 1649, in which Chmielnicki won many privileges for the Cossacks.
7. Latin for 'the way one sins, the way one is punished.'

Text: Opaliński, Krzysztof. *Satyry*. Ed. by Lesław Eustachiewicz. Wrocław: Ossolineum, Biblioteka Narodowa I 147, 1953, 23-29.

XI. Barbara Lubomirska, coffin portrait, second half of the 17th century

ŁUKASZ OPALIŃSKI (1612-1662)

A younger brother of Krzysztof, Łukasz Opaliński studied classical languages and literatures at the universities of Louvain, Orleans, and Padua. After his return to Poland, he was elected deputy, then marshal of the Chamber of Deputies (1638), and in 1650 Crown Marshal, taking part in major political and diplomatic activities of the state. During the Swedish invasion, he stood by King Jan Kazimierz, accompanying him during his temporary exile.

Łukasz Opaliński's major works were a political and social satire *Something New* (1652) and a literary treatise *The New Poet* (ca. 1661). In *A Conversation Between a Parson and a Country-squire* (1641), Opaliński criticized the Sejm and excessive privileges of the nobility. He also wrote in defense of Polish political institutions (*Polonia defensa contra Ioannem Barclaium*) and on Christian ethics (*De officiis libri tres*). *De officiis* was reprinted many times and used as a textbook in Jesuit schools.

The New Poet
(selection)

Coffin--the Measure of Things

    And to add to it, if these examples
    Will not provide you excellent counsels,
    Death itself will, because it brings to light
    That people in vain in this world delight,
5   Because death takes away everything here,
    As on its account all things disappear.
    Coffin the measure of things, while world's bliss
    Tumbles down into sepulchral darkness,
    Time destroys all, high rank and dignity
10 Must become subject to mortality.
    So why do we all these pleasures desire
    From which so quickly we have to retire?
    Why do we strive for all with such great pain,
    If so briefly as guests here we remain?
15 Why is that we would not rather prepare
    For another life, that gives man a share

Łukasz Opaliński

Of proper happiness and secure peace,
Which forever and ever will not cease.

Text: Vincenz, Andrzej. *Helikon sarmacki. Wątki i tematy poezji barokowej.* Wrocław: Ossolineum, Biblioteka Narodowa I 259, 1989, 307-308 (based on Łukasz Opaliński, *Wybór pism.* Ed. by Stanisław Grzeszczuk. Wrocław: Ossolineum, Biblioteka Narodowa I 172, 1959, 312).

JAN ANDRZEJ MORSZTYN (1621-1693)

Jan Andrzej Morsztyn was born near Cracow in a rich nobleman's family. He was educated at home and later studied in Leyden. As a courtier of Aleksander Lubomirski, Morsztyn travelled to France and Italy. For many years a deputy to the Sejm, he gained high offices, becoming a courtier to Władysław IV and Jan Kazimierz, and in 1668 Treasurer of the Crown. Opposed to the policy of King Jan Sobieski, Morsztyn was accused of treason and in 1683 escaped to France, where he died.

A court poet, Morsztyn excelled in disseminating Italian and French literary themes in his elaborate verses, filled with fanciful conceits. His love poems and songs, circulated in two major collections, *Dog Days* (1647) and *Lute* (1661), are teeming with bold comparisons and clever contrasts, inventive concatenations, and hyperbole.

Inconstancy[1]

Sooner one will bag the wind, sooner one will place
    Into his pocket tiny pieces of sunrays,
Sooner the blustering sea by threats he will calm,
    Sooner he'll grasp the enormous world in his palm,
5   Sooner without harm he'll put out fire with his fist,
    Sooner he will capture in the net cloudy mist,
Sooner, while crying, he will flood Etna with tears,
    Sooner the mute will sing, and one with insane fears
Speak wisely; sooner Fortune will show the same face
10   And death and laughter will live in one dwelling place,
Sooner the poet and vain dream tell a true tale,
    Sooner tears will not be fruitful for the angel,[2]
Sooner the sun will hide in a cave for the night,
    Peace will be in prison, men in desert abide,
15   Sooner all reason will perish and words will flee,
    Than any fair lady will ever constant be.

Notes

1. The poem was inspired by Giambattisto Marino, the main representative of Italian baroque.
2. The angel's tears will not help the unfortunate person for whom the angel laments.

The Fair Sex

A crocodile is bad, it deludes by crying,
    A siren is bad, for her voice is beguiling,
A serpent is bad, concealed deep in grass, it stings,
    Spring water is bad, though dazzling, a goitre brings:[1]
5 Yet the fair sex brings about much more casualty:
    With crying and voice, secretiveness and beauty.

Notes

1. Some springs, whose waters were deprived of iodine, could cause the goitre, a disease of the thyroid.

On His Young Lady

White is the polished Carrara alabaster,
    White is the milk sent from sheepfolds in a pannier,
White is the swan, with its white feathers covered,
    White is the pearl, with frequent stringing not tampered,
5 White is the snow, that freshly fell, still untrodden,
    White is the lily bloom in its freshness chosen.
But whiter still the face and neck of my lady
    Than alabaster, milk, swan, pearl, snow, and lily.

To the Same Lady

Your eyes are not eyes, but suns that shine bright,
    In whose glow all reason must lose its light;
Your lips are not lips, but rosy coral,

      Which capture every sense by their color;
5   Your breasts are not breasts, but a pure design
      From heaven, which our will in chains confine;
Thus the eyes, breasts, lips blind, bind, and confine
      Reason, sense, will with glow, color, design.

To a Young Lady

Hard is the iron smelted with great pains,
      Hard is the diamond, with no hammer stains,
Hard is the oak with old age petrified,
      Hard are the rocks, not heeding the sea tide;
5   You are harder, lady, who my tears mock,
      Than the iron, diamond, hard oak, and rock.

Safe Treasure

A thief will break into your Gdańsk coffers,
      A promised harvest will turn out much worse,
Lightning will burn down your barns and your rest,
      A poor debtor won't pay cash with interest,
5   The ruined peasants will not pay their lease,
      Grain barges will sink in a stormy breeze;
But what you have given to every friend,
      Fortune won't claim--it's surely your stipend.

Inconstancy

Your eyes are fire, your brow a looking glass,
      Hair--gold, teeth--pearls, skin--buttermilk[1] surpass,
Mouth is a coral, cheeks are lavender,
      While you, my young lady, with me concur.
5   But when we quarrel, your cheeks turn leprous,
      Mouth--a pit, cheeks--pale white lead[2] in excess,
Teeth--a nag's bone, hair--web of a spider,
      Your brow--a mangle, eyes--ashy powder.

Notes

1. The original phrase 'curdled milk' is not a complimentary description of a lady's skin in English.
2. White lead was used as an ingredient in paint, cosmetics, and medicines, all appropriate in this context.

To A Lady

Want to wed rich? You are wise. But the well to do
    Is not stupid; he won't marry but will buy you.

A Clever Maiden

A maiden once asked a doctor: When is it best
    To make love, when the sun rises or goes to rest?
The doctor replied: It will make the night sweeter,
    Whereas in the morning it will be much healthier.
5   I will then be following, she said, your counsel:
    When night falls for taste, in the morning to keep well.

Bee in Amber

In most transparent amber concealed visibly,
    It seems the bee is swimming in her own honey.
Treated with contempt when she lived under the skies,
    Now her burial and coffin bear a higher prize.
5   That's how for faithful work she's been given her pay,
    No doubt she herself wished to die in such a way.
Cleopatra ought not to flatter herself so,
    When an insect lies in a more splendid barrow.

The Wonders of Love
Sonnet

I nourish love with worry and thinking,
    Thinking with memory and covetousness,

I nourish lust with hope and comeliness,
    Hope with illusion and useless straying.

5 I fill my heart with pride and delusion,
    Pride with pretended delight and rashness,
    I nurture rashness with folly and smugness,
    Folly with anger and vile corruption.

I nourish worry with tears and with sighs,
10   The sighs with fire, fire with the wind indeed,
    The wind with shadows, shadows with deceit.

Whoever heard about such enterprise,
    That with this care about the others' greed,
    I'm hungry myself 'midst all these supplies.

To a Corpse
Sonnet

You lie struck dead, I am struck dead the same,
    You with the death bolt, I the love arrow,
    You have no blood, I have no ruddy glow,
    You have plain candles, I a hidden flame,

5 Your face is covered with a mourning shroud,
    In dreadful darkness my senses are trapped,
    Your hands are bound, while my mind has been strapped,
    Deprived of freedom, in irons throughout.

But you are silent, while my tongue whimpers,
10   You feel nothing, I can't deep pain forgo,
    You are like ice, I in hellish sunglow.

With time your body into dust scatters,
    And yet I cannot scatter in ash pyre,
    Eternal element of my own fire.

XII. *Autumn* (1684-1686) by Jerzy Eleuter Siemiginowski, Wilanów Palace

To a Butterfly
Sonnet

Carefully, butterfly! That fire is injurious!
   Beware of this candle, beware of this fair face,
   In whose glow gilded death secretly found its place,
   Do not be for your martyrdom so covetous.

5 You rush to your grave and deceitful obsequies,
   You draw near your own coffin and your dreams give chase,
   Hoping to be set free by what sets you ablaze.
   Ah! You have now lost your life, lover so hapless!

And yet you are fortunate that with an embrace,
10 After experiencing the desired pleasure,
   You parted company with your beloved candle.

O! If I could only by the same fortune's grace
   Die for the one for whom fires inside me kindle,
   And yet before that have our lips come together!

Texts: Morsztyn, Jan Andrzej. *Wybór poezji*. Ed. by Wiktor Weintraub. Wrocław: Ossolineum, Biblioteka Narodowa I 257, 1988, 69, 79-80, 105, 106, 107, 125, 145-146, 148, 149-150. Morsztyn, Jan Andrzej. *Wybór poezji*. Ed. by Maria Bokszczanin. Warszawa: PIW, 1963, 63, 87, 108.

WACŁAW POTOCKI (1621-1696)

Potocki was brought up and educated in an affluent Arian family near Biecz in southern Poland. He spent nearly all of his life there, managing his estate and serving as judge and deputy starost of Biecz. In 1638, Potocki took part in a military campaign in the Ukraine against the Cossacks, and later fought at Beresteczko in 1651, and against the Swedes in 1655-1656. Threatened with confiscation of his estate and banishment, Potocki accepted Roman Catholicism, yet since his wife remained true to Arianism, he did not escape persecution.

A versatile poet and publicist, Potocki compiled between 1672 and 1694 a collection of nearly two thousand anecdotes, trifles, and polemical poems, whose title aptly describes its nature: *A Garden, But Not Weeded, A Haystack, But Each Sheaf of a Different Grain, A Stand of Diverse Wares...*, or briefly *A Garden of Trifles*. His epic poem, *The Progress of the War of Chocim* (1670), is a chronicle based on the diary of Jakub Sobieski, father of the future king, which describes the heroism of Polish soldiers fighting against Turkish armies in 1621.

THE PROGRESS OF THE WAR OF CHOCIM
(selections)

IN WHICH OSMAN, TURKISH EMPEROR,[1] HAVING GATHERED ALL FORCES OF HIS STATES FROM AFRICA, ASIA, AND EUROPE, FAILED IN HIS VENTURE THANKS TO THE GRACE OF THE HIGHEST LORD, WISDOM OF VIGILANT AND FORESIGHTED COMMANDERS, AND THE BRAVERY OF POLISH KNIGHTS, AND HAVING LOST ONE HUNDRED THOUSAND PEOPLE, SOME IN THE FIELD, SOME ATTACKING OUR ARMY, SOME DEFENDING THEIR CAMPS, CONFIRMED THE OLD TREATY WITH THE POLISH CROWN, AND RETURNED *INGLORIUS*[2] TO CONSTANTINOPLE. HE SET CAMP AT CHOCIM IN THE YEAR 1621 OF OUR SAVIOR, ON THE THIRD DAY OF SEPTEMBER, LEFT ON THE TENTH OF OCTOBER. COLLECTED FROM VARIOUS MANUSCRIPTS AND DIARIES, AS WELL AS FROM THE NARRATIVES OF THE

OLD PEOPLE WHO WERE *PRAESENTES*,[3] BUT MOSTLY FROM THE ACCOUNT OF HIS HIGHNESS SIR JAKUB SOBIESKI,[4] COMMISSIONER OF THE KNIGHT ESTATE FOR THAT CAMPAIGN, FUTURE CASTELLAN OF CRACOW, APPROPRIATELY TRANSLATED IN VERSE FROM LATIN INTO POLISH FOR THE IMMORTAL GLORY OF THE POLISH NATION. YEAR 1670 OF OUR LORD, THE LAST DAY OF DECEMBER.

First Part

   First, before the Muse will pour out onto pages
Bloody deeds of Polish Mars for future ages,
Before I write down for the Poles to remember
Instances of the audacious Turk's procedure,
5 (Who arrogantly dared the old treaty to refute,
As in Hungary and Bulgaria claiming tribute)--
O God, who are praised by the lands, the seas, the skies,
Who rules a weak quill and the steel that terrifies,
Who avenges this house's last remaining part,
10 Where the oath is sworn with the lips but with false heart--
I implore You, deign to bless what this mortal hand
Wants to record for Your praise in the royal land:
Because it is the splendid work of Your right hand:
To destroy the pride of every haughty tyrant,
15 To confound the arrogant, to dust high thoughts smite,
Aided by those who depend on You for their might.
(...)

Fourth Part

(...)
The mountains and the banks of Dniester became white
(One could say fresh snow fell on the ground overnight),
As soon as the Turks stopped, in the blink of an eye
20 They pitched their countless tents stretching out far and high.
They did not set up a camp, they did not use cords,
But having taken lightly a handful of giaours,
Wherever they marched, they just stopped--feeling their might,
If they will not scare us, they will drown us in spite.

25 Nothing to keep them here, they don't want to stay long,
    The Vistula on their minds--how to bridge it anon?[5]
    The emperor himself took the upper hillside,[6]
    It is visibly boasting, it clearly shows pride
    That the monarchs of Asia, Africa, Europe,
30 Lords of three parts of the world, walk upon its top.
    (...)

    The chief janissary,[7] in peacock opulence,
    Puts in the front lines his fiery regiments,
    He has just now mounted a white Arab charger
    And glitters like a comet in a star cluster,
35 A feathery tuft overhead, samite silks shine;
    Above, flag with the crescent, an Ottoman sign.
    (...)

    Left and right of the janissaries stood in view
    Awesome creatures unknown to our eyes hitherto:
    Terrifying elephants, tusks and trunks beside;
40 Each carrying a tower with shooters inside,
    Thirty in each; wherever these angered beasts go,
    They cause destruction within the ranks of the foe.
    Cavalry units on the flanks, with their spears high,
    Look if the hideous giaour moves on them nearby
45 Or if they'll be told to move to where with fury
    A daring spahi[8] throws his lance at our army.
    You could not see cuirasses or any armor,
    Each attired in samite, in silk, and in feather;
    Enormous wings of vultures, plumes, panaches, crests,
50 Flutter above their heads, but they are all pretexts
    And paltry ornaments for showing here unfit,
    Since people use such things as scarecrows in millet!
    They have brought them all in, they put them on today,
    What for years they have looted and plundered away.
    (...)

55 At last Osman seeing our troops were mocking him,
    That he won't draw them out by any stratagem,
    He is ready to fight; he is getting reports,
    He sends the janissaries and all his cohorts
    Towards defenseless places and where our ramparts

60 Against pagans at the back had the lowest parts.
   He puts these ordinary hordes in front to fight
   And then drives forward countless crowds with all his might.
   They are now here, ready to leap over the moat,
   When our soldiers also of the danger take note;
65 So they fortify in brief words their confidence
   And stop the janissaries' first fiery advance;
   When the enemy comes close, they aim without fail,
   They shower him wherever he turns with lead hail.
   The pagan is falling down, shot in naked gut,
70 Never more destruction in a forest uncut
   Was brought about by impetuous Eurus[9] storms,
   Felling pines and tearing from trunks dry lungwort corms.
   They drop down their rifles, and like a herd ashore
   Throw themselves into the red sea of pagan gore.
75 They jump from the ramparts and if still have some breath,
   Under the victors' feet they are bleeding to death.
   So when chest strikes chest, when they step on others' toes,
   Then live pieces of flesh are flying between blows,
   Where the cutting broadsword comes down in a swift hand,
80 Reaching to the bottom, touching the soul of man.
   As when two water pots knock in a stream current,
   One of them will not be left without detriment.
   But when the iron pot fights with the pot of clay,
   It will smash it with its thrust without much delay.
85 The Pole has enough heart to face Turkish warrior,
   And when he is covered too with tempered armor,
   His chest shielded with plates, helmet guarding his head,
   Though he is stung, though slashed, he doesn't feel affected.
   The pagan carries naked belly like the lute,
90 A bare head, a thin neck can be cut to the root.
   He puts trust in numbers, but in such a melee,
   Is not able to fight nor can he run away.
   They could yell and scream at the top of their voices,
   While their stretched out veins were bursting into pieces.
95 And when the next enemy lumbers through death's door,
   Sweat blinds the eyes, the arm gets heavy in armor,
   But the prudent Chodkiewicz, as if from his sleeve,
   Gives them just in time the necessary reprieve.
   Three hundred men with Kochanowski have come in,
100 He has taken care of the prince's well being;

Weiher[10] draws near with his unit; some burn fuses
Against the Turks, others hold guns with cocked triggers.
They quickly attack the pagans straight at their sides,
Fire at them three times and blind them so much besides
105 That they begin to run away. And in this mess
Our men are stinging them, for their swords lost sharpness.
And when the sun is just reaching the lowest place,
The hetman forbids his men to give further chase,
He fears an ambush; the troops want the foe's defeat,
110 Yet with great jubilation he orders retreat.

Notes

1. Osman II (1604-1622), Turkish Sultan, was not yet eighteen years old during this campaign. His army of about one hundred thousand soldiers and twenty thousand camp followers lost about forty thousand people. He signed the peace treaty with Poland in 1621. Soon after he was dethroned by the janissaries and murdered.
2. *inglorius*--'defamed'.
3. *praesentes*--'present'.
4. Jakub Sobieski, father of King Jan Sobieski III, Castellan of Cracow, participated in the campaign led by Hetman Karol Chodkiewicz, and authored its description, entitled *Commentariorum belli Chotinensis libri tres* (1646).
5. They were already thinking of crossing the Vistula.
6. The sultan had his tent put up at the high point, from which he could observe the battlefield.
7. Janissaries were soldiers of an elite corps of Turkish troops, organized in the fourteenth century as the sultan's guard.
8. Spahis were Turkish cavalrymen.
9. Eurus--the east wind.
10. Jan Weiher commanded the German infantry.

XIII. Armour and pennons of Polish hussars

A Garden of Trifles

The World--a Prison

O, how miserable is this world's condition,
  Like a jailed villain, awaiting execution.
He awaits, doomed to die, for settling of the score,
  Morning or night--doesn't know when they'll knock on his door.
5 So then whoever's fate was ever to be born,
  Is already in jail, alas, a guard watching on.
He doesn't know day or hour from his cradle until
  His hair will turn gray, when death orders him to kneel.
He's waiting day and night, at dawn, in the evening.
10 What then is man's life? Death for which we are waiting.
  The incessant fear of death, which even much more
  Than death itself makes human hearts be dying sore.

What Man Cannot Conceal

Man can conceal everything without special art,
  Except: liquor in his head and love in his heart.
Although he keeps silent, though no one asks him twice,
  Barring other gestures, one soon reads from his eyes.

What Time Finds, Time Ruins

Someone said: Nothing more wise than Time. The other:
  Nothing more stupid. How then to solve this matter?
The former counted various trades and sciences,
  In which Time taught men and still shows influences.
5 The latter: kings, sages, mighty men, knights, nations,
  Castles, towns, palaces, which with great afflictions
Time left one unreliable thing to possess,
  Then drowned in lasting, irrevocable stillness.
You will ask: How can we this question clarify?
10   All things that came about with Time, will in Time die.

On My Poems

All those who read my poems or who listen to,
    Praise them, except for the poets who write them too.
They find fault with them, but I am not disheartened,
    I don't care about cooks, when my guests are content.

Shaved or Shorn

Man and wife crossing a footbridge over waters,
    Saw a man without a beard, who once had whiskers.
"Well, look here how our neighbor is shaved," the man said.
    The wife: "He is shorn, you can see it by his head."
5 So he said: "No, he is shaved." She said: "He is shorn."
    They kept squabbling about this matter for so long,
Until words came to blows; off the bridge he pushed her,
    She's already drowning, drinking from the river,
Her head under water, she's fishing for small fry,
10   And yet her fingers still keep shearing, her hand high.
When the neighbors found out about this incident,
    They ran to gape and saw that against the current
The man was searching; they all laughed. But he decreed:
    "There's no need to wonder, all goes down stream, indeed.
15 But this woman so adverse in all by nature,
    Even after death, I take it, floats up river."

Wise Answers

What is most ancient in the natural order?
    God. You ask why? For He has no progenitor.
What's most beautiful? The world; if you want to know,
    All things man calls beautiful in the world do show.
5 What's the wisest? Time is; it put all learning's store,
    Both of hand and mind into print for evermore.
What is the largest? Place; because all in your head
    That you find of large size in one place can be spread.
What's the fastest? Thought, for 'ere you finish a prayer,
10   Thought will cross the sky, land, sea, reaching everywhere.
What's the strongest? Death; for no one will break its bond.
    What's most terrible? Death; but not this--the second.

What's most uncertain? Death; it steals people away.
What's most certain? Death; it certainly comes your way.
15 What's most desirable? Death; for it does suspend
All the torments for which man dies by his own hand.

Man's Life

You have asked: What is the life of man on this earth?
    As your reply take two things of conflicting worth:
Look at the body, a flash tied to endlessness,
    If you look at the soul, age which is limitless.
5   Or instead: man's life is a fixed moment of time,
    Which ages' eternities are determined by,
From mother's womb to the grave it's a narrow strait,
    From body and soul's bond until they separate.
Where at each step, if he falls, a human being
10   Either life or eternal death finds awaiting.
Rarely anyone will reach his destination,
    So all matters have to depend on discretion.
He must treat every hour as if his last sojourn,
    Who wants to live with God, not with the devil burn.

Let the Drunk World Sleep
Third Poem on the Subject

The world is asleep, drunk with wine, it closed its eyes,
    The Babylon whore pours,[1] the devil wine supplies.
The world is asleep, resembling a dead tree trunk,
    From the winepress of God's wrath against its sins drunk.[2]
5 Not to wake it, the devil stands as a guardian,
    Warns from far with his finger, makes the dogs drunken.
First he puts in front of them a bucket of wine,
    So that they would slumber, in their pulpits not whine,[3]
Or their voices wouldn't be understood.[4] If instead
10   Some want to open their snouts, he tosses them bread.
Let one of them cry like a hound in the timber:
    A heretic! Wall him till death in a cloister,
Or behead or burn him! He wants to interfere
    In the world's sweet sleep? If so let him make it clear

15 To the hangman! While Sirens softly sing and play
   To make the world sleep more sweetly, he will still bay.

Notes

1. "Come, I will show you the judgment of the great whore who is seated on many waters, with whom the king of the earth have committed fornication, and with the wine of whose fornication the inhabitants of the earth have become drunk." (Revelation 17:2)

2. "Those who worship the beast and its image, and receive a mark on their foreheads or on their hands, they will also drink the wine of God's wrath, poured unmixed into the cup of his anger (...). " (Revelation 14:9-10)

3. "Israel's sentinels are blind,
      they are all without knowledge;
   they are silent dogs
      that cannot bark;
   dreaming, lying down,
      loving to slumber."
   "Come," they say, "let us
      get wine;
   let us fill ourselves with
   strong drink." (Isaiah 56:10, 12).
      'Sentinels'--prophets.

4. "The righteous perish,
      and no one takes it to heart;
      the devout are taken away,
      while no one understands." (Isaiah 57:1)

What the Eyes Cannot See, the Heart Does Not Regret
On the Eyes Getting Dim in Old Age

My eyes are filled with mist, glasses are of no use,
   I do not know why; probably old years' abuse.
Like an executioner beheading a felon
   Death first binds his eyes, first puts a cloth tightly on.
5 And yet why does he bind me, why my eyes cover,
   Since he has seized all they had to love forever?
Behead me, nothing in this world is worth eyeing,
   For this life has been full of pain, grief, and crying.

You have bound my eyes, nay, you rather plucked them free,
10   When you seized my children.[1] Nothing dearer to see.
Indeed, looking at others, when mine I think of,
   The eyes cause still more pain than when they were pulled off.
What will please the eye looking at spiritual
   Not physical life? All is sin and dreamlike all,
15 A bubble on water. In the blink of an eye,
   Nothing to lean upon, everything passes by.
You see water in the river, but it's different,
   That which you saw went down; so quickly are spent
Worldly things. You haven't today what you had last day,
20   They get older, until with time each will decay.
Time like a river runs its waters to the sea.
   The soil covers all these things that man's eyes can see.
Don't bind, open my eyes to the world of dolor,
   Let them look at the longed for end of this torture.
25 Fortune has already tormented much my heart,
   Why should I call death the tyrant of mortal part?
Don't drag from jail, from fire under sword, hook to square,
   Behead me at once, don't slaughter with long despair!
Open them, do not bind, let them see my sins' breadth;
30   They wouldn't cry for them in health, let them weep in death.

Notes

1. Potocki lost two sons and a daughter.

Texts: Potocki, Wacław. *Wojna chocimska.* Ed. by Aleksander Brückner. Kraków: Nakładem Krakowskiej Spółki Wydawniczej, Biblioteka Narodowa, I 75, 1924, 151-153.
Potocki, Wacław. *Wiersze wybrane.* 3rd ed. Ed. by Stanisław Grzeszczuk. Wrocław: Ossolineum, Biblioteka Narodowa I 19, 1992, 3-5, 13-14, 15-17, 132-133, 134, 137, 154, 206-207.
Sokołowska, *I w odmianach czasu smak jest,* 460-461, 464-465, 488, 492.

JAN SOBIESKI (1629-1696)

Jan Sobieski, King of Poland (1674-1696), was educated in the Cracow Academy and abroad. He spent some time at the French court and was married to Marie-Casimire de la Grange d'Arquein. During his military campaigns between 1664 and 1683, he wrote to her love letters, in which he also described his activities and major events of the day. His letters contain many words and phrases in French, the native language of his beloved 'Mariette.' His letter of September 13, 1683, was written directly after his victory over the Turkish army of the Grand Vizier Kara Mustapha at Vienna.

Letters to Marysieńka
Pielaskowice, on Tuesday, [June 9, 1665].

My darling, most beautiful wife, greatest joy of my heart and soul!

Your beauty, my gold maiden, got so much into my head that I could not close my eyes the whole night long. The Lord sees that I do not know myself if this *absence* will be bearable; so I begged Sir Koniecpolski to spend the whole night talking with me. Today it is just impossible to think either about food or about sleep. I can see that your graceful eyes enchanted me so much that without them it will be impossible to endure even a moment and I trust that *notre amour ne changera jamais en amitié, ni en la plus tendre qui fut jamais.*[1] It is certain that for a long period of time I have had a feeling that I cannot love with greater intensity and more; but now I admit that if not with greater intensity, as it is impossible to love with greater intensity, *je vous admire*[2] more and more, seeing perfection and the most kind soul in such a beautiful body. So for this reason, queen of my heart, rest assured that first the whole nature will turn around before the beautiful Astrée will see the slightest change in her Celadon.[3]

No messenger has returned yet from Warsaw. God permitting, I will be leaving on my journey tomorrow before dawn. They are letting me know from home[4] that the horde came to the Voivode of Ruthenia; the Voivode of Cracow has probably ad-

XIV. Interior of a Turkish tent captured at Vienna

vanced from Tarnopol to the Ukraine, Sir Sieniawski following him. So I do not know who will go now to the side of His Majesty,[5] for those who are more friendly are all in the Ukraine, while others are either on the other side[6] or will stay at home, watching the situation. (...)

Notes

1. 'Our love will never change into friendship and will never be more tender.'
2. 'I adore you.'
3. The names of heroes from the romance *Astrée* by Honoré d'Urfé.
4. Sobieski came from Ruthenia.
5. The king was Jan Kazimierz. Sobieski was at that time the Grand Marshal of the Crown.
6. Hetman Jerzy Lubomirski led the rebellion against the king in 1665-66.

In the Vizier's tents, September 13 [1683], at night

Only joy of my heart and soul, most beautiful and most beloved Marysieńka!

Our God and Lord, blessed forever, gave victory and glory to our nation, unheard of in the past. All the cannons, the whole camp, inestimable possessions have fallen into our hands. The enemy, having strewn the covered siege-trenches, field, and camp with dead bodies, is fleeing in disarray. Only today are our forces beginning to take camels, mules, cattle, sheep which accompanied the enemy, driving in front of them herds of Turks; meanwhile the others, especially *des renegats*,[1] on good horses and beautifully attired, escape from them to us. This is such an unexplicable thing that already today fears arose among common people here in the city and in our camp, as they concluded and could not find any other explanation but that the enemy was coming back. Gunpowder alone and munitions that he abandoned are worth more than a million. I also saw this past night the thing that I always wanted to see. Our rabble set gunpowder on fire in several spots; it looked as if the Judgment Day had arrived, but without any harm to people; we could see the clouds forming in the sky. Yet it is most misfortunate, because probably the losses reach about a million.

The Vizier barely escaped from all this, on one horse and in a single robe. I indeed became his successor because to a great degree all of his riches have fallen into my hands; it happened this way as one of his servants, who was in front of the camp and followed closely the Vizier, was bribed and showed us the tents, as large as Warsaw or Lwów within their walls. I have all the Vizier's insignia which they carry before him; the grand standard of Mahomet his emperor gave him for the war, which already today I have sent in the care of Talenti[2] to the Holy Father in Rome. Tents, all wagons came into my possession, *et mille d'autres galanteries fort jolies et fort riches, mais fort riches*,[3] and still I have not seen many things. *Il n'y a point de comparaison avec ceux de Chocim.*[4] Few quivers alone studded with rubies and sapphires are worth several thousands ducats. You will not be able to tell me, my dear soul, as the Tartar women used to tell their husbands coming back without booty that "you are not a brave warrior if you come back without booty," because the one who conquers must be in the front line. I also have the Vizier's horse with its saddle and trappings; the Vizier himself was pursued very closely but he saved himself. His *kiahia*, that is second-in-command, was killed, and so were many pashas. Lots of gold sabers and other military equipment are left. The night thwarted our goals and the fact that in retreat they were fighting fiercely *et font la plus belle retirade du monde.*[5] They left their janissaries in the covered siege-trenches, and they were put to sword at night, for such was the arrogance and pride of those people that when some of them were fighting us in the field, others were attacking the city, for what else could they do.

I estimate their forces, excluding the Tartars, at three hundred thousand: others estimate their tents alone at three hundred thousand and take the average of three men to one tent, which would give an immense number. However, I estimate at least one hundred thousand tents, as they had several camps. For a day and two nights they are taking them down, whoever wants to, even the city people came out, but I know that even in a week they will not take them all down. They left behind a lot of innocent people, local Austrians, especially women; but they were killing whoever they could. A lot of dead women lie here, but also a lot of the wounded who can still live. Yesterday I saw a three-year old child, a most charming boy, whose face and head had been horribly slashed by an infidel. It is indeed vile that the Vizier took somewhere from one of the Emperor's palaces an exceptionally beautiful ostrich; and even this one he ordered to be killed, so that it would not get into our hands alive. And what luxuries he had near his tents, it is hard to describe. He had baths, he had a little garden and fountains, rabbits, cats; he even had a parrot, but it was flying and we could not catch it.

Today I was in the city which could not have held out more than five days. The human eye had never seen such things that the mines have done there; they turned the fortified towers, terribly big and high, into awful rocks and ruined them so much that they could not stand any more. The Emperor's palace is completely ruined by cannon-balls.

All the armies, which did their duty very well, awarded this victory to the Lord and to us. When the enemy began to flee and was broken--it was my task to struggle with the Vizier, who brought all his armies against my right wing so that our center or main guard as well as the left wing did not have much to do and they sent therefore all their German reinforcements towards me--all the princes ran up to me, such as the Elector of Bavaria and Prince Waldeck, embracing me and kissing my face, while the generals were kissing my hands and feet; you can imagine the simple soldiers! The officers and all regiments of cavalry and infantry cried out: *Ach, unzer brave Kenik!*[6] They listened to me more than our men ever did. You can imagine this morning the joy of the princes of Lorraine and of Saxony (yesterday I could not see them as they were at the very end of the left wing, where I sent several regiments of the hussars to the forces of the Marshal of the Court); what about Starhemberg, local commandant[7]! All of them kissed me, embraced me, called me their savior. Afterwards I went to two churches. All the common people kissed my hands, feet, robes; others just touched me, crying: "O, permit us to kiss this valiant hand!" They all wished to shout "Vivat!", but one could see from their demeanor that they feared their officers and superiors. One group could not contain itself any longer and shouted fearfully "Vivat!", and I noticed that it was looked upon with disapproval. Therefore as soon as I finished dining with the commandant, I left the city for the camp, and the common people, raising their hands, led me as far as the gate. I see that the commandant seems to be at odds with the city council, for when they were greeting me, the commandant did not even introduce them. The princes came from all over and the Emperor informs us that he is one mile away; and yet this letter is not finished by the early morning, as they are not allowing me to keep writing and let my heart enjoy you.

Not a few of our people perished in this extremity; we are particularly filled with sorrow concerning those two,[8] about whom Dupont already told us. From the foreign troops, Prince de Croy is killed, his brother shot, and several important people killed. Padre d'Aviano,[9] who would not stop kissing me, says that he saw a white dove flying over our army.

We are leaving today for Hungary, pursuing the enemy. The Electors do not want to part from me. God's blessing is over us, for which we offer Him honor, fame, and glory forever! When the Vizier saw that he could not hold out against us any longer, he called his sons and cried like a child. Then he said to the Khan: "Save me if you can!" The Khan answered: "We know well the King, we will not defeat him and we have to think about ourselves so that we could save ourselves." (...)

Notes

1. *renegats*--Christians who became Turks.
2. Tommaso Talenti, King's secretary.
3. 'and a thousand of other small things, beautiful and expensive, but very expensive.'
4. 'There is no comparison with those of Chocim.' Sobieski was victorious in the battle of Chocim in 1673.
5. 'forming a splendid second line of defense.'
6. 'Oh, our brave King!'
7. Count Starhemberg was the commandant of Vienna.
8. Stanisław Potocki, son of the Cracow Castellan, and Andrzej Modrzejowski, Przemyśl Starost, died on the battlefield on September 12.
9. Marco d'Aviano, a Capuchin monk, was the Pope's envoy.

Text: Sobieski, Jan. *Listy do Marysieńki.* Ed. by Leszek Kukulski. Warszawa: Czytelnik, 1962, 28, 520-523.

ZBIGNIEW MORSZTYN (ca. 1628-1689)

Orphaned as a young boy, Morsztyn was brought up in an Arian community in Little Poland. In about 1646, he entered the service of the Radziwiłł family and remained in it until his death. He fought in major campaigns of the Cossack and Swedish wars. Beginning in 1657, Morsztyn carried out various diplomatic assignments on behalf of Bogusław Radziwiłł. After the law banishing the Arians from Poland was passed in 1658, Morsztyn settled in Prussia, where he administered the estate of Bogusław Radziwiłł's granddaughter and supported many impoverished coreligionists.

Only a few works, e.g., *The Famous Victory Over the Turks* and *Song In Distress*, were published anonymously during Morsztyn's lifetime. A major collection of his poems, *The Domestic Muse*, which included 113 religious *Emblems,* remained in manuscript and was published in 1954.

To a Virtuous Lady

A new miracle on this fair face shows:
    Today under snow a ruddy flame glows,
Snow does not dissolve in fire and the flame
    In violence to nature in snow doesn't wane.
5 Seeing then what nature can undergo,
    I burn up like a fire and dissolve like snow;
When I am between these elements thrust,
    I'll melt in a stream or burn into dust.

Song of Captivity[1]

I sing, even though misery
    And feelings depressive,
Close all around and worry
    A pitiful captive,
5   While great misfortunes thrive,
    I am barely alive.

   I sing to you, and yet my heart
     Without a single break
   Is by affliction torn apart
10   When constant sighs of ache,
      That mortify my soul,
      Must pour out in my dole.

   I sing, although my native land,
     This afflicted mother,
15 Whose soil was once so abundant,
     Whom no one could conquer,
      Has suddenly fallen,
      By the Swede is taken!

   I sing to you, and yet my songs
20   Ought to remain unknown,
   Let forest satyrs and let fauns
     In far-off groves intone;
      They should sing them again
      And in this way complain.

25 I sing, but many a current
     Of our Polish blood grows,
   While smoke high above to heaven
     From towns and hamlets flows;
      This land once vivacious
30   Is turning to ashes.

   I sing to you, but I don't leap,
     Such is my music's tone,
   Sadly, like a mother I weep,
     When she looks at her own
35   The most beloved children
      Back to earth now given.

   I sing, an yet so great many
     Of my dearest brothers,
   Were cut by sworded enemy,
40   While others in fetters
      Resembling my sad fate
      Are driven through jail's gate.

　　　　I sing to you like Niobe;
　　　　　　Left with her dead children,
45　Who in pitiful agony
　　　　　　Has turned into stone then.
　　　　　　　　Though my heart is singing,
　　　　　　　　In grief it is fainting.

　　　　I sing, though I'm affected by
50　　　　My miserable lot,
　　　Though in enormous grief I sigh,
　　　　　　Though as yet I can not
　　　　　　　　See end of slave travails,
　　　　　　　　And though my heart still ails.

55　I sing to you, but this singing
　　　　　　Will quickly give birth to
　　　Lamentation and complaining,
　　　　　　Flood of bloody tears, too,
　　　　　　　　In present bitterness,
60　　　　　　　It will bring more sadness.

　　　I sing, and yet my weary bones
　　　　　　Covered only by skin
　　　Are all dried up from the moans,
　　　　　　When greedy Parcae spin
65　　　　　　　The thread of existence,
　　　　　　　　Cutting my years' advance.

　　　I sing to you, and yet suck in
　　　　　　My tears, while I bewail
　　　Like a worrying pelican,[2]
70　　　　　　When the hunter will trail
　　　　　　　　His children unawares
　　　　　　　　Into treacherous snares.

　　　I sing, but the state of my head,
　　　　　　For most trivial reason,
75　Is hanging on the thinnest thread,
　　　　　　At every hour thereon,
　　　　　　　　At any odd moment
　　　　　　　　In this predicament.

I sing like a poor turtledove,[3]
80   When she lost her partner,
She sadly cries for her true love,
    For her dear protector,
        She carries her distress
        Through the far-off forest.

85 I sing, but my tenacity
        Suffered a heavy blow,
In such a long captivity
    I am just a shadow,
        When winds begin to play,
90   Like a reed I will sway.

I sing to you, and yet these coos,
    These coos that sadly flow,
Are thwarted in the morning dews
    By a tearful echo,
95   When over the valley,
        The rising sounds sally.

I sing, though only by water
    And by this bread alone
I have to live on in hunger,
100   To painful hardships prone.
        I look around to see
        If someone shows pity.

I sing to you, and yet my tears
    From the wounded heart's pain,
105 Which were veiled in its inner spheres,
    Just like an early rain
        Are profusely falling,
        And my song deluging.

I sing, though I nearly succumb
110   In fierce cold to freezing,
On the bare bench I have turned numb
    Without any bedding.
        This then is my repose
        Which a hard life bestows.

XV. Detail of the siege of Cracow, 1655

115 I sing to you, and yet my soul,
      Exposed to complaining,
  Exposed to this sorrowful dole,
      Does not like the singing.
          The plainsong that I hum
120   Floods of tears overcome.

  I sing, but I should howl instead
      At my confreres of yore.[4]
  When I was providing them bread,
      Many knew well my door,
125   My good deeds for these men
          Are today forgotten.

  I sing to you, and yet troubles,
      That have bothered me so,
  And constant fortune reverses,
130   Have changed some time ago
         All my joyful poems
          Into mournful laments.

  I sing, but I am like a stone,
      Where are my comforts now?
135 And who my possessions will own?
      The last remains somehow
         In ashes have been found
         And leveled to the ground.

  I sing and I will keep singing
140   Until the very end,
  Until for the final sailing
      In the boat I'll descend,[5]
         When from this world I'll fleet,
         The pallid shades to meet.

145 I sing, and yet I don't despair,
      Although I'm in such plight,
  Because the Lord is well aware,
      My Lord from the height,
         Who can do everything;
150   The help for me he'll bring!

Notes

1. On June 20, 1656, during the battle near Tyniec, Zbigniew Morsztyn was captured and imprisoned by the Swedes.
2. The pelican was a symbol of parental love. It was said that the pelican fed its children with its own blood.
3. The turtledove was a symbol of marital love.
4. This is an allusion to the Arians (Polish Brethren), who were in Cracow at that time. The Arians were the most radical champions of the Reformation in Poland. They rejected the concepts of the Holy Trinity and of original sin. They condemned serfdom, participation in war, and holding of office. For a fuller description of their philosophy, see Michael J. Mikoś, *Polish Renaissance Literature. An Anthology*, p. 19.
5. Charon carried the dead in his boat across Styx to Hades.

Epitaphs

For Captain Paweł Morsztyn, Killed at Batoh

In the field the bones of Paweł Morsztyn turn white,
He was a good knight. Why then did the soil not hide
Their bareness? So that the planets turning swiftly
Could look upon such gallant virtues constantly.

For Both Parents

Here the noble bodies of my parents were laid,
But their reverent souls to paradise were led.
Lord, as we inherit from them in this world here,
Let us share your life with them in eternal sphere.

Emblems

Emblem 8

The sick Bride asks the Bridegroom to feel her pulse.
Inscription: I am faint with love. (The Song of Solomon 2:5)

My heart that has been burned by the love fires
    Has turned now to ashes and to charred pyres,
O my dear Bridegroom, o love that's most true,
    It is sending a plaintive sigh to you.
5 Come and feel my pulse, see how from the fire
    That your holy torch did in me inspire
I glow almost like the wheels of the sun[1]
    That burn into dust Libyan soil in their run.
It's wonderful love and unspeakable,
10   The love by my mind uncontainable,
That you, dear Bridegroom, took for me the cross
    And suffered terrible wounds for my cause;
It kindles mutual love which in turn
    Although is not equal, yet it will burn
15 To such degree that I see myself dead
    But still alive in you, my Beloved--
It's neither life nor is it death outright,
    The difference between them is just slight.

Notes

1. The sun was often represented as a chariot.

Emblem 39

The Bride, seeking the Bridegroom at night, found him
  asleep upon the cross.
Inscription: Upon my bed at night
 I sought him whom my soul
  loves;
 I sought him, but found him not. (The Song of Solomon 3:1)

All day I run; I am gasping for air,
  I prick up my ears to learn anywhere
Of him I love, until I hear it said
That he was seen in his room on the bed.
5 I tiptoe lest I should cut in the bloom
  His sweet sleep, and yet my dearest Bridegroom
Isn't there and the spot he lay on feels chill.
  Did he vanish? Or run somewhere else still?
I search, I look, till I see him lying
10 Without a mattress, pillow or clothing
On the cross--pain, torture, and suffering
  Are his only sheets and his own bedding.
O my Beloved, is this then your repose?
Is this your rest--the cross and bloody blows?
15 Is that your sleep, is that your peaceful spell
  --With the devil and death a bloody duel,
For which you get ready well in advance
  And to my sinful soul give assurance
Through your cruel death, your mutilation,
20 Of blest life and eternal salvation.

Emblem 41

The Bride gives her heart to the Bridegroom and
turns the wheel so he can burnish and polish it.
  Inscription: Take away the dross from the
            silver,
        and the smith has material for
            a vessel. (Proverbs 25:4)

Bridegroom, in your holy hands I bequest
    The heart that was taken out from my breast,
So fouled by smoke when I, soiled, went astray
    And so disfigured by earthly decay.
5   Like a potsherd that was blackened by fire
      Or like a torch that was charred in a pyre.
    Polish it yourself so that it will be
      Clear as crystal, lucid as a ruby;
    While I will be turning the wheel alone
10   And sprinkle with bitter tears the grindstone.
    I know, know well, in the holy city

Zbigniew Morsztyn

        That you have founded, truly heavenly,
    Whose gates with pearls had been decorated
        And whose walls with precious stones created,
15 Nothing impure can be let anywhere.
        O deign to take me in your mercy there,
    With penitent tears I'll bleach my robes white
        And come forward at your grand wedding night!

Emblem 47

    A man cries looking at the sundial.
    Inscription: Are not the days of my life few? (Job 10:20)

How not to cry, not in worry cower,
    How can I not count each day and hour?
When they are being chased by fleeting time
    Faster than a runner off from his line.
5 The blacksmiths hammer, the craftsmen labor,
    People in the street to and fro scamper
And like the flies in the square mill around,
    Customs and townhall men are at work found,
The clock strikes the hours on a high tower,
10 And time doesn't come back, keeps running further,
And so the fleeting months race on their course
    Like the wind, like the clouds, while sharp scissors
The pitiless tyrant[1] holds in her hand,
    When the rest of the wool runs to the end.
15 Immortal Lord, who treat a millennium
    Just as a moment, prolong the consumed
Time of my life, for your omnipotence
    Can even move back the sun's wheels from thence[2];
As you once gave the sign of your mercy
20   To the sick king's cries and despondency
Through the shadow turned so my last breath
    Prolong and do not allow cruel death
To drag me to his snare, and the whole time
    I will spend praising your glory divine.

Notes

1. Parcae, collective name for the three fates in classical mythology, who weave the thread of human life. Atropos is the one who cuts the thread.
2. In Latin poetry, the sun was shown as a chariot.
3. "See, I will make the shadow cast by the declining sun on the dial of Ahaz turn back ten steps." (Isaiah 38:8)

Texts: Morsztyn, Zbigniew. *Wybór wierszy*. Ed. by Janusz Pelc. Wrocław: Ossolineum, Biblioteka Narodowa I 215, 1975, 31, 71-78, 79, 86, 284-285, 302-303, 308-309.
Morsztyn, Zbigniew. *Muza domowa*. Vol. 2. Ed. by Jan Dürr-Durski. Warszawa: PIW, 1954, 36-37.

WESPAZJAN KOCHOWSKI (1633-1700)

Kochowski was born in Gaj near Sandomierz, a son of an affluent landowner. He was educated in Cracow schools. From 1651 to 1660 he took part in the wars against Cossacks, Tartars, Muscovites, Swedes, and Hungarians. In 1660, he settled down in his native village. Three years later he moved to Goleniowy near Cracow, devoting himself to writing, while managing his estate and carrying out various civic duties. Appointed by King Jan Sobieski his official historian, Kochowski took part in the rescue of Vienna in 1683, describing it in a Latin memoir *Commentarius belli adversus Turcas* (1684) and its Polish versified paraphrase *God's Work or a Song of Vienna Delivered* (1684).

Kochowski excelled in historical works and poetry. He wrote in Latin four volumes of *Annales Poloniae,* which covered the times of King Jan Kazimierz and King Michał Wiśniowiecki. In *A Polish Psalmody* (1695), written to commemorate the victory at Vienna, Kochowski used the elevated biblical style to glorify the victorious king and praise the courageous deeds of Polish soldiers in their battle with the Turks. His *Non-idle Idling* (1674) is a large collection of historical, religious, and lyrical poems, including epigrams.

Song XVII
A Monument to the Brave Soldiers
Fallen on the Battlefield of Batoh With Their Hetman Marcin
Kalinowski,
Voivode of Czernichów[1]

    Not in a marble sepulcher,
        Nor a brick burial place,
    You are now resting forever
        In the wide open space.
5   O brave, undaunted commander,
        Followed by your legion,
    You should be honored forever,
        As long as Poland lives on.
    The Cossack units make headway,

10   Against the covenant--
    Yet you are loath to run away,
        O soldier most valiant.
    The hordes are attacking again,
        Loud "Alla!" ringing close,
15   They shoot off swift arrows like rain,
        From tightly strung longbows.
    Death brings no fear a brave soldier,
        He's not afraid of harm,
    Since fame for a Pole is dearer,
20   Than life's most precious charm.
    Although you knew what was to pass,
        Judged victory hopeless,
    And yet you like Leonidas[2]
        Displayed great manliness.
25   Virtue bowed to a big army,
        Polish troops defeated,
    And in eternal infamy
        In one pile they fell dead.
    But infamy had a high price
30   And the deed was valiant
    Though they did not spare their own lives,
        Fortune reversed its grant.
    Therefore you spirits virtuous,
        Rest with God forever,
35   Who suffered from hordes most vicious,
        At Batoh massacre.
    So for your everlasting fame,
        For virtue to resound,
    Our hands erected in your name,
40   This consecrated mound.

Notes

1. Marcin Kalinowski was killed on June 2, 1652, on the plain of Batoh (Batóg) on the River Boh, fighting with his soldiers against the Tartar and Cossack forces that violated the pact signed in 1651 in Biała Cerkiew.

2. Out of about 10,000 Polish soldiers, some 8,000 were killed, including prisoners. They are compared to Leonidas, king of Sparta, and his soldiers, who during two days held back the

Persians at Thermopylae in 480 B.C. before they were overwhelmed.

*A Curse on the Sons of the Crown
Who Break up the Diets*[1]

I

O, unheeding sons, for how much longer
    Will you with the vile fang your mother bite?
    Just to become known from her disaster,
    As of the Greek Herostratus they write.[2]
5   You bring to pass in your sacred shelter
    What the field Tartars[3] have not even tried,
    Even much more than from unfriendly Turks
    It's suffering from your viperous works.[4]

II

The mother deplores these unhapy days,
10   Which have brought upon her much infamy;
    Of former beauty and attractive ways
    She was stripped by the sundry enemy.
    Not so much the noise of the border frays,
    Have in twenty years caused her injury,[5]
15   Not the loss of Ruthenia, Ukraine,[6]
    As much as constant rows at home have been.

III

Smoleńsk in the north we did not regain,
    We forfeited too the unclaimed sectors,
    To leave Poland Swedes took in their domain
20   Livonia, won with blood of ancestors.
    The elector took Lębork, rich Draheim[7]
    And holds them with his administrators.
    The gluttonous Turk with empty entrails
    Is eyeing Kamieniec, his greed prevails.

IV

25 But we debate. If only these councils
    Could lift Poland up from its troubled fate!
    But private interests thwart, also quarrels,
    The Sejm was broken once for the salt spate.
    When the time comes to stop debating bills,
30 A member will say his veto won't wait[8];
    With no resolutions, the diet ends,
    While dear mother is left with no defense.

V

May he perish, be killed without pity,
    Who breaks up diets for private interest,
35 Let his head be cut with impunity,
    From book of life let his name be erased.
    If still alive, fall to adversity,
    And let the lack of bread give him no rest.
    Let the bad son, not mother, first pass away,
40 And let his carcass feed the beasts of prey.

VI

Poles, this is not how you were to deal
    With this precious diamond of liberty[9];
    Not to poison, but to adorn with zeal
    In loving concord, common amity,
45 But we make of our own body a meal,
    Breaking sejms for gain, self-will, hostility,
    Yet you that bring the Crown this disorder,
    Will not wash it off with holy water.[10]

Notes

1. The poem was written after the Sejm was broken up on November 5, 1669. According to the rule of the *liberum veto*, frequently abused at that time, any deputy was allowed to dissolve the Diet on behalf of the opposition.

2. To make his name immortal, Herostratus, a shoemaker from Ephesus, burnt the temple of Artemis (Diana), one of the seven wonders of the world.

3. Following the Polish military structure, some Tartar and Cossack units were led by the grand hetman ('buńczuczny,' named after a banner), while others by the field hetman ('sajdaczny,' named after a quiver), who was lower in rank. Bows and arrows, kept in quivers, were Tartars' standard weapon.

4. "You brood of vipers!" (Matthew 12:34)

5. Twenty years cover the period since the coronation of King Jan Kazimierz in 1648.

6. In 1654, by the terms of the Treaty of Perejasław, Chmielnicki, the Cossack leader, placed the Ukraine under the suzerainty of Alexis, the Tsar of Moscow. Soon after, Lithuania's White Ruthenian lands, including Smoleńsk, fell into the Muscovite hands.

7. In the Treaty of Welawa (Wehlau) and Bydgoszcz in 1657, confirmed in the Peace of Oliwa in 1660, the Elector of Brandenburg obtained Elbląg, Bytów, Drahim (Dreheim), and Lębork (Lauenburg) from Poland. In return, he withdrew from the alliance with Sweden. In the Peace of Oliwa Poland also lost a big part of Livonia.

8. The Sejm was adjourned because of the veto in 1670 and in 1671.

9. Kochowski refers here to the *liberum veto,* which was instituted to promote the principle of unanimity.

10. A reference to Mikołaj Prażmowski, the Primate of Poland, leader of opposition.

Polish Epigrams
In Our Language
Trifles

Gold Scepters
Insignia of the renowned Academy

The famed Academy has insignia of gold,
    But salaries, they say, are more from a lead mold.
Who teaches golden arts should be entitled to
    Not these paltry farthings, but to gold revenue.

5 Gold in the coat of arms, in title, is useless,
> When hard work fills the money chest with emptiness.

Old-fashioned Manners

Be god-fearing in church, but at school be humble,
> Valiant in war, gay at play, witty at table.

Requirements for Good Cheer

Salt, wine, and good will--to each banquet give flavor;
> Add the fourth one, a woman, and I will concur.

Pares ab Adam[1]

When Eve was weaving and Adam was tilling soil,
> Who was then a noble, who did as peasant toil?
So since Adam was our father, Eve our mother,
> From them we are equal brothers to one another.

Notes

1. *Pares ab Adam*--'equals as children of Adam,' was a popular saying that originated in England.

XVI. King Jan Sobieski and his family, after 1693

*The Proper Offering of Thanksgiving to the Giver of All That
Is Good--the Lord and God
or
A Polish Psalmody
Giving Thanks for God's Good Deeds
Written by a Most Humble Person
Anno Domini 1693
And Published Anno Domini 1695
in the Printing House of Jasna Góra in Częstochowa*

Psalm XXII

Domine, in virtute Tua laetabitur rex. Psalm 21.

*On His Departure for Vienna, to His Grace, Most Illustrious
Jan III, King of Poland*

1. O Lord, the king will rejoice in your strength, and in the deeds of your salvation you will give him great reason to be joyful.
2. Here the hero straps the sword to his side to fight in your name; he takes the heraldic shield[1] to wage the Lord's wars.
3. He is mounting a spirited horse and on the swift Pegasus sets off on his way; bestow, O Lord, good fortune to this knight of Christ.
4. Accept the desire of his heart, which he directed to you from the mountain he took to heart[2] and deign not to refuse him what he asked you for in front of the picture of your Mother.
5. For you come with your blessing to lift the fallen Christianity; keep giving him the strength to succeed, you that inspired in his mind the good will of deliverance.
6. When he gives his health and life for his brothers, accept O Lord this sacrifice, and bestow on him blessings.
7. For the beast that removes stars from the sky[3] opens his jaws against your people; help him, O Lord, to subdue this multiheaded hydra with his hand.
8. For nearly forty days this Goliath challenges God's people to fight and no one comes forward to resist this invader.[4]
9. The first born Eliab says nothing and others are struck speechless; bless, O Lord, David so that he will strike this impudent man's forehead with a stone.

10. For he has hopes in you and your strength, O the Most High! Let your hand destroy through this instrument the nations that hate you.
11. He that does not call with his tongue the sweetest name of Jesus, let him be cut down from this earth by the sword of the fighting king.
12. Strengthen, O Lord of the Hosts, his hands and straighten out the path to battle; and let the guardian angel protect his chest in danger with a strong buckler.
13. Advance happily, king, in the power of the Lord of the Hosts, who will go in front of you in a pillar of fire by day and by night.[5]
   Glory to the Father, and the Son, and the Holy Ghost etc.

Notes

1. King Jan Sobieski had a shield in his coat of arms.
2. Sobieski made a stop at the shrine of the Black Virgin in Częstochowa on his way to Vienna.
3. Kochowski refers here to the Turks and the crescent.
4. Goliath defied the Jews for forty days (Samuel I, 17:16).
5. "The Lord went in front of them in a pillar of cloud by day to lead them along the way, and in a pillar of fire by night, to give them light, so that they might travel by day and by night." (Exodus 13:21)

Psalm XXIV

Venite exultemus Domino. Psalm 95.

In Remembrance of the Rescue of Vienna Anno Domini 1683 on the Thirteenth Day of September

1. O come, let us rejoice in the Lord, let us sing to our Lord the Savior, let us come into his presence with thanksgiving, and let us praise his unspeakable goodness with songs and hymns!
2. For the Lord is a great God who creates everything and the mighty King, who can save the lost out of deepest waters.
3. He will, o desperate Vienna, tear you out from the hand of the giant strangling you and will smite the bloody beast opening its jaws against you.

4. He who assured Constantine of victory with the sign of the cross,[1] gives you as well a sure signal that with this sign you will soon be saved.
5. Lift your eyes towards the mountains and you will see numerous regiments with this banner coming to reinforce you.
6. Cast your eyes as far as you can at the sky-reaching, tree covered rocks from which bold eagles fly out with great speed to deliver you.
7. Now Kara Mustapha, the whelp of the Libyan lion,[2] having noticed the cross, begins to fear, and this Lucifer's heart full of pride issues orders to pull up the tents.
8. He has already taken off his splendid panache, either getting ready to set off on his way or to relieve his head, for which orders from Istanbul will soon come.
9. Proud pashas and commanders are filled with fear; they quickly set off when mighty columns withdraw in great confusion.
10. Cannons and big guns do not boom, but roar and the earth hurled up by mines[3] falls on them burying the living.
11. So move rapidly, besieged people, come and fall before the throne of the Most High; thank the Lord who created you and admire him, who for the second time gives you salvation.[4]
12. Yet today you will hear those who bring you rescue; do not harden your hearts with fear, but thankful for being saved, raise your hands to the sky.
13. Come out, the younger and those who can still carry arms, against the terrified enemies; and you, the old men and those who cannot fight, begin a triumphant hymn on the wall battlements.
14. Utter a joyful cry as if after a victorious battle and let Saint Stephen's tower grow bright in the fires of public joy.
15. Just as during the retreat of Suleiman from Vienna, when your fathers received help from the Lord of the Hosts.
    Glory to the Father, and the Son, and the Holy Spirit, etc.

Notes

1. Before the battle near Rome in 312, Constantine the Great was reported to see in the clouds a cross with the words "In hoc signo vinces." Kochowski writes in his *Commentarius belli adversus Turcas ad Viennam* that Polish soldiers found in a Hungarian church destroyed by the Turks a painting of God's Mother which escaped destruction, with the inscription "In hac imagine vinces." Kochowski interprets this event as a prophecy of the victory at Vienna.

2. Kara Mustapha, Turkish grand vizier, escaped after his defeat at Vienna to Belgrade, where he was strangled on the Sultan's orders.

3. A section of the Turkish camp was mined.

4. Suleiman the Magnificent (1496-1566), Ottoman sultan, after conquering Hungary, besieged without success Vienna in 1527.

Texts: Kochowski, Wespazjan. *Utwory poetyckie. Wybór.* 2nd ed. Ed. by Maria Eustachiewicz. Wrocław: Ossolineum, Biblioteka Narodowa I 92, 1991, 39-41, 176-179, 232, 281, 303, 420-422, 424-426.
Kochowski, Wespazjan. *Psalmodia polska oraz wybór liryków.* 1st ed. Ed. by Julian Krzyżanowski. Kraków: Krakowska Spółka Wydawnicza, Biblioteka Narodowa I 92, 1926, 105.

STANISŁAW HERAKLIUSZ LUBOMIRSKI (1642-1702)

Born into the family of the powerful magnate who led a rebellion against King Jan Kazimierz, Stanisław Lubomirski was educated in France, Spain, and Italy. He returned to Poland in 1662 and began his political career, becoming a deputy, Sejm Marshal (1670), and Grand Marshal of the Crown (1676). His residence at Ujazdów in Warsaw, with its own theatre, became a center of cultural and political activity.

Lubomirski's learning and literary tastes were extensive. He wrote in Latin and in Polish. His works included biblical paraphrases, e.g., *Tobias Delivered* (1683) and *Ecclesiastes* (1702), pastoral dramas, e.g., *Ermida, or the Shepherdess Princess* (1664), political treatises, e.g., *De vanitate consiliorum* (1699), and religious poems, e.g., *The Poems of Lent*.

Somnus

Primus[1]

With the down of swans the bed has been bestrewn high,
    Blissfulness covers it with delicate pillows,
The head sinks in as if in a sea that is dry,
    Immersed in the waves of the plucked geese it flows.
5 Here in the luxurious down sleep breathes a deep sigh
    And with a full breast it sings praises of repose,
The eyes have been sheltered by a green silk curtain,
    So that the rays of Phoebus would not filter in.

Secundus

Sentinels walk as if they were on cotton feet,
    When they are coming forward close beside the bed,
In opening the hinged door they are most discreet,
    The lips of each man are sealed, keep the words unsaid;
5 They cool with a fan the one who wakes in this heat,
    Darkening the windowpanes with draperies overhead,
The sun has not yet scattered here its rays of light,
    Even if it is burning with triple fire's might.

Tertius

Trouble and endeavors that cause anxiety,
    Discomforts, sorrows, despondency, and sickness,
Yearnings of the heart, sleeping inability,
    Weeping as well as laments, and whatever else
5 Could have caused a disruption of tranquillity,
    Are moaning outside the door chained and in distress,
While happy hours stroll along in lambskin slippers
    To make sure the first reveries would not disperse.

Quartus

Across the room, through a crystal duct of water,
    To bring more comforting sleep of which all are fond,
The spring is flowing with a delightful whisper,
    Its bottom is made not of stone but of diamond.
5 Sea goddesses are swimming along in leisure,
    Through a secret passage they reach the shade beyond,
Along the embankments mothers comb their long hair,
    Zephyr strokes their curly tresses with gentle care.

Quintus

Delicious honey plasters ripen in their combs,
    In a grove that surrounds a belvedere
A turtledove flies by, a lost mate it bemoans
    Who wanders in a far-away country somewhere,
5 A nightingale is chanting, not with vocal tones
    But more sweetly. If you look for paradise there,
That is where nature contains it in its smallness,
    To grant the sleepers most enchanting blissfulness.

Notes

1. *Somnus primus, secundus, etc.*--'first dream, second, etc.'

Sonnet on the Great Suffering of Jesus Christ

    Are throes suffered by God personified
    A triumph of love sublime and boundless,
    Or spoils of hell or graves of envious death
    Or the miracle of heavenly might?

5   Power, sway,[1] grief, fear, sweat, blood, death defied,[2]
    Betrayal, ropes, tears, judgment, unrighteous
    Slap on face and reeds used to give lashes,
    Pillar, thorn, cross, nail, gall, and opened side--[3]

    These are gifts of goodness, not punishment,
10   Not gifts but living founts of forgiveness,
    Not founts but the miracles of God's hand,

    Of the hand which released from its distress
    Happy salvation, for which hearts should send
    Offers of thanksgiving, o true goodness!

Notes

    1. "These are united in yielding their power and authority to the beast; they will make war on the Lamb and the Lamb will conquer them, for he is Lord of lords and King of kings (...)" (Revelation 17:13-14)
    2. "Death has been swallowed up
        in victory."
"Where, O death is your victory?
Where, O death, is your sting?"
"The sting of death is sin, and the power of sin is the law. But thanks be to God, who gives us the victory through our Lord Jesus Christ." (1 Corinthians 15:54-57)
    "(...) our Savior Christ Jesus, who abolished death (...)" (2 Timothy 1:10).
    3. Lines 5-8 constitute an enumeration, in which the Passion is described. This device was often used by Baroque poets. Cf. a similar rhetorical figure in *The Brevity of Life* by Naborowski, symbolizing passage of time.

The Poems of Lent

Coepit lavare discipulorum pedes[1]

    Let me as I should, God, have enough confidence
        To say that I doubted in your omnipotence,
    In being the lowest, yet eternal Sovereign,
        Also the Highest Priest, God, Creator, and King,
5   But when I see you before your disciples bow
        And washing their feet with your own holy hands now;
    What can you not do with the whole world, Lord of all,
        When being the greatest, you could become so small?

Notes

1. "He began to wash the disciples' feet." (John 13:5)

Tobias Delivered
(selections)

Sarah's Prayer[1]

    To you, o Master, I turn now my face
  Like a sunflower turning to the sun,
  To you, o Lord, my trusting eyes I raise
  Like a child looking for the pelican,[2]
5 To you in my heart and my thoughts I race
  Like a swift eagle, soaring to the sun.
  To you, then, like deer to the spring water
  My thoughts flow in, like the seabound river.

    Let me, O Lord, in harsh reprehension
10 That at present time I have to abide,[3]
  Be allowed to live free from oppression,
  For this I, wretched, my pleas to you guide,
  And if I cannot of your compassion
  Be deserving now, I ask you beside:
15 Take my soul away! Either I acquire
  The fruit of your mercy or I expire.

Notes

1. Tobit 3:12-15.
2. The pelican was a symbol of parental love. Cf. Zbigniew Morsztyn's *Song of Captivity*, l. 69.
3. "It is better for me not to hang myself, but to pray the Lord that I may die and not listen to these reproaches anymore." (Tobit 3:10)

The River Tiger

The river, quite similar to its name,
    Threatens with the bestial surname aptly:
The beast searches shadowy lairs for game,
    The river flows, in its dark bed ghastly,
5 So with a swift roar, as if to attack,
    Like the beast at its mouth it foams over,
In the plains it changes its mottled back
    With dense holms--like the stripes of a tiger.

A Quiet Moment Comes After a Storm

    A quiet moment comes after a storm,
Tulips blossom again after the snow,
After the dark night, the day takes its form,
A light beam comes back from night[1] in full glow.
5 The heart oft rejoices after tears swarm
And the time comes that fortune swore to show,
Even if one lost his way in a maze,
He will at the end reach the destined place.

    The compass that keeps drawing on the board
10 Will be closed up and put into its case;
The king moving on a complex chessboard[2]
Will come to checkmate,[3] although not apace;
An unchecked runner[4] will come to a stop,[5]
One who's lost in woods will reach open space,
15 After one turn, a star comes from the west,[6]
The swallow flies again to make its nest.

            The flame, having burned ashes in its blaze
        Will go its way for the highest sphere bound,
        Water will visit its winding valleys
20   And fall into the sea, ending its round,
        A glad pilgrim after long travel days
        Is greeted at home. So all things around,
        Even if they went as far as they might,
        End up where they started, at their first site.

Notes

1. The rosy beam returns from the place between the evening and the morning light, that is from the hours of darkness.

2. In the original, the chessboard is 'sage.' Lubomirski employs here a figure of speech, called *hypallage*, an interchange of syntactic relationship between two terms. It is the king who is sage, not the chessboard. Cf. l. 17, where the flame burns an object, not its ashes.

3. An ambiguous word in Polish, indicating both the end of a chess game and the reached goal.

4. Another ambiguity, as the word referred to a running person or to a horse.

5. The sonnet rhyme pattern of the original stanza (d e d e d e f f) is broken in line 13.

6. It was believed that the wandering stars revolved around the fixed stars, which in turn circled the earth.

Texts: Sokołowska, *I w odmianach czasu smak jest*, 577-578, 584-585.
Bukowski, *Biblia a literatura polska*, 277.
Vincenz, *Helikon sarmacki*, 411, 224-225, 225-226 (based on Stanisław Herakliusz Lubomirski. *Wybór pism.* Ed. by Roman Pollak. Wrocław: Ossolineum, Biblioteka Narodowa I 145, 1953, 80, 105, 157-158).

JAN CHRYZOSTOM PASEK (ca. 1636-1701)

Born near Rawa in Mazovia, Pasek received a scanty education in the Jesuit College. At the age of nineteen he enlisted in the army and for eleven years fought against Swedish, Hungarian, Muscovite, and Turkish forces. In 1667, after his marriage, Pasek settled on the estate of his wife near Cracow. In 1672, he fought against Turkey. Numerous brawls and lawsuits against his neighbors brought him court condemnation and later the sentence of exile, which was not enforced, however.

Pasek recorded his rich experiences in vivid and colorful stories, filled with amusing anecdotes and ribald passages. His *Memoirs*, unpublished until 1836, gained great popularity as a historical romance.

Memoirs
(selections)

The Year of Our Lord 1659

We began it propitiously, by the grace of God, still in Haderslev,[1] where we celebrated Shrovetide, though by no means with such gaiety as in Poland. The island of Als[2] still stood in our way and since it was at our rear, it was truly a great impediment for us: our retainers, while they lay in ambush, were kidnapped, our booty was taken, since its *praesidium*[3] was large. The Brandenburg army passed by Als with both cannons and infantry but as before they did not want to attack it or did not dare, for as they say: "Crows will not pick out crows' eyes.[4]" The Voivode[5] went one day to reconnoiter with 300 horses, *quidem*[6] for a ride; without a word he ordered the trumpet to sound so that everyone would be ready the next day to mount horses.[7] We did not forget this time about better preparations, as we told the retainers to put *ad victum*[8] into long sacks and set out. In one place we cut the ice with axes for the sea near the shore was still frozen, even though it was not very cold and the weather was fine; the dragoons on the other side did the same and it happened so quickly that the *praesidiarii*[9] did not realize it until we were already on the other side, for they were stationed in the town and in villages. The distance to swim was as from Warsaw to Praga,[10] but in the middle of the strait there was a place where a horse could touch bottom and rest, for it was about 30 paces long. So the Voivode crossed himself and went first into the water, the regiments after him, because there were only three of them, not the entire army, each soldier putting the pistols behind his collar and tying cartridge pouches to his neck. When he swam to the middle, he stopped and ordered each unit to rest, then to move on. The horses had already been trained to swim, any poor swimmer was put between the two good ones and was not allowed to drown. Fortunately the day was quiet, warm and without frost; it had already thawed a bit, but later it became bitterly cold again. None of the regiments had yet reached the shore, when the Swedes fell on us.[11] They began to fire, but the regiment that came out of the water instantly made a dash at them. The Swedes, seeing that even though we had just come out of the water yet our muskets were not soaked and could still fire and kill, took to their heels; those who came to their rescue, were cut off by our riders and then without thinking twice we took them straight on. The prisoners told us "we thought you were devils, not men." The Danish king requested that the local commandant be sent to him alive, for he had some great grievance against him; I do not know how he was greeted there. This job done, when the soldiers got into any warm dwelling, they would grab hold of anyone they could, be it man or woman, and tear the shirt of his back for a change of clothes. After combing the island, which was not large, only seven miles in all, several towns, a few dozen villages, the Voivode assigned a sensible captain, a Danish nobleman, as commander there, with newly enlisted men. For the ordinance read that right after we marched in with the army, officers of the Danish king would call for recruits and post them in the conquered fortresses. The Voivode, however, took for himself some one hundred good Swedes and spread them among the dragoons to make up for the losses they had suffered here and there, for it is normal that whenever wood is chopped, chips must fall. Then the army returned to its quarters, this time in boats. Just as the last year ended very well with the glorious conquest of Kolding, so the new one began quite luckily with so *gloriose*[12] capture of the island of Als.

Notes

1. Hederslev, a seaport in southeastern Jutland.
2. The island of Als, off the eastern coast of South Jutland, was captured in December of 1658, not in 1659.
3. *praesidium*--'garrison.'
4. Pasek implies here that the Brandenburg soldiers were not too eager to fight the Swedes, as both nations were of Germanic origin.
5. Pasek refers here to Stefan Czarniecki (1599-1665), leader of the Polish troops, and future Grand Hetman of the Crown.
6. *quidem*--'apparently, as if.'
7. Pasek does not mention that Austrian and Brandenburg infantry units took part in the attack on the island of Als.
8. *ad victum*--'needed for supplies.'
9. *praesidiarii*--'garrison defenders.'
10. Praga is a district of Warsaw, situated across the Vistula. The width of the strait was about 500 meters.
11. Pasek does not seem to be aware of an elaborate plan involving various units of the army attacking the island from different sides.
12. *gloriose*--'glorious.'

The Year of Our Lord 1680

We went to the pond; I stood on the dam and said: "Robak![1] I need fish for my guests, jump into the water!" The otter jumped in and first brought out a roach; I ordered her in the second time: she brought out a small pike; the third time, a pike the size of a platter, slightly hurt on the neck. Straszowski grabbed his head: "By God! What do I see here!" So I said: "Do you want her to bring out more? For she will carry them out until I have enough; if I need a tubful, she'll bring it, for her net costs her nothing." Straszowski said: "Now that I see it, I believe, but if somebody had told me, I would not have believed him." Straszowski grasped the offer *et consensit*,[2] seeing that this would not be any bother and he would be able to tell the king about her *qualitates*.[3] Before he left, I showed him all her skills, which were the following:

First, she slept with me in my bed, and she was so tidy that not only did she not make any mess in the sheets but did nothing under the bed; she would go to one spot where a pot had been put out for her and only there she would relieve herself. Second, she was such a night guard that God forbid anyone come close to my bed. She barely let my servant pull off my boots, and then better stay away, for she raised such a racket that I would wake up no matter how sound asleep I was. And when I was drunk and someone walked by the bed, she would trample on my chest squeaking until I woke up. And during the day she would sleep in such a fashion, sprawling anywhere, that even if I picked her up, she would not lift an eyelid, so much this creature trusted me! She did not want to eat raw fish or raw meat, for even when on a Friday or a fast day they would cook for her a chicken or pigeon but would not add parsley as was customary, she refused to eat. She understood like a dog: "Don't let them touch me!" If someone pulled at my coat and I said: "Sic'em," she would leap with an awful shriek, tear at his clothes, at his legs, just like my dog, the only one she loved, called Kapreol, a shaggy German dog, from whom she learned all this and other tricks as well. She lived in peace only with this dog, because it was a house dog and they travelled around together. She did not like other dogs and if any of them came in, she would at once bite it, even if it were the biggest greyhound. Once, Stanisław Ożarowski came to visit me, or rather travelling with me, he dropped in. I was glad to see him; the otter was also glad, as she had not seen me for three days, she came to me and couldn't get enough of joy and play. My guest had with him a nice greyhound bitch and he said to his son: "Samuel, hold on to the greyhound, so that she does not eat that otter." I said: "Don't worry, this little animal will not let anyone hurt it, even though it is small." And he said: "Are you joking? This greyhound will tackle a wolf, a fox will pant only once." The otter finished enjoying my company and saw a strange dog; she came up to the greyhound and looked her in the eyes, the greyhound looked back; the otter walked around her and sniffed her hind leg. Then she stepped back and went away. I thought: "She won't do anything more." We had hardly begun to talk about something, when the otter got up again from where she was stretching at my feet, and went quietly under the bench, came behind the dog again; when she bit her on the calf, the dog jumped to the door, the otter after her; the dog behind the stove, the otter after her. When the dog saw she had nowhere to escape, she jumped on the table, wanting to break through the window, but Ożarowski grabbed her by the legs. However, she broke two crystal wine glasses and after they let her out, she did not show herself to her master, even though he did not leave until the next day after dinner. The dogs were afraid of her everywhere. Even when we travelled, if a dog but sniffed her, she would shriek fiercely and the dog ran off at once. She was a great help when we travelled during fast days. Because as things are in this country, especially around here, you come to a little town and ask: "Can we buy any fish here?" They are amazed: "Where would we get them here from! We don't know of any." So when you rode somewhere by a river or a pond, and the otter was with you, you did not need a net. I got off the cart for a while: "Robak, into the water!" She would get in, bring out whatever fish was in the water, one after another, until I had enough. I was not as choosy as in my home pond and whatever she brought I took, except for the frogs, for she would bring them as well, since, as I have already written, she was not particular and she would take whatever she came across. So I and my servants fared well and sometimes a guest would have something to eat if several of us would happen to stay in one inn. People wondered: "I gave them orders to look for fish in such and such town, and nothing is available; where did your lordship get such excellent fish?" To this I would say that in the water. Sometimes even on a meat day my servants would say: "Oh, Good Sir, the fish are jumping in this pond here; let the otter go." So I would go with her, for she would not go with anybody but me, and she would carry them out; if a fish was good, like say a pike or a large bass, I would eat it myself, not only my servants, because I am ready to forego the best meat dish for a good fish. There was a problem with her on the road, for wherever we went people were astonished; they were coming in crowds as if we were carrying something from India; we had large audiences, especially in Cracow, for when I rode through the streets there, a crowd of all kinds of people accompanied me out of town. Once I went to a cousin of mine, Szczęsny Chociwski; Father Trzebieński was also there. He sat next to me at the table, and the otter was laying next to me on the bench; she had plenty to eat and was asleep, sprawled on her back, as that was her favorite position. The priest, after a while noticed the otter and thinking that it was a sleeve, he grabbed her to have a look. Awakened, the otter gave out a horrible shriek, caught his hand

and bit it; out of pain and fear the priest fainted and we barely managed to revive him.

Notes

1. 'Robak' means in Polish a 'worm.'
2. *et consensit*--'and agreed to it.' It is not clear what Straszowski agreed to.
3. *qualitates*--'qualities.'

Text: Pasek, Jan Chryzostom. *Pamiętniki*. Ed. by Roman Pollak. Warszawa: PIW, 1987, 19-20, 224-225.

ANONYMOUS

On Proud Masters

    I dismiss riches of a proud grandee;
        Those who scorn the poor mean little to me.
    With countless hamlets, from Noah descent,
        I still will not regard him as decent,
5   Why would I, poor man, do what I uphold,
        I wear a gray coat, for him cloth of gold.
    Law and nature put us in the same ward,
        A squire with a few men equals a lord.

On Youth and Love

    It is hard with a bridle swift youth to restrain,
        Often a rider falls down, oft a steed will strain.
    Fire, which is being smothered, will quickly grow bright,
        Love burns much stronger when it is put out of sight.

Twelve Songs on the Siege of the Bright Mountain of Częstochowa
(selections)

Song I

1

    I sing the godless war and the tyrant,[1]
    Who without respect for Holy Infant
    Launched an assault against the Bright Mountain,
    When King Charles was fighting the Sarmatian,
5   He renounced treaties and broke commitments,
    Defying the pledge and God's commandments.

2

You that have come to be the Polish queen[2]
And built up the palace on this mountain,[3]
Virgin, help me, and from the sapphire sky,
10 Where the empyrean stars are shining high,
Turn down towards me your eyes in earnest,
Put the gift of grace into my dull breast.

3

Remind me, Virgin, sitting in glory,
In the robe made of sunray embroidery,
15 How Northern Lucifer set out to fight
Against your castle here with his whole might,
How he wished to wreck it, destroy, plunder,
Erase to the ground, your virtue conquer.

4

Sarmatian land, you trembled in this war,
20 When you were watching it, steeped in the gore,
Now feel triumphant for this holy site
Would not succumb to the enemy's might;
You see noble Christian, my descendant,
Why throughout the world it's so eminent.

5

25 There's a splendid rock in Little Poland,
Than other peaks by miracle more grand,
The work of the Lord's works, it is called Bright,
In Częstochowa always had its site;
Which because of its form and graceful whole,
30 Gives pleasure to man's eyes and to his soul.

6

A miracle, not a mountain, for while
It has normal uses and ornate style,
That is not all; for from it the Lord sends

His lavish graces towards various lands,
35 Whence He works wonders, pours gold rain from its height,
That's why it's more worthy and shines more bright.

7

And it is even shining with more light
With the miraculous painting inside,[4]
Depicted from beautiful Mary's face
40 By pious Luke in a circle of rays,
Who used the brush with utmost gentleness
Drawing on the table made of cypress.

Notes

1. In 1655, the Swedish army of King Charles Gustavus X (1622-1660) overran Poland, violating the 1635 Treaty of Stumsdorf. On November 18, 1655, the Swedish mercenary troops attacked the Paulite Monastery at Jasna Góra (the Bright Mountain), the shrine of the venerated Black Madonna. Heavily fortified and heroically defended, the Monastery held out for forty days against the attacks. The successful defense of the Monastery was ascribed to the protection of the Holy Virgin who saved the shrine from the invading Lutherans. In 1656, when the whole nation rose against the invaders, Charles Gustavus and the major units of his army were threatened with total defeat and retreated.

2. On April 1, 1656, King John Casimir of Poland, who returned from exile, made a vow in Lwów Cathedral, placing the country under the protection of Our Lady of Częstochowa and declaring her Queen of the Crown of Poland.

3. The Jasna Góra Paulite Monastery was founded in 1382 on the site of a small wooden church.

4. According to legend, the picture of Our Lady had been painted by Saint Luke the Evangelist on a wooden plank which had served as a table-top in the house of the Holy Family in Nazareth. The icon, eastern, Byzantine in its contents and western European in its form, was brought to Częstochowa in 1384, becoming before long the object of the cult and the goal of pilgrimages.

Fame

All things that exist must surely perish,
    But man's good name years won't impoverish.
Cities, castles, and houses count for naught.
    Fame has no fear of time or any blot.

Time Destroys Everything

Time ruins everything, greedily swallows all,
    Nothing endures for long here, things will never stall.
The sea recedes from its shores and rivers get dry,
    While mountains will fall down, even those very high.
5   Little things I will mention: the imposing skies
    Will burn suddenly, for every thing on earth dies.
Death by his law takes anything that comes his way,
    And the time will come when this world passes away.

Running to the Stable

When I was running, I, a humble maid,
To this poor stable, a small boy, shepherd,
Wanted to outrun me with his musette,
And yet I grasping my violinette

5   Managed to play first, lively, merrily,
And the Maiden looked at me graciously,
Holding in her arms her beautiful Son,
I handed Him bread and a little bun.

I also brought apples in a basket,
10 Be so good and take them, my little pet,
I will sing for You, I will play for You,
If You are so kind and will listen to.

My dear little lamb, squeezed in the corner,
Why were You put to lie in the manger?
15 Why are You here in these swaddling clothes bound
And with the humble beasts of burden found?

>   Great is Your love and Your humiliation
>   That will in heaven uplift our station.
>   Allow us if You please to follow You,
> 20   And Your example always keep in view,
>
>   Contempt, mortification, and Your cross.
>   Our life's delights derive from that source,
>   And with this music let's always please You,
>   Both here, dear Jesus, and in heaven too. Amen.

Texts: Sokołowska and Żukowska, *Poeci polskiego baroku*. Vol. 2, 598, 599, 680-682.
Sokołowska, *I w odmianach czasu smak jest*, 645, 646, 660-661.

II. ENLIGHTENMENT

INTRODUCTION

HISTORICAL BACKGROUND

The political and economic crisis, caused by constant warfare which had devastated Poland since 1648, deepened in the eighteenth century. Surrounded by the militaristic absolute monarchies of Russia, Prussia, and Austria, the once powerful Republic of Poland and Lithuania became a pawn of foreign interests, a campground for invading armies. The three kings who ruled the Republic during its last hundred years of existence were placed on the throne by foreign powers.

The sixty-six year's reign of August II (1697-1733) and of his son August III (1733-1763), called by historians the Saxon era or the "Saxon night," brought still more ruin and humiliation to the country of eleven million people, inhabiting a territory of 282,000 square miles. In the election of June 1697, a French candidate, Prince François Louis de Conti, was proclaimed the king but was unable to claim the crown, as the Saxon and Russian armies installed August II, the Elector of Saxony, on the Polish throne in Cracow after a brief civil war. The new alliance of Saxony, Poland, and Russia, formed against Sweden at the outset of the Northern War (1700-1721), proved disastrous for Poland. In 1700 Charles XII of Sweden invaded the Republic and by 1702 occupied large parts of the country, including Warsaw, Cracow, Poznań, and Wilno. He deposed August II and installed Stanisław Leszczyński as the new king of Poland in 1704. But when the Swedish army was defeated at Poltava in 1709, the victorious tsar Peter the Great was able to restore the throne to August II and to intervene at will in Polish affairs. The 1715 political and military conflict between August II and the majority of the Polish nobility, united in the Confederacy of Tarnogród and determined to remove the Saxon king from Poland, was arbitrated by the Russian envoy Grigorij Dolgoruki and the resulting agreement was ratified in 1717 by the Silent Sejm, surrounded by Russian troops. The Saxon army was ordered to leave Polish territory, the Polish army was reduced to

24,000 men, and the Commonwealth of Poland and Lithuania was left defenseless.

The weakness of the king and of the Sejm caused in turn a paralysis of central government. During the reign of August II eight Sejms concluded their deliberations, but ten were broken up, and during the years of August III, only one Sejm was completed, while thirteen were broken up. No legislation could be passed, no taxes imposed, as important decisions concerning the government of the country were relegated to the local dietines, which were controlled by powerful magnate families.

The influence exercised by the princely noblemen who ruled their own domains, to mention only the Czartoryskis, Potockis, Radziwiłłs, and Branickis, was derived from the possession of large estates, hereditary fortunes, and lucrative offices. The families had their own armies, entered into their own alliances, and employed thousands of lesser noblemen to advance their interests in the courts and in the legislature. They developed their own factories, enlarged their estates, and when wars, natural disasters, and falling agricultural prices reduced their profits, they demanded more effort from the burghers, peasants, and tenants. They fiercely protected their privileged status and cared little about the nation's depleted finances, stagnant economy, and impoverished towns. They enjoyed their 'golden freedom' to the full and some of them were not averse to enter into collusion with foreign powers in order to advance their goals.

This short-sighted expediency became particularly visible during the election and reign of August III. Initially the Saxon's chances to ascend to the Polish throne were tenuous, as more than 13,000 votes were cast in favor of electing Stanisław Leszczyński king. But just as in 1697, the Russian and Saxon armies entered the country, allowing a handful of noblemen to elect August III King of Poland. The invaders quickly overpowered a confederation of the noblemen that supported Leszczyński, forcing him to flee the country, disguised as a peasant. The ensuing European War of Polish Succession (1733-1735) ended with the recognition of August III.

The choice could not have been worse. The indolent king lived in Dresden, while his minister Heinrich Brühl governed in Warsaw. August III treated Poland as a source of funds for his Saxon treasury and was unable to stop the Russian and Prussian armies from marching across the Republic and looting at will. While the king and many of his subjects were "eating, drinking,

XVII. King Stanisław August Poniatowski, coronation portrait by Marcello Baciarelli

and loosening their belts," the country was drifting, sinking gradually into anarchy.

But just as a sick man in his death-throes rallies in the last hour, so did Poland struggle valiantly to recover. The seeds of regeneration were planted by the twice deposed king Stanisław Leszczyński and other enlightened men. The exiled king and educator, whose court at Lunéville in Lorraine attracted many of his countrymen, published an influential treatise *A Free Voice Insuring Freedom* (1749), in which he presented a sound plan of reform for Poland. Stanisław Konarski, a Piarist[1] who spent some time in Lunéville, was the founder of the Collegium Noblilium, a school that offered a modern curriculum, and the author of *On the Effective Method of Deliberating* (1760-1763), a seminal document for political reform. Bishop Józef Andrzej Załuski, another resident of Lunéville, founded with his brother a collection of more than 300,000 books and manuscripts, opened it in Warsaw in 1747 as the first modern public library in Europe, and gave it to the Republic in 1771.

Prospects for the improvement of the Republic's political condition following the election of 1764 were not promising. The new king Stanisław August Poniatowski (1764-1795) was imposed on the nation by Catherine II of Russia and Frederick II of Prussia, two intractable enemies of Poland. Poniatowski served as a deputy in the Sejm and Ambassador to Russia, became Catherine's lover, and when he was elected under the watchful eyes of Russian soldiers in Warsaw on September 6, 1764, he was perceived by many countrymen as a mere puppet king.

Yet the young monarch, who received a thorough education and spent many years in France and England, surprised his supporters and detractors by launching an ambitious program of political reforms. Within a short period of time, King Stanisław initiated many administrative and economic changes. His goals were to modify the constitution, strengthen the central government, reform finances, and modernize the army. He encouraged the development of industry and commerce. What is more, King Stanisław distinguished himself as an educator and a great patron of learning and the arts. He established the new institutions which trained military and administrative cadres, and initiated the publication of the periodical *Monitor*, which informed the public about social and political issues of the day.

The sweeping process of Polish national regeneration alarmed Russia and Prussia. In October 1767, Russian troops

XVIII. Tadeusz Kościuszko

surrounded the Confederate Sejm and blockaded Warsaw, arrested four prominent deputies and deported them to Russia. The Russian envoy Repnin demanded that five cardinal principles barring any substantial reform be accepted by the Sejm, guaranteed them in the name of Catherine, and thus placed Poland formally under Russian protectorate.

The aroused patriots were not ready to submit to these humiliating conditions. In February of 1768, a group of noblemen formed an armed Confederacy in Bar to defend faith and freedom. They were led by Michał Krasiński, Józef Pułaski, and his brother Kazimierz Pułaski, who eight years later fought and died in the American War of Independence. The confederates battled against the overwhelming Russian forces for four years, but were unable to avert an impending disaster. On August 5, 1772, Russia, Prussia, and Austria signed an agreement which deprived Poland of one third of its territory, justifying their rapacity by "a total dissolution of the state" and "a factious spirit breeding anarchy."

This act of international aggression was accepted virtually without any protest in Europe. Frederick II, who recommended that Poland should be eaten "like an artichoke or a head of cabbage--leaf after leaf, town after town," disclosed that it was always in his interest to see Polish matters in a state of disorder. Some years later, Catherine II found herself irritated by the Poles who exceeded all the follies of the National Assembly in France. In response Voltaire, the celebrated proponent of the Enlightenment and renowned defender of the oppressed, praised the King of Prussia for his ingenious idea of partitioning Poland and the Empress Catherine for sending the Russian army to Poland solely to champion the cause of religious toleration--all this flattery in exchange for generous gifts of furs, gold, and china from the two grateful despots.

In spite of Poland's enormous losses and precarious political situation, the movement of national rebirth was not brought to a halt. In 1773 the King appointed the Commission for National Education, the first ministry of education in Europe, whose goals were to reorganize the school system of the whole country. Other new ideas introduced by the King and his patriotic collaborators were turned into legislative acts by the Sejm. The Four-Year Sejm, which convened on October 8, 1788, constituted itself into a legal Confederation ruled by the majority of votes, thus eliminating the *liberum veto* (free dissent), a destructive tool of the minority opposition. It passed a resolution increasing the army to 100,000 men, imposed taxes on the lands owned by the gentry and the Church, and granted new rights to the burghers.

The crowning document of the Four-Year Sejm, indeed of the entire reform movement, was the Governmental Statute consisting of the preamble and eleven articles, known as the Constitution of May 3, 1791. This first European constitution, modelled on the American Constitution of 1787, was drafted by King Stanisław August, Stanisław Małachowski, Marshal of the Sejm, Ignacy Potocki, Chairman of the Constitution Commission, and Hugo Kołłątaj, an influential thinker and member of the Commission for National Education. Committed to the supreme goal of "securing our liberty, and maintaining our Kingdom and our possessions," the Constitution framers granted the Sejm the major legislative and executive authority, limited the king's power, confirmed new privileges for the burghers, and placed the peasants under the protection of the government. They also proposed substantial economic, legal, and social reforms.

It is not surprising that this proud declaration of independence and the rights of man was hailed in France, England, and America, for as Karl Marx wrote "this constitution stands against the background of the Russo-Prusso-Austrian barbarity as the only work of freedom which Eastern Europe has ever produced." Nor is it surprising that the three partitioning powers saw this attempt at reform as a dangerous challenge which had to be suppressed without any delay. As in the past, they responded with violence.

The pretext used by Catherine to attack Poland was provided by a faction of the Polish noblemen who opposed the Constitution. They signed the act of confederation in Saint Petersburg on April 27, 1792, which they subsequently called the Confederacy of Targowica, and promptly appealed to the Russian Empress to intervene in defense of their "golden freedoms." The Russian army entered Poland, but was initially repelled by the Polish forces, led by Józef Poniatowski and Tadeusz Kościuszko, the hero of the American War of Independence. When the combined Russian and Prussian armies advanced towards Warsaw, the King lost heart, declared his access to the Confederacy of Targowica, and ordered Polish troops to stop fighting. In 1793 Russia and Prussia signed the second agreement of the partition of Poland, which gave Russia 100,000 square miles of the eastern provinces and Prussia the whole territory of Great Poland, Gdańsk, and Toruń.

Yet the Poles were not ready to put down their arms. The country was seething with conspiratorial activities and on March 23, 1794 Kościuszko arrived in Cracow, where the next day he proclaimed the Act of Insurrection and swore to use his powers of the Commander-in-Chief to defend the integrity of the country, regain national independence, and establish general liberty. On April 4, Kościuszko's small army of four thousand soldiers and two thousand peasants armed only with scythes defeated the Russians at Racławice. On April 17 the shoemaker Jan Kiliński led an uprising in Warsaw that freed the capital, while Colonel Jakub Jasiński defeated the Russian garrison in Wilno and General Jan Dąbrowski fought against the Prussians in Great Poland. On May 7, Kościuszko proclaimed the Manifesto of Połaniec, which eliminated peasants' servitude and reduced their obligations.

When the Prussian and Austrian troops joined the Russian army, the situation of the insurgents turned hopeless. On October 10, 1794, the Poles were defeated at Maciejowice by the Russian army led by Alexander Suvorov. Kościuszko was wounded and taken prisoner. On November 4, Suvorov's army stormed Praga, an eastern suburb of Warsaw, and massacred thousands of civilians. Warsaw capitulated. The city was sacked, many works of art and the Załuski Library were sent to Saint Petersburg.

In 1795, the discredited King was forced to abdicate and departed to Grodno, then to Saint Petersburg, where he died in 1798. The three aggressors divided among themselves the remaining territories of the Republic, stipulating in the secret document of the partition that the name of Poland should be forever suppressed. The state ceased to exist and Poland disappeared from the map of Europe.

But the news about Poland's demise was premature. Generations of Poles were sustained by the legacy of their splendid past, heroic resistance, and noble Constitution, which gave them faith that "Poland has not lost her life yet, inasmuch as we live."

This faith was severely tested during the long ordeal of the Poles' stateless existence. The vision of free homeland became particularly intense during the Napoleonic era, when Polish soldiers followed the victorious Emperor, believing firmly that to resurrect Poland they had first to defeat the coalition of the common enemies. Already during Napoleon's first Italian campaign of 1797 General Jan Dąbrowski formed the Polish Legion, followed by two more in 1798 and 1800, which distinguished themselves by their bravery and spread throughout Europe the cry for Poland's liberty. It did not matter in the long run that they were used by the French dictator to advance his imperial ambitions and that many of them perished far away from their native land. In 1807 some territories taken by the Prussians were returned to the Poles and formed the free Duchy of Warsaw.

Further hopes for the restoration of the Polish state were dashed when Napoleon's army was defeated in Russia and Józef Poniatowski, the valiant commander of the Polish army, perished covering the French army's retreat at the Battle of the Nations at Leipzig on October 19, 1813. When Napoleon fell, the fate of Poland was left in the hands of the victorious allies. In 1815, at the Congress of Vienna, Prussia, Russia, and Austria again carved up Polish territories, this time into five artificial parts. But they were also compelled to create a Kingdom of Poland, a rump state of about 80,000 square miles with over three million inhabitants. Even though the executive power in the Kingdom was in the hands of the tsar, the new state had a liberal constitution, the name of Poland was restored, and Polish national aspirations and culture flourished almost unabated.

CULTURAL BACKGROUND

Even though both August II and August III were interested in art, their patronage in Poland was limited to a few residences embellished in the new Rococo style. Only a handful of works from their reign have survived to this day, e.g., the Saxon Garden or Saxon Palace, whose colonnades still stand, guarding the Tomb of the Unknown Soldier in Warsaw. Much more enterprising were the aristocratic families, such as the Bielińskis, Mniszechs, Sapiehas or the powerful minister Brühl, who built richly decorated palaces in the capital. Gradually, the other munificent patrons introduced the new style throughout the country, as the Branickis erected their splendid residence in Białystok, the Lubomirskis in Rzeszów, and the Potockis in

XIX. Old Audience Room in the Royal Castle of Warsaw

Introduction

XX. "The General View of Warsaw from Praga" by Bernardo Bellotto (Canaletto), 1770

Radzyń. They also supported the construction of ornate Rococo churches, e.g., Saint George's Church in Lwów, designed by Bernard Merderer, and the Church of the Missionary Fathers in Wilno, known for their elegant lines and expressive wooden figures of the saints, as well as of public buildings, e.g., the Town Hall in Buczacz, another masterpiece of Merderer.

Yet it was primarily the magnanimous patronage of King Stanisław that provided the impetus for the revival of intellectual life and for the flourishing of the arts. The King surrounded himself with educators, scientists, artists, and poets, and established permanent institutions to advance his ambitious plans. When the Jesuit Order was dissolved, the King and the Sejm used some of the remaining Jesuit wealth to endow the Commission for National Education, giving it a broad mandate to reform the whole school system, train teachers, prepare textbooks, and introduce new programs that would emphasize the teaching of the Polish language, mathematics, nature, history, law, and civic studies. In 1765 the King founded the School of Cadets, which during its thirty years of existence prepared over one thousand officers, among them Tadeusz Kościuszko, Julian Ursyn Niemcewicz, Jakub Jasiński, and later the Engineering Corps of the Crown, which trained builders of fortifications. He set up the astronomical observatory and the office of cartography, which under the leadership of Charles Perthées, the principal cartographer, carried out the project of mapping the whole Commonwealth.

The spirit of scientific inquiry characteristic of the Enlightenment spread throughout the country. In 1743 the Societas Physicae Experimentalis, one of the first scientific societies in the world, was established in Gdańsk. New laboratories and observatories were set up at the University of Cracow, which was reformed by Hugo Kołłątaj, and at the University of Wilno, reformed by the astronomer Marcin Poczobutt-Odlanicki. Jan Śniadecki, an eminent mathematician and astronomer, chancellor of Wilno University, and his brother Jędrzej Śniadecki, a chemist and biologist, propagated the new empirical methods and wrote seminal treatises and textbooks. Jan Krzysztof Kluk authored a three-volume *Dictionary of Plants,* the first systematic description of Polish flora, while Stanisław Staszic, the founder of the Warsaw Society of the Friends of Learning, crowned his scientific researches with the study *On the Natural Resources of the Carpathians and Other Mountains and Plains in Poland.* Prince Józef Aleksander Jabłonowski, the enlightened Palatine of Nowogródek, who devoted his whole life to numerous scientific projects, directed the task of compiling an atlas of Poland, which was published by Giovanni Rizzi Zannoni in Paris in 1772.

King Stanisław, a man of excellent education and exquisite taste, was influenced by the French philosophy and culture as well as by Italian art. Throughout his life he commissioned new projects and collected precious works of art in his galleries and libraries. He organized the Royal Academy of Painting and the first permanent theatre, the forerunner of the National Theatre. Soon after his election, the King invited to his court distinguished artists and employed them in the reconstruction of the Royal Castle and Łazienki Palace.

The restoration of the Royal Castle and its interior was carried out by Jakub Fontana, Victor Louis, Domenico Merlini, and Jan Kamsetzer. The showpiece of the new royal residence was the magnificent Knights' Hall, embellished with six large paintings associated with important historical events, e.g., the Prussian homage and Jan III Sobieski's victory at Vienna, by the royal painter Marcello Baciarelli, and twenty four busts of illustrious Poles sculpted by André Le Brun and Giacomo Monaldi. For the rebuilt Marble Hall, Marcello Baciarelli executed twenty two oval and rectangular portraits of the Polish kings, a large full-length portrait of King Stanisław in coronation robes, and the plafond which depicted Fame celebrating the achievements of the Polish monarchs. André Le Brun made a cartouche with the coats of arms of Poland, Lithuania, and the King, surmounted by allegorical figures representing Peace and Justice. Other paintings by Baciarelli decorated the walls and ceilings of the Old Audience Chamber and the Royal Bedchamber. A special room designed by Domenico Merlini was decorated with twenty two views of Warsaw and Wilanów by Bernardo Bellotto from Venice, also known as Canaletto, who painted not only the monuments of architecture, the most famous picture representing "The General View of Warsaw from Praga," but also street scenes, teeming with courtiers, officers, burghers, and peasants. For the furnishings of his chambers, the King ordered furniture, damasks, mirrors, clocks, and vases, mostly in French classicist style.

Nearly all of the King's artists who worked at the Royal Castle, together with Jan B. Plersch, Franciszek Pinck, and

XXI. The Temple of Sibyl in Puławy, 1798-1809

Tomasso Righi, were also engaged in the transformation of the Baroque bath-house designed for Stanisław Lubomirski by Tylman of Gemeren into the splendid Łazienki Palace on the Water, the King's favorite summer residence. After a series of reconstructions, the architects, sculptors, and painters converted a small pavilion into an original Classicist building of great harmony and unity, which reflected the King's personal taste. The artists permanently decorated most of the interiors with stucco and paintings as well as with marble and bronze statues of Roman emperors, kings, and allegorical figures, among which the symbolic *Mars requiescens* represented the god of war in repose and *Polonia reflorescens* the flourishing Poland. They built the Gallery and the Portrait Study for the royal collection, which included six paintings by Rembrandt and many other masterpieces.

Other painters and architects, both foreign and Polish, were active at the royal and magnatial courts. Gianbattista Lampi painted portraits of the statesmen active in the Four-Year Sejm, while Józef Grassi depicted the military heroes Prince Józef Poniatowski and Tadeusz Kościuszko. Jan Norblin, associated with the family of the Czartoryskich in Puławy, created a veritable album of realistic sketches of people of various origin and station from villages and small towns, including impoverished noblemen, Cossacks, Jews, craftsmen, and beggars. He also painted dramatic pictures of contemporary events, e.g., "The Proclamation of the Third of May Constitution" and "The Slaughter of Praga." His disciples, Aleksander Orłowski and Michał Płoński, who painted realistic scenes from the lives of common people and became influenced by Rembrandt, were the precursors of the Romantic style. Zygmunt Vogel drew watercolor views of palaces, parks, and monuments of Polish architecture during his artistic journeys throughout the country.

Architects Szymon Zug and Efraim Schröger, who built mostly for the Warsaw burghers and aristocrats, adhered to the early Classicist style. Jan Kubicki, the designer of the Belweder Palace, popularized the traditional style of the Polish manor house, while Christian Aigner, a professor of architecture at Warsaw University, built large classical buildings of the Radziwiłł Palace and Saint Aleksander's Church in Warsaw as well as the Temple of Sibyl and the Gothic House in the Puławy Park.

The Puławy residence became the major center of national tradition and artistic life after the partitions. Prince Adam Czartoryski and his wife Izabela restored the palace, designed the English gardens, created a collection of Polish artefacts and works of art, cultivated theatre, and supported literature, finding in Franciszek Kniaźnin a court poet and chronicler, who wrote after Poland's downfall that "we were not without a homeland, for we still had Puławy."

Many elegant palaces and villas in the style of Italian Baroque and French classicism were built throughout Poland, for example in Natolin, Sierniki, Kozłówka, Nieborów, and Arkadia near Łowicz, often with elaborate romantic gardens. Artistic crafts flourished during this period, especially traditional embroidery and weaving, produced in Grodno and Słuck, ceramics from the manufactures in Baranów and Ćmielów, glass from Naliboki and Urzecz, and porcelain from Korzec.

Music, mostly opera, was cultivated at the royal court in Warsaw as well as at the courts of Maciej Radziwiłł in Nieświerz and Michał Krzysztof Ogiński in Słonim. Both magnates were accomplished composers and musicians, who replaced foreign adaptations with their own works. In 1778 Maciej Kamieński composed and staged the first national opera *Misery Made Happy,* which was received with great enthusiasm by the public in Warsaw.

The crowning achievement of this period was the opera *A Supposed Miracle or Cracovians and Mountaineers* by Jan Stefani and Wojciech Bogusławski (1794), which introduced many native folk songs and dances. Staged on the eve of the Kościuszko Insurrection, the first night performance turned into a political manifestation and was banned after three performances by the Russian authorities. When the Insurrection was put down, Michał Kleofas Ogiński, who led his own unit and decided to fight for the country's independence abroad, composed one of his popular polonaises, entitled *Farewell to the Homeland.* Ogiński's melancholy dances and Maria Szymanowska's piano compositions of nocturnes, mazurkas, and waltzes were the harbingers of Chopin's Romantic music.

Introduction

LITERARY BACKGROUND

The crucial role in transplanting various strands of eighteenth-century Western thought to Poland was played by Stanisław Konarski, who laid the groundwork for the revival of political life and education. He coedited a corpus of Polish laws *Volumina legum* (1730-1739), presented a program for transforming the political system, and offered a plan for a thorough reform in education. To this end, he wrote *School Regulations*, founded the Collegium Nobilium, and authored textbooks and plays. Konarski's beliefs, expressed in his call "through the reform of education to the rebirth of the homeland," were put into practice by the Commission for National Education and echoed throughout the literature.

Many of Konarski's ideas were adopted by King Stanisław. The King supported poets, historians, and publicists. He met with prominent writers at his Thursday Dinners in the Royal Castle or Łazienki Palace, and discussed with them new ways of promoting literature and knowledge. Interested in Western philosophy and literature, the King encouraged translations of Locke and Pope as well as of Montesquieu, Voltaire, and Rousseau. It was mostly through these texts that the seminal Enlightenment ideas on natural religion, tolerance politics, and education, which originated from Locke's *Essay Concerning Human Understanding*, reached Poland. The propositions that men were created equal and that they could attain the state of well-being and happiness through education had considerable influence on political and social life.

The interest in new ideas, in the written word, was cultivated by the newly reformed schools and by the popular press. The goal of the influential weekly *Monitor*, launched by the King and modeled on Addison and Steele's *Spectator*, was to improve the readers' manners, minds, and morals. Periodical essays in the *Monitor,* many of them authored by its editors Franciszek Bohomolec and Ignacy Krasicki, dealt with philosophical ideas and literature as well as with light matters, e.g., characters, fads, and foibles. A literary weekly *Pleasant and Useful Amusements,* an unofficial organ of the King's circle, edited by Jan Albertrandi and Adam Naruszewicz, promoted classical and Polish literary tradition, introduced neoclassical literature, and served as a forum for many beginning poets. Numerous other publications in

Polish and foreign languages circulated in Warsaw and in the provinces. *The National and Foreign Gazette* supported the patriotic party, *Warsaw Gazette* attacked the Enlightenment ideology, while *Wilno Courier* and *Warsaw News* reported daily events.

Many new ideas emanated from the stage of the theatre, which gained great popularity in the eighteenth century. The public royal theatre, established in 1765, was directed by a Jesuit priest Franciszek Bohomolec, who polished his craft by staging didactic comedies in a Jesuit school theatre, one of fifty seven theatres of this type active throughout the country in 1756. Many of his plays written for the public theatre were adaptations of popular comedies by Molière, Destouches, and Goldoni. In his Collegium Nobilium, Stanisław Konarski propagated French classical tragedy in the tradition of the Piarist school theatre. Another popular playwright Stanisław Zabłocki wrote glittering comedies in verse, e.g., *The Fop Suitor* and *Sarmatism,* Julian Niemcewicz authored an original comedy *The Return of the Deputy,* which showed a conflict between two opposing political parties during the Four-Year Sejm, and Alojzy Feliński dealt with a historical theme in the tragedy *Barbara Radziwiłł.*

Theatre life was stimulated during the long career of Wojciech Bogusławski, an eminent actor, director, and playwright. Bogusławski staged major works of European drama in his theatres and founded the national opera. He organized the professional and artistic life of the public theatres in Warsaw as well as in Cracow, Lwów, Lublin, Wilno, and other cities. In 1811, he established the first drama school in Warsaw. Bogusławski saw the theatre as a major platform for expressing the ideas of the patriotic party. In 1794, he wrote and staged a comic opera *A Supposed Miracle or Cracovians and Mountaineers,* which told a story of two hostile groups of peasants and contained an undisguised call to arms on the eve of the Kościuszko Insurrection.

The literary reformers Konarski and Bohomolec were also active in promoting the Polish language in education, literature, and the cultural life of the nation. In his treatise *De emendandis eloquentiae vitiis* (1741), Konarski stressed the utilitarian function of Polish and called for creating a clear, simple, and concise instrument of communication. In *A Discourse on the Polish Language,* Bohomolec compared the flowery style and macaronisms of the Baroque period with the lucid diction of

Kochanowski and postulated that the proper use of the vernacular would bring about significant cultural changes. Jan Śniadecki defended the purity and clarity of the vernacular in his studies *On the Polish Language* (1815-1816) and *About the National Language in Mathematics* (1814).

In 1783, the Commission for National Education passed a statute that established Polish as the sole official language in schools. The Society for Elementary Books, under the leadership of Grzegorz Piramowicz, commissioned new textbooks and grammars. Onufry Kopczyński wrote *Grammar for National Schools* (1778-1783), several textbooks, as well as a study *On the Spirit of the Polish Language,* while Józef Mroziński authored *Basic Rules of the Grammar of the Polish Language* (1822).

The most important lexicographic works were Michał Trotz's three-volume *New Dictionary* of Polish, German, and French (1744-1764) and Samuel Linde's *Dictionary of the Polish Language* (1807-1814). Linde's monumental six-volume work was based on about 800 literary texts dating from the sixteenth to the eighteenth century and included numerous quotations as well as comparative etymologies from Slavic and other languages.

The language described by Linde underwent many changes in the second half of the eighteenth century, assuming virtually its modern form. It abandoned several back vowels, making the phonological system more simple. The past perfect tense became rare, the declensions, especially of the numerals, more uniform.

The greatest changes took place in lexicography, as Latin, French, and German words entered the Polish language in various fields of the humanities and sciences. Thus, the cultural terms *bilet*, "ticket"; *adres,* "address"; *afisz,* "poster" and the military *avant-garde, détachement, depôt*, came from the French, while *parostatek,* "steamship"; *czasopismo,* "periodical"; *światopogląd,* "world view" were derived from the German "Dampfschiff"; "Zeitschrift"; and "Weltanschauung."

Questions concerning literary style were taken up by Konarski and Bohomolec in their textbooks and manuals of rhetoric. In 1762 Wacław Rzewuski wrote *On the Art of Writing in Verse,* an original poem concerning poetry and style. Filip Golański discussed various theoretical issues in poetics in his treatise *On Rhetoric and Poetry* (1786), adapted from Dubos, Rollin, and Batteux, and Franciszek Dmochowski described them in his didactic poem *The Art of Poetry* (1788), based on Boileau's *L'Art Poétique.* Translations of Horace's *De arte poetica*

(1780) and Pope's *Essay on Criticism* (1790), presented major conceptions on the critical evaluation of poetry in a systematic form.

The major literary style that emerged in Poland was based on the principles of classicism. In 1819, Jan Śniadecki summarized the position of classicists in the following way: "Let's listen to the teachings of Locke in philosophy, to the rules of Aristotle and Horace in literature, and to the laws of Bacon in the sciences of observation and experimenting." He also named Boileau and Dmochowski as the codifiers of model classical rules.

Neoclassicism was rooted in rationalism, relied on reason, and advocated balance, harmony, and lucidity of style. It used as its models the French writers of the seventeenth century, mainly Corneille, Racine, Molière, and La Fontaine. Neoclassical literature was didactic and political, as it aimed at improving the state and its citizens, and relied on satire to achieve its goal of evoking laughter or indignation.

Polish satirists did not give free rein to virulent derision, as many writers were clergymen. Konarski, Bohomolec, Krasicki, Zabłocki and others, even though they intended to bring about change and attacked moral vices, displayed moderation and maintained the traditional values of Polish literature, namely its religious and historic inspiration.

The most representative figure of the period was Ignacy Krasicki. Moderate and dispassionate, Krasicki wrote brief, lucid, and witty poems. He was primarily a moralist whose didactic bend found most resonant expression in fables and satires. His mock-heroic poem *Monachomachia* makes good natured fun of monks and their way of life. Krasicki's *Fables*, concise and simple, are allegorical stories depicting in a dramatic fashion the wicked ways of the world. His *Satires*, for example, *Drunkenness* and *The Fashionable Wife*, are refined sketches of characters and of their weaknesses. On the other hand, Krasicki's didactic treatise *Mister Pantler* portrays a virtuous nobleman who lives in peace with himself and in harmony with the world.

The same lightness of style and elegance of form was displayed by Stanisław Trembecki, who wrote fine narrative fables and melodious occasional poems, e.g., *To Madame Kossowska When Dancing*. Kajetan Węgierski, a satirist and translator of French literature, mocked people of different walks of life, including his fellow poets whom he accused in *A Letter to Rhymesters* of writing panegyrics.

Traditional religious inspiration of the Polish literature was visible in the poems of Elżbieta Drużbacka, the author of edifying romances, for example, *Penance of Saint Mary the Egyptian, Penance of Saint Mary Magdalen,* and *The Description of Saint David's Life.* Konstancja Benisławska's collection of *Songs Sung for Myself* grew out of her reading of the Bible, particularly of the Psalter, and reflected her profound spiritual, at times mystical, sentiments suggestive of the Baroque.

Attention devoted to the individual's inner life was characteristic of literary sentimentalism. In Poland, the movement was advanced in the treatise *On Rhetoric in Prose and Poetry* (1782) by Franciszek Karpiński, who called on poets to use their creative imagination for expressing emotional life of the heart. Karpiński's religious songs, pastoral lyrics, and patriotic poems, to mention only *Night Song, To Justina,* and *The Lament of the Sarmatian*, are imbued with the feeling of love and foreshadow preromantic poetry. In a similar way, Franciszek Kniaźnin, closely associated with the center of national culture at the court of the Czartoryskis in Puławy, excelled in eclogues and love poems, e.g., *The Looms* and *To Love.* Alojzy Feliński's popular *Hymn* combined religious and political issues, while Kazimierz Brodziński, the author of an influential treatise *On Classicism and Romanticism As Well As On the Spirit of Polish Poetry* (1818), wrote A *Shepherdess's Song* and *The Raszyn Field,* in which he described a historical battle of 1809.

Moved by the critical situation of the country, many other poets turned to national history in order to extol Poland's glorious past and comfort their readers. Adam Naruszewicz, a lyrical poet and satirist, wrote a patriotic poem *Voice of the Dead* after the first partition and, encouraged by the King, the six-volume *History of the Polish Nation* (until 1386), for which he gathered numerous documents, used critically to show the rich heritage of the Polish people. Wacław Rzewuski, an author of patriotic poems, also wrote two historical tragedies: *Żółkiewski* and *Władysław at Varna.* In the same vein, Julian Niemcewicz, who lived through the tumultous years of partitions, wars, and insurrections, wrote the plays *Kazimierz the Great* and *Władysław at Varna,* as well as *Historical Songs.* He kept a diary in which he described major happenings of his eventful life, among them the Battle of Maciejowice, his captivity in Russia, and travels in America. Kajetan Koźmian's major works were an epic poem *Stefan Czarniecki* and *Memoirs.*

One of the most original historians was Jędrzej Kitowicz, who excelled also as a diarist. His *Description of Customs During the Reign of August III* gives a detailed and unembellished picture of Polish culture, including religion, schooling, occupations, offices, housing, furniture, dresses, entertainments, and other topics, while the *Diaries or Polish History,* which cover the period from 1743 to 1795, provide a vivid and minute description of contemporary events.

Among the writers who took an active part in public life, the most prominent was Hugo Kołłątaj. An ambitious politician influenced by French radical thought, Kołłątaj became one of the leading reformers. Many of his ideas presented in *Several Letters by the Anonym* and *Political Law of the Polish Nation,* which contained a thorough program of reorganizing the state, were implemented in the Constitution of 1791. Stanisław Staszic, another political writer and scientist, commented on public and social problems in his *Remarks on the Life of Jan Zamoyski.* In *Warnings for Poland,* Staszic offered his plan for the salvation of the country, which was based on the fundamental principles of the rights of all citizens.

Occasional literature flourished during the times of upheavals. Battles fought by the Confederates of Bar (1768-1772) inspired many anonymous poems extolling the patriotic ideals. In his poem *To the Nation,* written just before the Kościuszko Insurrection in 1794, Jakub Jasiński called on his compatriots to fight for freedom. In 1797, Józef Wybicki wrote the *Song of the Polish Legions in Italy,* which became Poland's national anthem, and Cyprian Godebski described their saga in his 1805 *Poem to the Polish Legions.* Many other popular songs which were preserved in oral tradition linked important historical events with national literature.

Notes

1. The Piarist Order was founded in Rome in 1597. In Poland, Piarists established schools for poor children. They competed with the Jesuits and after 1773 took over many Jesuit schools.

CHRONOLOGICAL TABLE

1697	August II installed on the Polish throne
1700-1721	Poland takes part in the Northern War
1704	August II deposed, Stanisław Leszczyński elected as the new king
1709	August II reclaims the throne
1717	The Silent Sejm
1733	August III elected king
1733-1735	The European War of Polish Succession
1740	The Collegium Nobilium established by Stanisław Konarski
1747	The public library established in Warsaw by Bishop Załuski and his brother
1760-1763	*On the Effective Method of Deliberating* published by Stanisław Konarski
1764	Stanisław August Poniatowski elected king
1765	Three important institutions established by the king: School of Cadets, the political periodical *Monitor*, and the National Theatre
1768	The Confederacy of Bar formed against Russia
1772	Defeat of the Confederates in Częstochowa. First partition of Poland
1773	Establishment of the Commission for National Education
1775	Establishment of the Society for Elementary Books

1788-1792	The Four-Year Sejm
1791	Proclamation of the Constitution
1792	Confederacy of Targowica and Polish-Russian war
1793	Second partition of Poland
1794	The Kościuszko Insurrection Victory at Racławice Defeat at Maciejowice Fall of Warsaw
1795	Third partition of Poland Abdication of Stanisław August Poniatowski, the last king of Poland
1797	Polish Legions organized in Italy
1806	Napoleon's campaign in Prussia
1807	Formation of the Duchy of Warsaw
1813	Napoleon's defeat at Leipzig, death of Józef Poniatowski, commander of the Polish Army
1815	Creation of the Kingdom of Poland

STANISŁAW KONARSKI (1700-1773)

Stanisław Konarski, born in Żarczyce near Kielce, lost his parents in infancy. He was brought up by his uncle and educated in the Piarist school in Piotrków. In 1715 he joined the Piarist Order, continued his studies, and taught. In 1722 he went to the Piarist College in Warsaw, where he taught rhetoric and began to publish his Latin poems and panegyrical speeches. In 1725 Konarski was sent to the Nazarene College in Rome and in 1729 to Paris. During his studies abroad, Konarski became acquainted with Latin and French literature as well as with new methods of education. Between 1730 and 1739 he coedited a compendium of Polish laws *Volumina legum,* took part in political debates, and taught in the Piarist colleges in Cracow and Rzeszów.

In 1740 Konarski founded the Collegium Nobilium, a model school, and began a process of reforming Polish methods of education. He presented his program in *Ordinationes (School Regulations,* 1754) and wrote numerous textbooks and grammars. In 1746 he began to write his four-volume major work *On the Effective Method of Deliberating* (1760-1763), in which he depicted the chaos of Polish political life and presented his proposals for a reform of the parliamentary system.

*On the Effective Method of Deliberating or
On Upholding the Ordinary Sejms*[1]

Part I
(selection)

In Which the Great Need for Ordinary Sejms Is Discussed, Beginning With Many Methods of Upholding Sejms, But All of Them Are Found Inadequate

1

All innumerable misfortunes and harm to the Republic come solely *ex mala consiliorum forma*[2]

XXII. Stanisław Konarski

The great concerns of the homeland which require counsel are innumerable, innumerable are dangers which should be averted. The Republic is like a house or like an old, big ship, which either has not been properly looked after for a long time or has been patched up superficially here and there, heading directly towards ruin and destruction, unless it is thoroughly repaired. Everyone will find in it something important and in need of great improvement.

Some people wish to look first into administration of justice, on which all kingdoms stand as if on a strong foundation, and to reform tribunals[3] and courts, which are becoming more and more unjust. Some constantly advocate supporting greatly weakened powers of the Republic, on account of whose weakness we suffer unbearable contempt and harm from foreign states, and establishing defenses appropriate to the dimension of such a large state.[4] Some call for adequate regulation of treasury and public revenue, depleted with clear detriment to the Kingdom. Others suggest ways of bringing trade to full bloom, which in this rich country does not even have one thousandth of its vigor. Some others see a great need to properly reorganize laws, of which many require regulation, updating, and execution, and find more effective methods of executing them, so that they are not written just to fall prey to moths.[5] Still others have a lot to complain, justly or not, about the courts. For some, it is deterioration of the coin[6] and public destitution; for others, lack of workshops and factories needed throughout the country, causing every year an outflow of big sums of money abroad; for some others, the ruin of cities and little towns; for still others, serfdom and heavy burdens imposed on the ploughman, who can barely breathe: these are great and urgent matters for reform. Some wish to uproot widespread crime, equally unbearable. Others see clearly the woes of the noble estate, which does not have means for education of its sons and then for apprenticeship when they grow up, thus forcing them to accept degrading service.[7] For some, the problem is the severely weakened and virtually scorned and subverted authority of the senate; for others, the considerable and frequent conflicts with the clergy[8]; for others, the foreign and local factions; for others, the ugly disorders at diets and dietines; for some others, the elections so essential in each voivodship, but not held[9]; for some others, the indescribable afflictions of interregnums and national disasters[10]; for some others, the oppression brought by foreign armies[11]; for still others, the loss of the Kingdom's borders and provinces[12]; for still others, various great misfortunes of the homeland, and the pain grips and hurts the heart suffering for its nation.

All of these are without a doubt true and deadly afflictions, there are thousands more, if one wanted to count them in detail. We would be glad to relieve the homeland of each, we propose to cure all, we would like to find an effective prescription for every last one. But what can be done when all of us only complain, and do not set about offering solid means of salvation. "As things are, Rome is dying of a strange malady. Disapproval of what has been done and indignant complaint are universal. Opinion is not divided at any point, there is open grumbling even to the stage of loud groaning, but nobody comes forward with a remedy. This is because we think resistance is bound to be suicidal, while we see no end to concession except destruction."[13] What is more, in this disorder and confusion life became almost odious, even for many decent and great people in their own country. "The times are such that everyone considers his condition miserable and he would not like to see himself where he is, where he resides. And truly, I consider it a great misfortune that we live in Rome. Not only is it more difficult to see with one's eyes misfortunes of the homeland than to hear of them, but also here we are closer to all dangers and events than if we were absent."[14] And we rightly complain about immutable decrees of nature and Providence, about being born in times so miserable for the homeland, not peaceful, or about living to see them. We congratulate those who do not see any more this disorder, this disgrace of the nation. "But I am thoroughly sick of life, nothing but misery of every kind. Nobody is more miserable than I am (says the Roman consul),[15] Catullus is supremely to be envied, not only in the dignity of his life but also now that he is dead."[16]

But we complain in vain about the ways of Providence, as it is always willing to help those who want to help themselves, and in vain attempt to count the innumerable misfortunes of the Republic. We will not find, I assure you, any remedy for all of them together or each one separately until we cure one deadly disease, from which all others, as many as they are, are derived. "Nobody will clean putrid and unhealthy streams without first cleansing the infected source from which they all flow."

I remember a conversation with a respected minister of the Republic, a man filled with lofty sentiments and wishing his homeland well, whose opinion, shared by many leading and most important people in the country, was: "Whatever is wrong in our state, that to this date cannot be reformed, all of this comes from one contaminated source: *ex mala consiliorum forma.*" His statement spurred me to collect all reflections about that truth, even if somewhat long, and not so much to show the way of reforming our bad form of counsel, but to present it in this book, following the opinions of such respected and wise men.

First of all, it is an unquestionable and obvious thing that no kingdom can stand without good counsel. It is clear that we cannot reform and cure those Tribunals, those weak military forces of the Republic, those revenues of the treasury, those trades, those ruined cities and little towns, those countless disorders and lawlessness, in any other way but through the counsel. And when this counsel does not work, everything must happen in a slap-dash manner, and must eventually collapse. For if one property, one private and small home cannot function well without counsel, how can a kingdom function well and govern itself without counsel? In all human societies the government and counsel are the soul of everything. The government cannot exist without counsel. Counsel is the leader and light of a good government. Charles the Great ordered to have it written on the representation of the world: "With authority and counsel." And I add about counsel what the Roman consul said about laws: "Without which no house, no city, no country, no human race, no nature, nor the whole world can stand."[17]

Therefore all states that exist under the sun, large and small, always have wise and effective counsel. Every day monarchs deliberate in their offices, as much as is required, and at once make decisions. Their edicts or decrees, ordinances, laws, decisions on various matters, appear virtually without interruption. At the end of each year, they grow into big volumes, similar to royal laws. Free republics have several appointed days in a week for their assemblies, where without delay they deliberate and decide about everything. Everywhere, they deliberate about everything in advance, everywhere decisions in all matters are required and prompt. Our Sejm assembles only every two years and just for six weeks, but we do not really have Sejms: several years pass, dozen or so, even several decades, and we cannot have an ordinary Sejm, which is our highest assembly. No wonder that left without this counsel we lose everything, everything deteriorates, more and more.

It went so far that this most wise Roman consul, statesman, and politician could predict from the unhappy circumstances of his time what would happen next. He says: "I augur not from the flight of birds, not from the stars, as astrologers do, but I have different signs which I observe. My signs are those circumstances and times in which we live; our augury about the future should find credence with everyone."[18] I can say too, in the situation in which we are, it is proper to make inferences about the future. Who does not see that without counsel and assemblies we will become more unfortunate, we will descend into greater disorders, and finally we will approach and overstep the bounds leading to, heaven forbid, our final ruin.[19]

Notes

1. Regular Sejms, known also as 'ordinary' or 'six-week' Sejms, were called every two years on the first Monday after September 29 for six-week sessions. Extraordinary Sejms were called only in emergencies for two or three weeks.
   During the reign of August II and August III, twenty four Sejms were broken up. In this work, Konarski suggests various ways of reforming the Sejm. He uses the word 'rada' ('counsel') to refer to the interchange of opinions in a deliberative assembly as to what ought to be done as the result of this process.
2. 'From a bad form of counsels.'
3. Tribunals, supreme courts for the nobility, were considered particularly corrupt.
4. The size of the army, established by the Sejm in 1717, was 18,000 men for Poland and 6,000 for Lithuania. Konarski was aware that in reality it was impossible to field an army larger than half of the prescribed size.
5. The first effort to reorganize laws was undertaken by Konarski and Jędrzej Załuski in 1731. The codification of laws was carried out by Andrzej Zamoyski between 1776 and 1780.
6. Polish coins were steadily losing value, because, for example, their gold edges were trimmed off or they were forged by the Prussians. The 1761 Sejm which was called to reform the monetary policy was broken up.
7. Education of noblemen's sons generally ended in Jesuit or Piarist schools. After graduating, the boys were usually sent to serve at the courts of big lords and magnates, becoming dependent for promotion on their patrons.

8. These conflicts concerned taxation of Church properties by the state.

9. These were elections for local offices, mostly in courts. When dietines were broken up, local administration was paralyzed.

10. Konarski is writing about the double election of August III and Stanisław Leszczyński, and the war of succession, won by August III, with the support of the Russian army.

11. During the reign of August II and August III, Poland was plundered by Saxon, Prussian, Swedish, and Russian armies.

12. Beginning in the seventeenth century, Poland suffered territorial losses to Sweden, Russia, and Prussia. In 1737, for example, Poland lost Curlandia.

13. Quoted from *Cicero's Letters to Atticus*. Ed. by D.R. Shackleton Bailey. Vol. I. Cambridge: Cambridge University Press, 1965, II, 20, 3.

14. Cicero, Liber VI, *Epistola ad Torquatum*.

15. Cicero became a consul in 63 B.C.

16. Catullus, author of lyrical poems and political lampoons, died in 54 B.C., before the outbreak of civil war (49-48 B.C.). Cicero, *Ad Atticum*, II, 24, 4.

17. Cicero, *De legibus, liber III*.

18. Cicero, *Epistola ad Caecinum, liber VI*.

19. The last sentence is a paraphrase of a thought from Virgil.

Text: Konarski, Stanisław. *Pisma wybrane*. Vol. I. Ed. by Juliusz Nowak-Dłużewski. Introduction by Zdzisław Libera. Warszawa: PIW, 1955, 106-111.

ELŻBIETA DRUŻBACKA (ca. 1695-1765)

Drużbacka was born most likely in Great Poland, and educated at several magnates' courts. Married ca. 1720, she was widowed in ca. 1735. She administered two villages, visited the courts of the Sieniawski, Sanguszko, Czartorski and Branicki families, and wrote poetry, admired by her contemporaries. At the end of her life Drużbacka settled in the convent of the Bernardine Nuns in Tarnów.

The only work published during her lifetime was *A Collection of the Spiritual, Panegyrical, Moral, and Wordly Rhythms* (1752). She was the author of a fairy tale *The Story of Prince Adolph* and a romance in verse *A Christian Story of Princess Elephantine Eufrata* (1769), adapted from French texts.

On Proud Narcissus
fleeing from the love of the nymph called Echo[1]

In vain you come out to fight with love, Narcissus,
In vain you joust with it garbed in steel cuirasses,
In vain you trust arms, a triangular rapier,
When the naked child can by ruse win it over;
5   In a short time one dart
        Will hit the brave man's heart.

Flee to the hills, woods, dark forests, and wilderness,
In this hunting you will find that joys are useless;
Love will follow you and it will vex you beside,
10 It'll teach you to pay homage and will curb your pride,
        Abandon the wild game,
        Fall in love with this dame.

Just show me a hero who in his fearlessness
Was not overcome by love that is victorious.
15 Each weapon, even forged of hard steel, will shatter,
It will get easily through helmets and armor.
        Mars's work and hardship
        Love will change to courtship.

Through trenches and bridges, field-works, walls, and each gate
20 Love walks without hindrance, its road is always straight,
There has not yet been a fortress in existence
Which would not be captured by love's skilled experience.
        The builder built in vain,
        Love crossed borders again.

25 Love will find a hermit in a deserted den
And light in cold flint the fires in the spark hidden.
So the one that was touched when the flint took its aim
Turns into a flare that is bursting into flame.
        The holy bones disperse
30   And turn into cinders.

Love hides under the lowered hoods with readiness,
Where not to be recognized, it will wear a dress
Of modesty, but when it finds its usual role,
It counsels to raise the hood and comfort the soul.
35   It will allow the eye
        Everything to espy.

It's in vain vestal virgins promise solemnly
To hold vigils by day and by night mindfully;
For when natural sleep covers a virgin's eyes,
40 An eager spark will often from the fire arise,
        Till the vow is broken,
        It blames the victim then.

Love will blemish and efface beautiful crimsons
Colored by modesty and virtue's paragons,
45 So that no painter of glazes and of lusters
Will know how to restore the substance of colors;
        The hues became now plain,
        As disgrace left its stain.

Love comes to the garden that's enclosed by a fence
50 Of golden marital league, though it makes no sense
For it to mar God's judgments; but this house mistress
Makes concealed openings in solid enclosures,
        Hence great devastation
        In new vegetation.

55 Love will also warm those who in their senile years
   From natural warm feelings to white snow traverse,
   It will gain its end, if in rotten mold aglow
   It will find less fire, more smoke, when inside it'll blow.
             The happy devil grins,
60   Each time the old man sins.

   Here is a clear proof, impertinent Narcissus,
   That the entire world homage to love professes;
   People feel it, beasts feel it, all that lives can see
   The might of the lady whose rule no one will flee.
65   Abandon stubbornness,
             Embrace submissiveness.

   Go there, I wish, where Echo's voice is calling you.
   Often instinct follows fortune's fate for those who
   Obedient to heaven's will and man's counsel
70 Put in them the hope of their happiness to dwell.
             Those who act in this way
             Will never go astray.

   But the one who strides boldly, looks down at others,
   Will fall into a hole or into deep waters,
75 When Narcissus scorned the nymph, rushed to the fountain,
   He swallowed his own tears and drank of death therein.
             Thus in shame he ended
             His combat with Cupid.

Notes

1. The nymph Echo fell in love with Narcissus, a beautiful youth, but was rejected. Narcissus was punished for his cruelty by becoming enamored of his own image in a fountain. He tried in vain to approach this beautiful object, became desperate, and died. He was changed into the flower that bears his name. Cf. Ovid, *Metamorphoses* 3, 342-510.

Text: Kostkiewiczowa, Teresa and Zbigniew Goliński. *Świat poprawiać--zuchwałe rzemiosło. Antologia poezji polskiego Oświecenia.* Warszawa: PIW, 1981, 30-32.

WACŁAW RZEWUSKI (1706-1779)

Rzewuski was born into a magnate's family in Rozdole. He was educated in a Piarist school and travelled extensively, spending much time in France. He reached the positions of voivode of Podole (1737), of Cracow (1762), and of Grand Hetman of the Crown (1773), playing an important part in major events of the period.

Rzewuski wrote political poems and speeches as well as historical tragedies, e.g., *Żółkiewski* (1758), comedies, e.g. *The Eccentric* (1760), and collections of poems. He was influenced by Molière's comedies and Boileau's *Art poétique*, translated Horace and the Psalms.

On the Equality of Earthly Happiness
(selection)

    Let's abandon errors and let's despise
    Views of the crowd and thoughts that masses prize,
    And let's give, what people grant but a few,
    Happiness to all in servitude, too.
5   Claiming that all estates have equal fate,
    Let's put the throne and soil in one blest state.
    We'll sing praises which are due to heavens
    That wished we all shared happy providence.
    Purest of goddesses, dame without sham,
10   Honored by sages, scorned by common man,
    O Truth! Sovereign queen of every science,
    Accept my verse, a gift of subservience.
    I will not present it to Apollo
    Nor in sacrifice on Parnassus show,
15   My verse will be worthy and happy, too,
    When it becomes your own, when it is true.
    God our father, from one mother of men,
    Made out of dust, we are all their children.
    Each of us is brought forth in the same way,
20   Each gives up his soul and passes away.
    After death all the mortals turn to dust,
    Body to the earth, soul to God entrust.

In life too God's might gave everybody
Same functions of soul, senses, and body.
25 Why wouldn't joy come in an even measure
Before Parcae[1] push us out forever?
Why aren't we treated fair by happiness,
One man getting naught, the other excess?
I don't know the reason why our father
30 Unequal joy to his sons would offer.
Having made all people from the same clay,
Give some happiness, cause others dismay?
And having tied happiness to the crown,
Ploughs and plots of land with curse weigh down? (...)

Notes

1. Parcae were three goddesses who determined the course of human life.

A Grove

You that cool us down in the sun's shimmer,
Drying off our wet foreheads in your shades,
Embellished by nature in the mirror,
Calm water crystal, with trees, flowers, blades;
5 That show us beauty of lost paradise
In part at least, o grove, divert my eyes.

Nature forms here walls made of little trees,
Embellishing them in green leaf decor,
Beautiful branches fashion canopies,
10 She profusely lays flowers on the floor,
Just as there's music inside palace doors,
A nightingale sings here and water soars.

Dishes of a cook unpaid for her toil,
Fruit in abundance from many a source,
15 The earth prepares, the sun brings to a boil,
The trees then offer them to visitors.
Nature is happy for they are eager,
The feast goes on from June to November.

She gives them drinks that come out of the sea,
20 Then they return there, passing through the earth,
The lively springs that run incessantly,
Refreshing us more than other waters;
Drink them as you wish, even bathe with zeal,
You won't leave drunk from such a lavish meal.

25 You, grove, divert me from my deep sorrow,
Soothe cruel fate with hope of happiness,
From Iris's[1] affection I'll well know
That joyous days will replace my sadness;
Ere your leaves are blown off by Autumn's gale,
30 Let wishes of my bliss come to prevail.

Notes

1. Iris was the messenger of the gods and the goddess of the rainbow. She was the wife of Zephyrus, the west wind.

Text: Kostkiewiczowa and Goliński, *Świat poprawiać*, 46, 49.

FRANCISZEK BOHOMOLEC (1720-1784)

Bohomolec joined the Jesuits at the age of seventeen, studied philosophy at the Wilno Academy, and after several years of teaching was sent to Rome, where he read theology (1747-1749). At the Jesuit College in Warsaw, he directed the school theatre, supplying it with his own comedies. Bohomolec was also an editor of prose and poetry, e.g., by Kochanowski (1768) and Lubomirski (1771). As a publisher, he founded and edited the *Warsaw News, Warsaw Courier,* and most importantly, the *Monitor* (1765-1784), to which he contributed hundreds of articles.

In five volumes of his comedies (1755-1760), written for Jesuit, royal, and public theatres, Bohomolec imitated the French plays, mainly by Molière, but adapted them to Polish customs and color.

To Sir Gregory
A Drinking Song[1]

Now call for wine, my most dear Gregory,
Let us forget we have any worry!
Let Annie[2] sit down with all of us too!
Your health, brother, here's to you!

5   The moment your hand will touch the bottle,
Your heart will be free from any trouble;
So let's clink our glasses and call anew:
Your health, brother, here's to you!

This wine's not bad! To you, my Greg, most dear:
10 My friend, let's be glad while we can and cheer!
All dull thoughts and troubles should say adieu!
Your health, brother, here's to you!

Look, this wine's vigorous power is clear:
My heart is already full of good cheer.
15 Down with small cups! In tumblers have a few!
Your health, brother, here's to you!

MONITOR.

No. I.

Ridendo dicere verum quid vetat:
HORATIUS.

Piſać, niepiſać, trwałem czas niejaki w tey rozdwojoney myſli, odwazam ſię piſać, y puſzczam ſię na wſzyſtkie niebeſpieczeńſtwa, krytyki. Tych, wielu nawet, ktorzy y bez przeczytania ganić będą. Jak gdybym ſię na to patrzył, Nadchodzącą widzę ſcenę. Przyjezdza kawaler z Tych (co to niedoſzedł Francuſa , a wyſzedł z Polaka) z Wizytą zrana do Damy, przeziera ſię w Zwierściedle, proſi o kawę; poſtrzega Ten Papier leżący na Gotowalni, krzyknie z podziwieniem: Coz to za Szpargał? proſzę Mcia Dobr. Jakiz to Tytuł; *Monitor*, o czym ze to piſze, pewnie nas ſekować chce ten Jegomość przeſtrogami niepotrzebnemi, zachęcać moze do applikacyi, wytykać Inkonweniencye w kraju dziejące ſię. Niepſuy ſobie WMPani Dobrodzieyko Oczy nad tym, lubom nieczytał, założył bym ſię, ze nic do rzeczy; Mam Ja tu potrzebnieyſzy daleko Papier, godzien rozwazania; ieſt to Projekt y ułozenie Pana Salwatora do przyſzłych Redut; juz tedy według wyrokow Galantoma, Monitora czym prędzey krają na papieloty. Dla rozerwania Melancholii wſtępuie z Przyjacielem do Winiarza Prozniak, lezy Kuryer Warſzawſki na ſtole, przy nim *Monitor*, pociągnowſzy wąſa, woła na Kompana: P. Władyſławie, a to kiz Diabeł, *Monitor* coz to ſię znaczy, niedopierom ze Szkoł wyſzedł, y w tych prawda, bardziey Piłki, jak Łaciny pilnowałem, ale zdaie mi ſię coś, jak przez Sen, ze to *Monitor a monendo*, *moneo* przeſtrzegam, y od czegoz on to ſtrzeze, od Ognia? Nad Relikwiami kwartowey Flaſzy w koncie Zabawny, przybył dla roznych Sprawunkow do Miaſta Jm. Xiądz. Wikary Pytającego ſię ciekawość w ten Sens uſpokaia. Ten, ktory piſze, o grozliwych bez rządu kraiu Naſzego Konſekwencyach, chce nas przeſtrzegac, y podobno zamyſla obiaſnic czaſem; *quid ſit honeſtum, quid deceat Civem in vita Publica*, y iakie ſą Jego powinnoſci; ale obeydzie ſię bez Jegomości fatygi, od wiekow te użyſkiwanie

And you, our dear Annie, Greg's better half,
Join us at table, be cheerful and laugh:
Amuse yourself with us, have one or two!
20 Your health, brother, here's to you!

The bottle's empty, let's have a jug now!
Vivat[3] our whole company anyhow,
Vivat little Matt[4] and our friendly crew!
Your health, brother, here's to you!

25 Little Matt's a bungler, does not like wine,
For him the girl is like a true gold mine:
Let's leave him in peace, let's drink alone too!
Your health, brother, here's to you!

Let's bring back ancestors' immortal skills,
30 Away with tumblers, those flawed utensils:
Let's drink in goblets, old fashion make new:
Your health, brother, here's to you!

Well now, Greg, you are more advanced in years,
You know wine is like milk for the elders;
35 Sip one and with youngsters you'll sing on cue:
Your health, brother, here's to you!

Notes

1. The word 'kurdesz' in the Polish title of this popular poem was of Tartar origin, meaning 'brother' or 'brotherhood.' It became the name given to a drinking song and also a dance. Grzegorz Łyszkiewicz, to whom the poem was dedicated, a prominent merchant and banker, was Mayor of Warsaw.
2. Annie was Gregory's wife.
3. *Vivat*--'long live.'
4. Matthew, Gregory's son.

From *The Monitor*
16, 1765

Invited to dinner by a good friend, I found the whole house in confusion. I asked for a cause, they whispered in my ear: "Madame had a dream that she lost a tooth." I could barely suppress my laughter at this story, but not wishing to make the hosts angry, I did what I could to show that I was a participant in the general sorrow. Madame came in; as soon as she saw me in a black robe,[1] she exclaimed: "I just said we were facing some misfortune." We sat at the table, the host said that on Monday he was taking his son back to school. "Ah, God forbid!--she said--did you forget, my husband, that Monday is the Feast of the Holy Innocents?" I sat as if on needles in my black robe; they asked me to pass the dish, I jumped to my feet and knocked over the salt shaker. Madame moaned, barely right in her mind, and said to her husband: "Remember, my heart, two years ago, on the eve of Saint Bartholomew's, our neighbor had also spilled the salt and the same day we learned about locusts in Podolia and then two weeks later a barn was set on fire by a thunderbolt. Our deceased paternal uncle had knocked over the salt shaker two days before his death; I said right away that he would die and that's what happened. God save us from that, but to my mind all seems to indicate that we will soon be crying." I could barely manage to sit still in the midst of these fatal prophecies, but as I gathered that Madame was looking at me awry and the host, to please her, began to make a wry face, I slipped out from that awful house without saying good bye, filled with pity at Madame's weakness of mind and her husband's harmful indulgence.

Notes

1. Bohomolec was a Jesuit priest.

Texts: Chrzanowski, Ignacy. *Historia literatury niepodległej Polski (965-1795) (z wypisami)*. 13th ed. Warszawa: PWN, 1983, 487-488, 489-490.
Kostkiewiczowa and Goliński, *Świat poprawiać*, 56-57.

JEDRZEJ KITOWICZ (1728-1804)

Kitowicz was born in Great Poland, attended Warsaw schools, and served at magnates' courts. In 1768 or 1769, he joined the Confederates of Bar and fought in many battles. In 1771 he entered the Warsaw Seminary, became a priest, and held positions at several parishes.

Keenly interested in history and politics, Kitowicz recorded important events in the *Diaries or Polish History*, edited in the last years of his life. His most important work, *Description of Customs During the Reign of August III,* published posthumously in 1840, in which he attempted to present a systematic picture of the Polish customs, changing rapidly in the times of partitions, is considered today an authentic historical and social document.

Diaries or Polish History
(selection)

On the Polish King

Stanisław August Poniatowski, after abdicating his crown in Grodno, was taken to Saint Petersburg where on the twelfth of February 1798, he died of a headache which he had suffered for several days before his death. He confessed before dying to Father Jurcewicz, his chaplain, received from him the last absolution, and began to say with him the acts for the dying, but having repeated several words after the priest, when he was unable to speak any more, he was taken under doctors' care, who bled him twice, then applied a vesicatorium,[1] and in this way did away with him.

It was also generally known or supposed that he died of a cold, assisting in an important ceremony of a Russian rite of blessing the Jordan, that is some river by this name, which the Russians celebrate on the three kings' day, when it is usually the coldest. So assisting in this ceremony for three hours or rather assisting the tsar who did not wear a fur coat, Poniatowski, also without a fur coat, caught a cold and from that time on his health began to deteriorate. Finally, others were of the opinion that his life was shortened by poison so that it would be no longer necessary to support with expensive outlays that unneeded king deprived of his kingdom.

Whichever reason brought him close to death, all issued forth from the lost kingdom: headache from the worry and shame eating up his insides, cold from slavishly flattering the tsar, poison on account of removing an idle person from Saint Petersburg.

Several days after his death the tsar gave him a most magnificent funeral. First, during religious rites in the Marble Palace,[2] where the king lived and died, his body was displayed to the public on a state bed. On the day of exportation, two senators approached the dead king, lifted his head, on which the tsar put a crown, and then sprinkled his body with an aspergillum, which was handed to him by the archbishop or the Russian metropolitan. Then all bishops and senators sprinkled him with the same aspergillum, passed from hand to hand according to rank. After this aspersion, the body was placed in a casket, put on the funeral carriage, and led to the Catholic Church, the tsar riding his horse by the casket with his drawn sword reversed. Senators and Russian ministers surrounded the casket, led by the Russian and Latin clergy singing, at times the band playing. Knights in silver armor, the best military regiments, horses draped in funeral cloth led by hand were marching in that procession. The emperor's retinue in mourning, the king's in gala robes, combined into a strange mixture of sorrow and mirth, followed the casket; eighteen thousand soldiers were drawn up on both sides of the street from the Marble Palace to the church.

The interior of the whole church was decorated in black with cloth of silver, the *castrum doloris*[3] was lavishly adorned with various designs, the deceased man's escutcheons, and white eagles. The tsar truly did not overlook anything that could have made this funeral the most splendid, doing whatever his strange fantasy prompted him, among which the first place should go to crowning after death the head deprived of the crown during its lifetime and using holy water to consecrate the king's body with his unconsecrated hand.

Soon after we learned from the people who came from Saint Petersburg that the funeral for Poniatowski did not cost the tsar even a penny; on the contrary, it brought quite a lot of money to his treasury. That came to pass in the following fashion: the tsar, in return for the funds spent on the said funeral, imposed a contribution on all the voivodships that were detached from the Polish Crown and the Great Duchy of Lithuania and came under his rule after the last partition, a ruble for each homestead. 692,828 homesteads were detached according to the list by Moszyński, secretary of the Grand Duchy of Lithuania, deputy from Bracław, who laboriously drew it up from treasury registers of both nations and presented it to the attention of the Sejm in Warsaw on April 19, 1790. So the tsar took 692,828 rubles, explaining that it was the funeral of the king of Poland and the Grand Duchy of Lithuania and therefore both the Poles and Lithuanians should cover the costs. Let's note now what costs the tsar had in this funeral and what cost him nothing at all: he incurred costs for candles, lamps, decorative painting and carving, church tapestries, catafalques, caskets, masses, which in the schismatic city, without a lot of Roman Catholic clergymen, could not have been numerous, and finally he might have had some costs for exentering and balsaming the body, funeral dinner and alms for the poor; about those two points we did not hear anything, but let us indulge in admitting them. All of this could not cost more, even if it were most lavish, than three hundred thousand rubles, so the second part, more than half of the collected taxes became the tsar's profit and reward for his effort. (...)

So then Stanisław Poniatowski, considered the wisest contemporary monarch in Europe, ended his life most abjectly and shamefully. And the opinion based on the play of letters in the anagram of the name 'Poniatowski,' repeated throughout the nation: "He'll fool the world," came to pass, but only in the second case of the said name, that is *in genitivo*: 'Poniatowskiego'--"the world will fool him"[4], which indeed had happened. Had he lived in a peaceful age, ruled in a state safe from his neighbors, the people could not have wished for a better king. For as a matter of fact he was most learned, very intelligent, fluent and engaging in spcech. He loved arts and sciences, tried his best to improve crafts and arts, and made useful reforms of the old, bad laws. In addition, he was kind, approachable, pleasant in conversation, also patient and forgiving, when faced with the libels, which he ordered to be collected and brought in 'for snacks,' and with which the Poles fed him to the teeth, as they say, at each Sejm. These virtues were worthy of a throne, but of a peaceful and safe one. On such a throne, he could pass for a most excellent monarch. But as soon as the monarchs laid plans to partition Poland, Poniatowski ceased to be a useful king. The state finding

XXIV. Bird's eye view of the Łazienki Royal Palace and Theatre in Warsaw

itself in these circumstances should have had a warrior, a king brave enough for all contingencies. Yet Poniatowski was a coward, milk-sop, immersed in pleasant life, but still trying by all means to die a king on any decent piece of land. (...)

Łazienki Palace near Warsaw, built and decorated at the cost of millions, was the apple of his eye and the abyss devouring his treasures for constantly new varieties of decorations and structures according to his passing fancy. The fear of losing them, as well as the throne, threatened by the Russian envoy Bulgakov,[5] compelled him to renounce the Constitution of the Third of May, even though he swore on it solemnly, and accede to the Confederacy of Targowica. He usually moved from the Warsaw Castle to Łazienki for his summer residence, followed by performers of comic plays, opera, and other entertainments. There he sailed on canals in a large boat, there he promenaded in far-extending groves with a retinue of women and courtiers, there he had a mirror wall built near his boudoir bed, so that his eyes could help those members working on procreation, feeling no doubt that under the master's eye every job proceeds more efficiently.

He abhorred drunkenness; to quench his thirst he drank water and at the table a glass of wine. It must have been an important occasion for him to allow himself to drink a big glass of wine. He ate only once a day at four in the afternoon; he ate well and when he was in a good mood, his language at the table was coarse. Gentle in public conversations, he was hotheaded in the privacy of his home: he swore to no end, cursed others with dirty words, a simple man could not do better, and he would give it to his servants right on the nose for any inconvenience, most often to Ryx, his chamberlain and most efficient minister of amorous pleasures. And since lumps and blows from the king were never healed without good compensation, that is why Ryx would often lay himself open to them. He liked flattery and praise a lot, that is why he was never short of flatterers, extolling his reign to the skies in words and letters.

He looked at the entertainments of the common folk as if they were great events worthy of royal attention. That is why noblemen, knowing the king's taste, when he visited them, would entertain him with peasant weddings that were just taking place or were acted out. The king would approach a group dancing in the open air, listen with pleasure to love songs, and encourage the country boys to indulge in the most intimate caresses with the girls.

The city of Warsaw offered the king a splendid view of a similar kind soon after his coronation. A boat on the Vistula was decorated with pennons, flags, rugs, and other festive ornaments. Six maidens of great beauty were put in it. Bare to their navels, they represented the sea sirens, singing for the king on the shore and luring him to join them. After this maritime exercise, the sirens had the good fortune of finding themselves in strict *incognito* in the royal chamber, where the king, having tasted an inside piece of each fish, granted them monthly salary wages, paid for a long time for this and similar gratifications.

But one should also tell the truth that the king was giving a lot for pious deeds, to hospitals, orphans, poor monasteries, being generous, even extravagant. And when his income did not correspond to expenditures, he would contract small and big debts, wherever he could. His brokers would run wherever they could smell money with the ready royal cyrographs even for five hundred red zlotys[6] and less. The king combined the royal treasury with the crown treasury, separate before then, and in this way often took from the Republic considerable sums and also exceeded his income established by the Sejm. And when all these sources were dried up, he would go to the rich monks, threatening them with the appropriation of monastic possessions for having no ownership or with other perils, until they were truly afraid. "You have to give, you have to give, the king is in need, your properties are ill-gotten, you will lose them, if you don't give"--this was a general formula to frighten the monks.

However, all these defects and injustices would have counted for naught, if he had not lost Poland, for if he had not the heart to defend her, he should have renounced the throne just after the first partition of the country according to the rules of an honest man's conscience and character. He would have descended from it then much more commendably, out of heroism rather than forced to later, but that unfortunate desire to reign blinded him and brought him to a shameful end.

He expressed belief in the Roman Catholic faith, as he was born in it and bound to the throne by the law *Rex catholicus esto*.[7] Every year on Holy Thursday he confessed publicly, knelt near a priest sitting in the middle of the church in front of the grand altar, received Holy Communion, washed the feet of twelve poor people and served them when they sat at the table in his chambers, attired in new clothes and shoes and furnished with generous alms. He listened with exemplary modesty to the Holy Mass in the castle chapel and also to the sermons delivered in an elevated and refined style by Lachowski and Witoszyński, court preachers famous for their eloquence. On the more solemn holy days he attended High Mass in the Warsaw Collegiate Church or at the missionary church in Krakowskie Przedmieście Street,[8] where he established the custom of awarding the Order of bishop Saint Stanisław. (...)

On the other hand, because of Poniatowski's dissolute life, willing association with persons without faith and decent manners, abolition in the courts of the register *arianismi*,[9] established against heretics and godless people in the past, and failure to observe the fasts, he brought upon himself the suspicion of being a Catholic only in appearance, a libertine in his heart. Nonetheless good fortune protected his name in this matter and maybe favored him with saving his soul, as he died like the Catholic, as was shown above.

Notes

1. Plaster vesicatorium or 'emplastrum vesicatorium, made of a powder from Turkish flies Cantharides, was applied in order to absorb harmful fluids from the patient's body and to relieve him from bad humours.

2. The Marble Palace in Nevsky Prospect was built by the Italian architect Rinaldi between 1768-1785 as a gift of Catherine II to her lover Grigorij Orlov.

3. The catafalque.

4. In Polish: Poniatowski--'*on okpi świat*,' Poniatowskiego--'*okpi go świat.*'

5. Yakov Ivanovich Bulgakov was Catherine's ambassador in Poland.

6. Polish currency at the time.

7. The king should be Catholic.

8. At present Saint Cross Church.

9. *Regestr arianismi*, retained in the courts against the Arians after they were banished from Poland in the seventeenth century, stipulated that they and other dissidents could be liable to prosecution.

Description of Customs During the Reign of August III

About the Education of Children Over the Age of Seven
(selections)

Even though some children of more receptive minds below the age of five years old were initially taught to read at home, in general they were not sent to school until they were seven or over.

For those who lived in towns, their first school was a parish school, at the church or cathedral, depending on its location. It was rare to find such a school at a church in the country. Therefore a nobleman who lived in the country, before he sent his children to school, first had to teach them to read at home, hiring a teacher for this purpose, if there was nobody qualified for this service in his household.

Boys were taught in parish schools, while girls were sent to matrons whose occupation was to teach them to read in Polish, knit stockings, and do all kinds of sewing. Daughters of more affluent people were taught German and French, which already began to be fashionable. Daughters of magnates were taught all this by governesses at home and also writing and dancing by teachers.

Boys in parish schools were taught reading from a primer and beginning Latin from an Alvar or Donat grammar book.[1] Catechism, that is teaching of religion, was first among all other subjects. (...)

On Public Schools

Those trained in the rudiments of Latin in parish schools were sent to public schools, Jesuit or Piarist, which in whatever city they were located, were so large that in some of them about one thousand pupils were enrolled. All burghers, noblemen, and the biggest lords sent their children to schools; education and discipline were equal for all, whether they were sons of a lord or a poor squire, nobleman, burgher or peasant. The young lords, on equal terms in their school duties with the poorest, had the privilege of sitting at school in the first row, unless they were poor scholars and would go *ad scamnum asinorum*.[2] That was the desk by the stove, called by this name because it was for those who did not want to learn. And if even this demotion did not help the lazy pupil, they would put a straw crown on his head. As a last spur to learning they would take this pupil wearing his crown to all other rooms, calling after him: *asinus asinorum in saecula saeculorum*,[3] but this last and unbearable humiliation rarely happened, for if someone reached the straw crown, he would sweat and labor over his books with all his might, so that he would not be taken around and soon would get out of the donkey desk, ceding the straw crown to the peg where it always hung when there was no head to put it on. Lazy pupils looked at it as if it were a fearsome object, while the good ones as if it were a joke invented to make one laugh.

Education was divided into levels. The first level at Jesuit schools was called *infima*[4] and was divided into *infima minor* and *infima maior*[5] although in both they covered almost the same material: agreement of adjective with noun and the cases of nouns as well as the tenses and moods of verbs, with only one difference, namely in *infima minor* they selected the compositions which were easier, in *infima maior,* more difficult, and in addition, smaller children coming to school were sent to lower *infima*, bigger to higher *infima*. At Piarist schools of this level, the school was called *parva*,[6] but they taught there the same things as in either *infima* in Jesuit schools. After *parva* there was grammar, in which both Jesuit and Piarist schools had the same levels, that is: grammar, syntax, poetics, rhetoric, philosophy, and theology, to which hardly any students advanced, unless they already felt, when at school, the vocation to become men of the cloth. Those who did not have that spirit ended their schooling with philosophy, and often with rhetoric.

Grammar taught them to put together small and short sentences using simple expressions. Syntax taught ways of embellishing simple speech with various figures and modifications of words. Poetics taught the length of Latin words, which of them should be pronounced short and which long, also how to write Latin and Polish poems, most helpful in enlarging the mind. Pupils acquainted with Latin from their study of syntax, their minds enlarged by poetics, advanced then to rhetoric, the art of speaking well and at length on any matter and of expressing their thoughts well either in a discourse or in writing. This is very useful for everyone in any walk of life, and that is why education of school children considered this its main goal and made every effort in this area. Philosophy professed an art completely different from the instruction described above, but I have to apologize to my reader for not giving him thorough information about it, for I did not study it, having ended my education with three years of rhetoric. As far as I know about that discipline, it occupies itself with studying of nature, which means all created things, causes and effects, inferences and conclusions, unfailing truths, but I forgot to mention first, that this discipline starts with teaching certain terms, by which it is possible to express matters briefly and accurately in other sciences. This field was divided in normal instruction, both Piarist and Jesuit, into: dialectics,[7] physics, logic, and metaphysics;[8] an hour of mathematics was offered to some pupils several times a week.

And in the public academies, that is general ones, as those in Cracow, Zamość, and Wilno, besides the subjects just mentioned, there were additionally: mathematics of all kinds, astrology, geography, geometry, cosmography,[9] and also: jurisprudence, medicine, and those academies were called *universitates*. As for philosophy in general, it had no more than two patriarchs: Aristotle and Saint Thomas, for in all disputes those who engaged in discussions expressed themselves only either *iuxta mentem Aristotelis* or *iuxta mentem divi Thomae*.[10] Those who adhered to the opinion of Aristotle were called *peripatetici*, and those of Saint Thomas were called *thomistae*.[11]

It was the Piarists, who about 1749 or a little later first dared to publish in a political calendar some fragments from Copernicus, proving that the earth revolves and the sun is stationary.[12] As soon as the Jesuits noticed it, they did not fail to use against the Piarists, their unyielding enemies, their best minds, the best they had, but additionally stirred up other religious orders against them on account of this hypothesis or opinion contrary to the old learning. There was a great commotion in all schools against the Piarists, similar to a levy en masse; they were publishing books challenging such opinions, invited the Piarists to debates, and tried to harm them as much as they could in this matter. But the Piarists, having time and again taken out a new excerpt from the present leaders of philosophy: Copernicus, Descartes, Newton, Leibnitz, achieved this that all schools accepted *neotoris* or *recentiorum*,[13] according to which the earth revolves around the sun, not the sun around the earth, just like a roast revolves around the fire, not the fire around the roast; that there is no color in things, for those hues which we see in them--white, black, green, red, yellow--depend merely on the eyes and light, of which a great proof, for example, is an apple, green in daylight, but seemingly dark blue by candlelight; that pain, itching, and other feelings do not occur in the body, but in the soul, because the body does not feel anything without the soul.

Nota bene. It seems to me that just as the body does not feel without the soul, the soul does not feel without the body; the organ does not play without an organist and an organist without the organ; and if feeling is not in the body, but in the soul, the sound is not there, either. (...)

Notes

1. Alvar and Donat were popular Latin grammar books, written by Emanuel Alvarez (1526-1582), a Portuguese Jesuit, and Aelius Donatus, a Roman grammarian (IV c. B.C.). Both texts were outdated and criticized by reformers.
2. Latin for 'the donkey desk.'
3. Latin for 'donkey of donkeys forever and ever.'
4. Latin for 'the lowest.'
5. Latin for 'lower' and 'higher.'
6. Latin for 'small.'
7. Dialectics was the art of logical thinking, correct ways of reaching the truth.
8. Metaphysics dealt with science of the first principles and causes of existence.
9. Cosmography or general astronomy dealt with the description of the universe.
10. According to Aristotle or according to the divine Saint Thomas.
11. Latin for peripatetics and thomists.
12. Stanisław Duńczewski wrote about the Copernican system in 1748, while the first Piarist account by Antoni Wiszniewski appeared in 1754.
13. Neotoris was a Polish term for a new philosophy preceding the Enlightenment.

Texts: Kitowicz, Jędrzej. *Pamiętniki czyli Historia polska*. Ed. by Przemysława Matuszewska. Warszawa: PIW, 1971, 668-675.
Kitowicz, Jędrzej. *Opis obyczajów za panowania Augusta III.* Ed. by Maria Dernałowicz. Warszawa: PIW, 1985, 56-59.

ADAM NARUSZEWICZ (1733-1796)

Naruszewicz was born in an impoverished nobleman's family in Polesie and at the age of fifteen entered the Jesuit Order. He studied at the Wilno Academy and abroad (1758-1762), mainly in Lyon, and then taught rhetoric, history, and French in the Warsaw Jesuit College. In 1770 he became King Stanisław's court poet and confidant, participated in the Thursday dinners, meetings of the Warsaw cultural elite at the Royal Palace, and edited *Pleasant and Useful Amusements,* an influential literary weekly (1770-1777). After the dissolution of the Jesuit Order in 1773, Naruszewicz received numerous benefices and titles from the King. In 1788 he was appointed the Bishop of Smoleńsk, in 1790 the Bishop of Łuck. After the King's access to the Confederacy of Targowica, Naruszewicz withdrew from the political life.

Naruszewicz was a prolific writer. He authored panegyrical poems, odes, eclogues, fables, and satires as well as tragedies, biographies, and translations from Latin and French. Between 1780 and 1786 he published six volumes of his monumental *History of the Polish Nation From the Times of Its Conversion to Christianity* (another volume was issued in 1824), which was based on new sources and covered not only political history, but also various aspects of national life and culture.

To the Stream

Clear small stream running in the forest free,
In many matters I agree with you:
One impulse always takes you to the sea,
While mine leads me along the same path, too.

5   Your soft murmur tickles sweetly our ears,
It doesn't frighten with terrible rumble:
I, full of grief, which dries up my senses,
Only God knows if I ever grumble.

The earth holds profuse waters in its womb,
10   Yet with you they are unable to rank:
The fire, which will penetrate my heart soon
Is as clear as the silver of your bank.

XXV. The Church of the Nuns of the Visitation in Warsaw, 1755-1761

When ruthless winds shake the realm of Neptune,
Your lively waters flow in sweet shadow:
15 When I'm attacked by the wrath of Fortune,
To spotless conscience my shelter I owe.

Beautiful Daphne, standing on your shore,
Looks at her charms reflected in a glass:
While in my heart, as if in pure spring's core,
20 I see myself, this view will longer last.

Your current doesn't hide sly pits that ensnare,
My mind does not catch anyone to fool:
All is seen in it, just look anywhere;
And everyone reads my heart to the full.

To a Sad Friend

My dear John, don't worry yourself at all!
What God ordained by a changeless decree,
Putting around it the eternal wall,
Man's thought will not reach, his eye will not see.

5 The sailor should not fret with every wave,
Unable to steer, black mists cast a veil,
When the wet death hurls itself on his nave,
If he made ready, before he set sail.

No one will escape fickle accidents,
10 For Fortune treats us as a mere plaything:
Before golden hours, the bright dawn ascends,
While the evening strikes with a swift lightning.

There is, however, at least a short lull,
The wind isn't always blowing with great force.
15 He'll cast anchor, before water gets calm
And you hold on to good hope on your course.

A vicious slander has to break its neck,
Foul wrath will kill itself with its own bane:
A dart from the sky will some neighbors wreck,
20 The fiend will soon take others to his reign.

Voice of the Dead[1]
(selection)

From Helicon[2] grounds covered with flowers,
Left among murky cypress trees alone,
When I looked at moss overgrown marbles,
Lamenting over effaced lines in stone,
Of your years, o kings, mute testimony!
A voice from the grave spoke these words to me:

"You that my nation's story wish to write[3]
And the deceased want to see with your eyes!
Clotho[4] doesn't hold us so much in sleep's might,
Having stripped us of our frail bodies' guise,
That we would lose the better part of life:
We lived, are living, and will stay alive.

Placed in the circle of eternal sphere,
From high we look at earth's inhabitants,
The sounds of your sorrows have reached us here,
Where having built impassable ramparts,
The Maker detached essence from untrue,
Allowed us to know, you to seek virtue.

Why do you complain, you errant nation,
Blaming your lot on foreign abuses?
Look for ill fate in your dissipation
And grieve at its deplorable uses.
No country tempted a foreign power,
That did not first itself become weaker.

Having torn a bond of peace and concord,
Which was once lodged in the highest power,
You dispersed like a shepherd's feeble horde,
Without a head, rule, council, defender.
To public good your hearts became adverse:
What's left are flatterers or slanderers.

But then disorder grew its thousand heads,
Tying up monarchs' arms, now motionless,

It robbed people, enhanced private profits,
Claimed bestowed lands as family largesse,5
35 Under guise of seeming independence,
It limited kings, multiplied tyrants.

The homeland hasn't recovered to this day,
Anarchy reached from head to limbs beneath;
Peasants lost their means, crafts suffered decay,
40 Themis6 put her harsh sword into its sheath:
Priest turned to collect, lord would make a row,
King for appearance, soldier just for show.

Jagiellons' and Piasts' sacred possessions,
Have shabbily become the prey of pride,
45 They embellished idlers' slothful mansions
Or were squandered on table pleasures outright;
Gone are the spoils taken from kings' bowers,
The wind broke up their castles and towers."

Notes

1. Naruszewicz wrote this political elegy in 1778, blaming the Poles for the fall of their country. The poem initiated 'the poetry of the grave' and was one of the first manifestations of pre-romantic poetry in Poland.

2. Helicon, a mountain in Boetia, not far from Parnassus, was dedicated to Apollo and the Muses.

3. Naruszewicz began to write his *History of Poland* in 1775.

4. Clotho was one of the Parcae, three goddesses of classical mythology, who determine the course of human life.

5. The author refers here to the practice of converting the properties given by the king for life ('starostwa') into hereditary possessions.

6. Themis was a personification of justice.

Balloon[1]

Where only the Eagle in its swift flight
    Chases startled birds far away,
And the fire dart shot by Jove in his spite
    Runs fast through the airy byway,

5 A pair of unique men, most audacious,
  By overcoming nature's laws,
 Repeat the grand failed course of Icarus
  And reach nearly to heaven's doors.

 Swollen with breath of a hot metal vein,[2]
10 The sphere is guiding the light boat,
 The rudder is its fate, the threads its chain,
  It challenges the winds afloat.

 The vastness of a grand establishment
  Elevated by golden pride
15 Is changed into a scattered settlement
  Of base ruin by earthly eyesight.

 King, Chief, Senator, hard working peasant,
  Whether a ruler or tiller,
 Crawls hidden in a poor clay embankment,
20 Like vermin in a small cluster.

 The Vistula current most sonorous
  Is barely trickling far below,
 Transformed into a stream of rare smallness,
  As if drawn in a child's tableau.

25 You that came here to see a rare toy,
  What miracles can your minds see?
 You imagine spells and the devil's ploy:
  A wise man will think differently.

 Although nature protects itself with care
30 With a steel wall in triple line,
 The human reason passes everywhere,
  Undaunted, through labor and time.

 Fortified by them, it did even more,
  Sending boats to the stormy sea,
35 It wrested from the depths most precious ore
  And taught rocks to jump about free.[3]

 The elements of wild power submit
  To his bold-spirited command,

              The water leaves behind its stagnant pit[4]
40   And mountains lie flat overland.

         When the Sarmatian's hand grasped without fright
              The rudder on a pleasant day,
         Although soon abandoned by wind and light
              He slowly flies up and away.

45   You will conquer everything, noble Boat,
              Unyielding to a hostile plight,
         Your airship will be of immortal note,
              Much more famous than Blanchard's flight.

Notes

1. The poem was written to commemorate the balloon flight by Jean Pierre Blanchard over Warsaw on May 10, 1789. Blanchard, a pioneer of balloon aviation, flew from Dover to Calais in 1785.
2. The balloon was filled with gaseous substance.
3. Man was able to blow up rocks, using explosives.
4. Water is pumped up.

Satires

Satire IV

The Corrupt Age

O tempora, o mores! [1]

     Laugh for show, but don't feel an ounce of merriment.
     Be fearful of your own wife and of your close friend.
     Do good deeds, but don't receive any gratitude.
     Serve long, but say adieu to any pay for good.
5   Don't show anyone fully what is in your heart.
     Make a loan and later litigate it in court.
     Love without response, work with no reward in sight.
     Wait in court till you die, before you claim your right.
        In truth, there's no sincerity under the sun:
10   All people speak sweetly, their hearts filled with venom.

All things turned around, all things are out of control:
A rare couple stays faithful to conjugal role,
Vileness gripped the minds, base gain took lust in its hold,
For naught God, king, homeland, so long as you have gold,
15 Self-interest covered with virtue sly maneuvers.
Tell the truth, you'll be counted among intruders.
A frank man is called a fool, innocent--a gull;
Shame to live among the mean, not being their pal.
Each man fashions conscience out of his own desire
20 And blesses open crimes dressed in righteous attire,
Deaf to all things when it comes to private matter,
Black and white, ice and fire he'll fain put together,
He forces his mind to praise what he wants to do;
A wolf who wished to eat a sheep found a cause, too.
25 Once obedient wishes always followed reason,
Nowadays reason follows their riotous throng,
It will not take for itself any other guide,
Only this which it likes and concerns it beside.
   A true scoundrel, whose proud nose no one dares to tweak,
30 Thinks that statutes are written only for the weak,
That poverty means guilt, and he who has power,
Is an angel, though he lies, fights, breaks word of honor.
He can do what he wants, if he just wins the game:
With the rich a crime changes its nature and name.
35 I'm a robber, someone told the world conqueror,
For only one vessel sails under my banner,
But you are a hero whose fame forever lasts,
Who decked the sea with a floating forest of masts.
As if only he were guilty altogether,
40 Who against justice could not find any measure,
But the one before whom the courts kneel and shudder,
Even if he killed many, it does not matter.[2]
It's a master who feeds on the tears of yeomen,
An outright fraud who is called a politician,
45 A slanderer calls himself eager without shame,
A slothful man--calm, for sluggishness he'll disclaim,
For them all transgressions are virtues in pure state,
That are slightly adorned with outward gilt by fate.
Harass, cheat, lie boldly--you'll surely be master;
50 Cowed innocence cries wistfully in the corner.
Golden apples hang there on the trees much too high:
Food only for many a vile crow and magpie,

That fill up their bellies with this lovely offer,
While industrious ants die below them of hunger.
55 Once honor closely followed virtue at each stage,
Hellish smiths reforged the golden into iron age.³
If one wants to do something and finds it is hard,
Let him just claim falsely he has a change of heart,
Let him simply try to use pretty words and praise,
60 I assure he won't go wrong in his greedy craze,
And when his cherished hope is fulfilled thereafter,
He will become a foe of his benefactor,
And the one who once fawned to gain his confidence,
Will take off, vile dissembler, when bad times commence.
65 Somewhere far off in the world kind love will wonder.
We chase happiness just as swallows chase summer.
Everyone thinks only how to be affluent.
You have a friend, for you gave him a big payment;
And a wife, but you paid dearly to her father;
70 Your brother loves you, because he fleeced you earlier;
You praise a deft servant; I believe it indeed:
He must serve you deftly, for he robs you with speed.
And the fair sex almost loses its heart to you,
Yet your treasure chest is almost without a sou.
75 Whatever they are, all people will show favor,
Just give them food, drink, clothes and supply with silver,
But when the funds are gone, all who swore allegiance,
Will keep from your house, though it's dry,⁴ at safe distance.
  There's no sincerity, I repeat, any more,
80 We just delude ourselves with the outward decor.
Poor is that friendship that's based on declaration;
A saint who clasps his hands, sighs without cessation;
A humble man who bows, a sage who with boldness
Talks excessively among ignoramuses.
85 And throughout all this, to avoid pricks of conscience,
It's just enough to be free from shameful offense.

Notes

1. "What an age! What morals!" (Cicero, *Oratio in Catilinam*, I, 1. *Speeches.* Tr. by Louis E. Lord. Cambridge, Mass., Harvard University Press, 1969).

2. This anecdote about a pirate and Alexander the Great was told by St. Augustine, *De Civitates Dei*, IV, 4.

3. This metaphor refers to mythological stories about a golden, silver, bronze, and iron age, the last one filled with rapacity and crime.
4. Even though the roads are dry; after spring and fall rains, it was difficult to travel on country roads.

Satire VI

A Gaunt Man of Letters
(selection)

Who will be surprised that this age is still silly?
Rarely will they read books, they will buy them rarely.

--And so what will you say, my learned but poor sire?
Two years are gone by and still in the same attire
And same coat I see your literary figure?
Your fame did the earth as well as the clouds cover,
5   Sure you were fed milk in the crib by the Muses,
Yet I see from fame it is hard to get new clothes.
I do not ask about your food and home address?
It is said that close to the manure Parnassus[1]
Apollo's spirit puffs up your empty belly,
10 Up to the ears in debt, purse without a penny.
Meanwhile your writings come out fast off the presses,
You're barely able to endure all the praises,
That you're a rich sugar crop bee, our paragon,
Also our darling, and the eye of Helicon,
15 Flower, pearl, canary, sun of the Polish land...
--Don't torment me with your jokes, my dearest friend.
I'm punished hard enough, lost all my resources,
For I relied on patrons and printing houses.
Those houses will take from your purse the last farthing,
20 While the patrons reward you only with bowing.
These days reason doesn't sell, one has to swallow all,
If the world is to see it on paper withal.
Many complain: a lazy Pole is loath to write,
But no one will reach into his pocket outright.
25 There are not those effective incentives of gold,
A swindler or a lackey will get more to hold;

He pays court to noblemen or he entertains,
Since for his line of work many gifts he obtains.
And you, poor wretch, after you have paid the printers,
30 Either burn your writings or give them to dunces,
So that a housewife can, when silly Billy comes
From school, put it under the raisin cake for crumbs.

Notes

1. Parnassus, mountain in Greece sacred to Apollo, the god of sunlight, prophecy, music, and poetry, and to the Muses. Our man of letters resides near a dunghill.

Texts: Naruszewicz, Adam. *Liryki wybrane.* Ed. by Juliusz Gomulicki. Warszawa: PIW, 1964, 65-66, 68, 164-165, 190-191. Naruszewicz, Adam Stanisław. *Satyry.* Ed. by Stanisław Grzeszczuk. Wrocław: Ossolineum, Biblioteka Narodowa I 179, 1962, 44-48, 63-65.

IGNACY KRASICKI (1735-1801)

Ignacy Krasicki was born into a magnate's family of moderate means in Dubiecko near Sanok. He was educated at the Jesuit College in Lwów, in the Saint Cross Church Seminary in Warsaw, and in Rome. In 1764, he became the chaplain of King Stanisław August and gradually gained numerous benefices. In 1766, Krasicki became the bishop of Warmia and in 1767 senator of the Republic, participating actively in major political and intellectual debates. In 1795 he reached the position of archbishop of Gniezno. In the last years of his life, Krasicki withdrew from political activity and devoted much time to preparing for publication his *Works* (1803-4).

Krasicki was a poet, essayist, novelist, comedy writer, and translator. He debuted in 1764 as a co-founder of *The Monitor,* to which he contributed more than two hundred articles. In 1774 he wrote the poem on *Sacred Love of Our Cherished Homeland,* and next year a mock-heroic poem *The Mousiad,* followed by *Monachomachia or the War of the Monks* (1778) and *Antimonachomachia* (1780), two satirical poems about ignorance and idleness prevailing in monastic orders.

Krasicki is best known for his masterful *Fables and Parables* (1779), *New Fables* (1803), and *Satires* (1779). His fables, for which he borrowed the subjects from various ancient and modern poets, to mention only Phaedrus and La Fontaine, are concise and dramatic, written in simple language and elegant verse. In his *Satires,* didactic and moralistic, Krasicki condemns the vices of the age, drawing a gallery of rogues, rakes, and hypocrites.

Krasicki's story of *The Adventures of Nicholas Doświadczyński* (1776) is the first modern Polish novel, depicting the life and experiences of a young man. In a moral treatise entitled *Mister Pantler* (1778), Krasicki shows the virtues of a model citizen. He was also the author of a historico-philosophical novel *History Divided Into Two Books* (1778), an epic poem *The War of Chocim* (1780), comedies, and letters.

XXVI. Ignacy Krasicki

Monachomachia
or the War of the Monks
(selections)

Song I

A civil war I sing and reconstrue,
A war that's cruel, without arms or sword,
Of the barefoot knights, scantily clad, too,
By their manliness are they only shored.
5   The war of monks ... Your laughter please subdue,
Human frailty in mercy finds support.
Or laugh if you will, in spite of this fun,
I shall still tell you what the monks have done.

Within a town, which will remain nameless,
10 As it will not provide you any clue,
Within a town, or else this emptiness,
A worthy home for a peasant and Jew,
Within a town, for courts and offices,
Were in an old castle, vile bareness, too,
15 There were three taverns, of four gates traces,
Nine monasteries and scattered small houses.

So in this splendid country capital
Reverend senselessness settled for long;
Under the cover of an old temple
20 Fattening its true worshippers on and on.
From everywhere flocked the faithful people,
The air was filled with an admiring song.
Holy simplicity, who'll sing your praise!
Rule here for ever! But let's move apace.
(...)

25 The one who runs along this earthly way
And feeds herself only with human plight,
The witch of Discord[1] who in bygone day,
Found fleeing Paris on the Ida height,
When she perceived the monks' sweet Heaven's bay,
30 She groaned in anger and stopped in her flight.
Seeing peaceful men and their happy fate,

The stings of bristling snakes hissed at quick rate.

She shook her torch, at once the sparks of flame
Have fallen over the roofs and towers,
35 They pierced throughout the sprawling mansion frame,
They crept into the most tiny corners.
There where silence forever held its reign,
Disturbance rises and clamor sounds fierce.
Ferocious passions strike the minds at once,
40 The monks wake up from their lethargic trance.
(...)

Song V

(...)
Hyacinth runs in, it's a new matter!
Place of dispute is a war field instead:
They wound and inflict pain on each other,
Our peaceful knight got hit right on the head,
45 He sees restraint won't safeguard him ever,
So valiant, in giving back freehanded,
He tucked up his sleeves, he pulled up his frock,
He tore off two cowls with a single knock.

Sandals and slippers and belts are flying,
50 Widespread clamor terrifies and stuns all.
For Hyacinth this noise became numbing,
He'd like to dodge a fight with all his soul,
So cursing those unhappy times therein,
He let the cowl remnants on his ears fall.
55 He was slipping out ... when he fell down hard,
Hit by famed father Zephyr's wine tankard.

Gaudentius roared like an enraged lion,
When he saw Hyacinth fall to the ground,
Fired up with new ire, he charged anon,
60 He would not forgive any monk around:
The master[2] with his chair was overthrown,
The counselor's[3] cowl he grabbed in one round,

Luke, who was wounded, curled up underneath,
Meanwhile Cleophas lost his last three teeth.

65 He hurled away all the plates and glasses,
Even the mugs were cracked on hardened heads,
He grabbed the book behind the arrases:
"The Host of Newly Recruited Affects."[4]
This is his shield, from the lists he rushes
70 Of the knights exhausted by long contests.
So once a famed strong man from Palestine
With a bone slayed many a Philistine.[5]
(...)

Song VI

(...)
The wine cup was put in a special place;
The prelate unveiled this reliquary.
75 It dazzled their eyes with its ornate grace,
Its shining metal gilt and silvery.
Plenty of liquor can get in this vase,
Its size shows it is extraordinary.
Exquisite sculpture on the top, beside
80 Four seasons were engraved on every side.

The eyes are feasting on this splendid vase,
The battle and council are forgotten.
Then father Casper rushes in apace,
His black eye a proof that he was smitten.
85 The doctor[6] in normal tones states the case
To go to war with a mug, his intent.
"With the full one though--the prelate agrees--
The vase will stop them, the wine will bring peace."

In need a miser will give assistance:
90 Brother Chester, red, on the portly side,
Carries huge jugs, all can smell the fragrance,
Of the wine that during fast and Shrovetide
The doctor drank, who during indulgence
Shared drops with brothers, himself well supplied,
95 Chester poured a jug in the vase and groaned,
The prelate smiled inside, the doctor moaned.

Whose health were they drinking now, you inquire?
I don't know, but if I were there perchance,
I would drink yours, venerable prior,
100   Yours, who thanks to your glorious performance
Are master and father to each friar
And make known by your exemplary stance,
How a righteous mind avoids all that's foul,
It's virtue that makes the monk, not his cowl.[7]

105   Read and permit your friars to read too,
Let each of them laugh out with innocence,
None will accept this reprimand as true,
None will be shocked, I have a hopeful sense.
True virtue doesn't fear a probing review,
110   Let vice bemoan and grieve in penitence.
He who boldly feigns, should recant his writ:
You read and judge. No praise, I will burn it.

Notes

1. The Greek goddess Eris, Roman Discord, was the daughter of the Night. She was snaky-haired and held a torch in one hand, a dagger and snakes in the other. In Virgil's *Aeneid,* referred to in the next line, she appeared as Allecto.

2. The function of an honorary master was to arbitrate disputes.

3. The counselor was in charge of several monasteries of the same denomination and advised the provincial superior.

4. The book, written by Hilarion Falęcki, was published in Lwów in 1739.

5. Samson killed a thousand Philistines with the jawbone of a donkey (Judges 15, 15).

6. The doctor was in charge of the monastic school.

7. *Cuculum non facit monachum*--'A cowl does not make the monk,' was a popular medieval proverb.

Diverse Poems

4. Sacred Love of Our Cherished Homeland

O sacred love of our cherished homeland,
Only noble minds can be moved by you!
Baneful poisons taste good at your command,
No disgrace to bonds and chains will accrue.
5   You grace with honored scars the cripples' band,
You plant in the mind the delights most true,
So long as one can help you and stand by,
We don't mind misery, don't mind to die.

19. Gravestone of a Peasant

Here lies the one who fed enlightened noblemen,
In a simple grave dug in sod, a poor villein,
His gravestone above him does not lie, no proud heir
Propped up a metal coffin with rich columns there.
5   Buried modestly, just like other village men,
His wife shed tears over him, so did his children,
The memory of his name is lost undoubtedly,
If he stole like the lord, he would hang on a tree.

Fables and Parables

Preface to *Fables*

There was a youth who led a temperate life,
An aged man, devoid of gall and strife,
A rich man, who shared with the poor his grain,
An author, much pleased when others won fame,
5   A tax man who didn't steal, a cobbler dry,
A soldier who didn't brag, a rogue of fight shy;
A public servant who didn't think of gain,
A poet, too, who checked his fancy's reign.
Why is it a tale? All this can occur!
10 True, but I'll put it in the fables' corner.

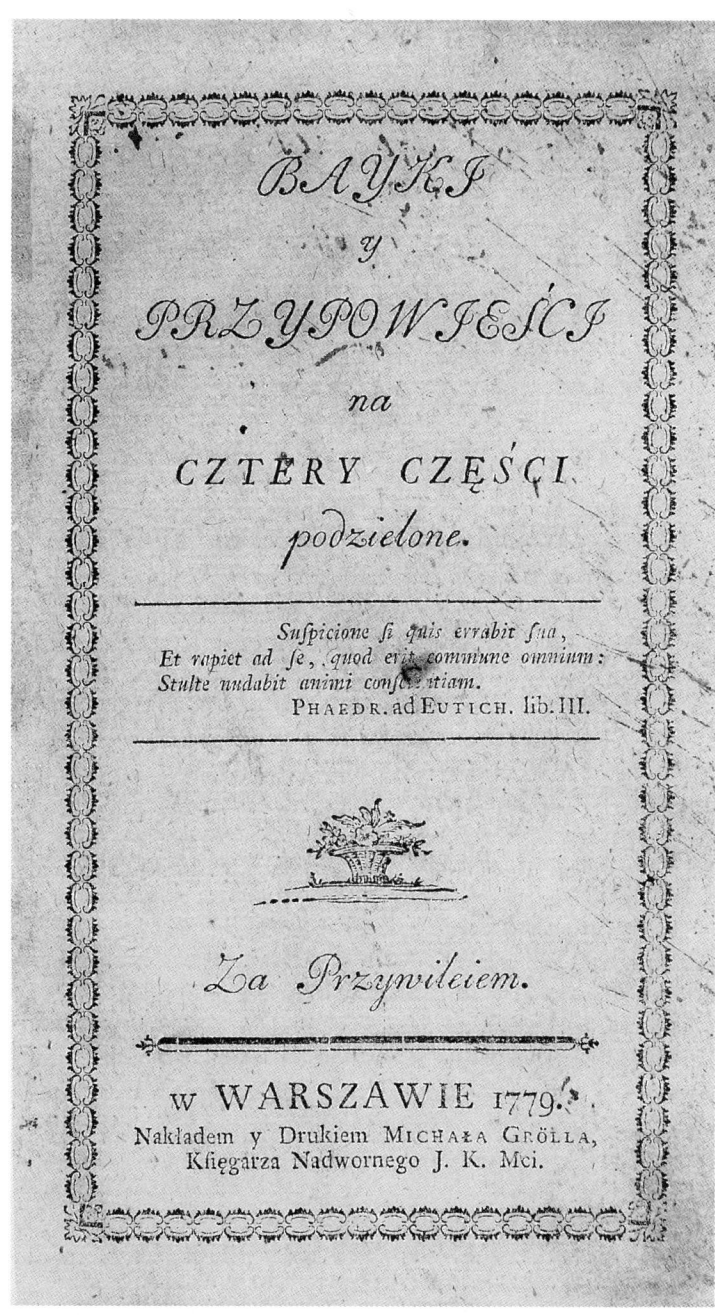

XXVII. Title page of Jan Krasicki's *Fables and Parables*, Warsaw, 1779

Part I

8. The Rat and the Cat

"They burn incense for me"--bragged the rat to his kin,
Sitting on the altar during Mass offering.
Suddenly, when he coughed because of intense smoke,
The cat jumped out, snatched him, and killed him with one stroke.

18. Son and Father

Each age has its bitter side and ills of its own:
A son pored over books, while his old father groaned.
One had no free rein, no leisure had the other:
Son cried he was young; I'm too old, cried the father.

20. The Mouse and the Cat

On account of a book the mouse ate once whole,
He convinced himself fully that he knew it all.
So he told his friends: "I will end your agony,
I will convert the cat, you just rely on me!"
5   So they sent for the cat. Always ready, the cat
Showed up immediately to engage in a chat.
The mouse began a speech; he listened with care,
He sighed and cried ... The mouse, seeing his mood was fair,
Became even more absorbed in zealous preaching,
10 Stepped out of his hole--suddenly the cat caught him.

21. Birds in a Cage

A young siskin asked an old one: "Why do you cry?
Better comforts in cage than in the field nearby."
The old said: "I'll forgive you, for here you were born;
Once free, today in the cage, that is why I mourn."

23. The Oak and the Pumpkin

When the right time to get ripe finally arrived,
The pumpkin asked of the oak how long he had thrived.
"Hundred years." "It took me hundred days, as you see"--
Said the pumpkin. The oak said: "In vain you mock me;
5   You are fair, it's true, for show, your fame is show too,
However, you will perish as fast as you grew."

Part II

5. The Animals and the Bear

Animals kept fighting under the old lion.
When a peaceful reign was promised by his scion,
They were all rejoicing. A bear sat quietly,
Asked why he kept silent, he answered directly:
5   "Let us wait for a while with this joyful report,
Till the claws of the young lion are not so short."

6. The Stream and the Fountains

The force of water in the clamorous fountains
Was envied by the stream purring in their presence.
The pipes burst, which gave abundant water supply,
The stream flowed just as before, the fountains got dry.
5   Unspeakable joy replaced earlier torture,
The stream found out that art could never match nature.

9. The Bear and the Fox

Thinking that his companions he would entertain,
The bear, as was his custom, told stories inane.
Bored by these fables, when all slumbered unaware,
A wolf got cross with a fox for praising the bear.
5   Said the fox: "I'm concerned about saving my skin:
His diction is clumsy, but his nails cut right in."

15. The Marriage

Thank heavens! I saw once an old fashioned couple,
A very happy marriage, polite, amiable.
Their steadfast life had been by many admired,
Too bad a week after nuptials the man expired.

17. Two Dogs

"Why do you sleep inside, while in cold I must tug?"
A chained dog posed this question to a portly pug.
"Why? I will very quickly this secret explain--
Said the pug in response--You serve, I entertain."

18. A Friend

"I am calling upon you, Arist," said Damon,
"Come to my help in this extreme situation.
I love beautiful Irene. Her parents and she
Are not yet persuaded to accept my plea."
5   Arist said: "You know quite well, you I most commend,
How deeply I am in favor of you, dear friend.
I'll see them for you." Indeed, he was no idler:
He went, he met with Irene, and he married her.

Part III

1. The Elephant and the Bee

The weak should never show anger towards the strong.
A bee who relied on her sharp sting all along,
When she saw a big elephant graze in the grass,
Not heeding her at all, though close by she would pass,
5   Intended to punish him. What then transpired
When she stang him? He didn't feel it, she expired.

4. The Child and the Father

A son wouldn't learn, his father used a rod in ire.
When he left, the enraged son threw it in the fire.
Soon stubborn Johnny earned a whipping once again:
The father found no rod--he whipped him with a cane.

6. The Bigot

A bigot was by her maid servant offended,
At the time when her prayers were almost ended.
So she turned towards the maid with an angry hiss,
Saying just these words: "... forgive us our trespasses,
5   As we forgive those"--she beat her without pity,
Please save us, Lord Almighty, from such piety.

13. The Stream and the River

The swift stream whose waters across a lovely valley flow
Reproached the mighty river for moving too slow.
The river said: "Before the morning lights will flee,
You speedily, I slowly will run to the see."

16. The Master and the Dog

A dog barked at a thief, all night long he'd labor;
They beat him the next day for waking the master.
He slept soundly the next night, the thief did not hark;
He robbed the house; they beat the dog for he didn't bark.

20. The Eagle and the Owl

An eagle stayed at night with an owl on a tree,
Feeling sorry that only then the owl could see.
The owl thanked him for his compassionate display.
Afterwards, well before the first light of the day,
5   A hunter stole 'neath the tree. The owl cast a glance
And hurried to the eagle to warn him at once.

They escaped death; and the eagle went on to tell:
"If you had not been blind, I would not now feel well."

21. The Inkstand and the Pen

The inkstand on the table argued with the pen,
Who authored the book that was just written.
The one who wrote it came in, laughed at both tattlers.
How many such inkstands and pens are on this earth.

23. The Nightingale and the Goldfinch

A finch told a nightingale, quietly seated,
"Too bad you sing briefly." The other retorted:
"What nature has granted me, I use faithfully.
Better briefly, but well, than for long and poorly."

26. The Wagon Driver and the Butterfly

A wagon got stuck in the mud, could not budge at all,
The driver and horses were too tired to haul.
A butterfly, sitting on the wagon right then,
Deeming he was a burden in crossing the fen,
5   Thought: "Compassion is not a bad habit today."
He flew off, told the man: "Go with God on your way."

Part IV

3. The Lamb and the Wolves

He who looks for spoils will always find a pretext.
Two wolves swooped down upon a lamb in the forest.
They closed in to kill the lamb. It said: "By what right?"
"You're tasty, weak, in the woods!" They ate it forthright.

4. The Turtle and the Mouse

Because he was closed in his shell in discomfort,
The mouse pitied the turtle. The turtle's retort:
"You may have palaces, I have my cramped small home.
True, it is not splendid--it's tiny, but my own."

7. The Penitent Wolf

A wolf succumbed to scruples. He led a knave's life,
So in order that his penance could fully thrive,
He gave up meat. Eating vegetables a few days,
He ran into a friend on his hunting forays.
5   One must help one's neighbor; for useful assistance
He ate a chunk of meat--one shouldn't scorn a pittance.
He came upon a lamb walking alone next day,
Wished to warn it, scare it, by chance put it away.
Next day, seeing a calf not walking with a cow,
10 He killed it--such transgressions one mustn't allow.
Seeing an old bull grazing with cows the next day,
"Let it suffer no longer"--he ate it right away.
And so fully deprived of the world's sustenance,
Skinny while sinful, he gained weight doing penance.

26. The Wise Man and the Fool

The fool asked the wise man: "Of what use is the brain?"
The wise man kept silent; bothered by him again,
He told him: "It's useful, one of my suggestions,
In refusing to answer such stupid questions."

28. The Stubborn Oxen

Mischief has nice beginnings, but a sad ending.
The oxen did not want to walk in yoke in Spring,
They would not bring the harvest to the barn in Fall,
With no bread in Winter, the farmer ate them all.

New Fables

Part I

15. Children and Frogs

    Near a lake
        Before the night break
    Boys were running about
    For the frogs looking out:
5   If any came in sight,
    A rock hit it outright.
    One frog, bolder by nature
    Stuck out its head higher
    And said: "Boys, stop this play, it is a big mistake,
10   For you it's fun, for us life itself is at stake."

Part II

12. The Heron, the Fish, and the Cray-fish

An old heron, as one can often find,
Became slightly crooked and slightly blind,
When she wasn't able to fish any more,
The following ruse she set out to explore.
5 She remarked to the fish: "You do not know,
But it is concerning you above all."
      So they wished to find out,
What they should fret about.
       "Yesterday
10   At the end of the day
I could overhear the fishermen plot:
It is a lot of work to have them caught
With the fishing rod or using the net:
Let us drain the pond, all of them we'll get,
15   They won't have a chance to get by,
     When the pond turns out to be dry!"
The fish cried, to which she gave an answer:

"I am deeply grieved by this disaster;
But for this evil there's a remedy:
20 We'll find another place for you ready.
    There is a pond not far away,
    In which you can quite safely stay.
    Although the first pond they will drain,
    In the second you can remain."
25 "So you move us there"--the fish said.
The heron seemed to wince with dread;
At last she allowed herself to be swayed,
    She came to their aid.
She took one at a time in her beak, as if carrying
30   And slowly each fish devouring,
At last she fancied to taste some cray-fish.
One of them, just when he was taken to the bush,
Saw her treachery, revenge at once attempted,
Grabbed her by the neck so hard that she was strangled.
35   She fell dead on the spot:
    That is a traitor's lot.

13. The Peasant and the Calf

It's not hard to kill, it's hard to kill well--
    This lesson the fable will tell.
A peasant led to market a calf on a rope,
    On the forested ravine slope,
5 At night the storm came down, and when the wind whistled,
In the dark he spied a wolf by its eyes that glistened.
He grabbed the club; he swung it not thinking enough,
Instead of the wolf that ran off, he killed his calf.
Doctors, it happens not just in the forest thick!
10 Medicines--the club, wolf--sickness, the calf--the sick.

Part III

15. The Torch and the Candle

A candle was once put next to a torch aglow.
When it, very proud, made of its brightness a show,

Someone said: "You only share in the other's might:
A candle is one thing; another the torch light."

Part IV

1. The Crow and the Fox
(from Aesop)

    He is often deceived,
    Who wants to be flattered.
The crow had a big piece of cheese in his beak;
    The fox, appearing meek,
5 Came over to him and said: "Brother dear and true,
I never cease to marvel when I look at you!
        Your eyes are so bright!
        They blind with their light!
        How can one secure
10   Such a good figure?
        And feathers so fine!
        All alike, they shine.
    And if I am right,
    Your voice--pure delight."
15 So the crow opened his beak and burst into song,
The cheese fell out, the fox caught it, and ran along.

Satires

6. Drunkenness

"Where've you been?" "I can barely walk." "Sick?" "I'd say so.
I never coddle myself a great deal, you know.
But then my headache is really very bad."
"You were happy yesterday, so now you are sad.
5 The headache will be gone, what happened, tell me, pray,
After a tasty snack, it's nice to drink, they say."
"O no, it is not nice, my friend! He should be damned
Who made up this proverb. I'll tell you what happened.
I got drunk the other day at my wife's nameday,

10 I didn't mind it. We had to celebrate this day
   Most solemnly. A good neighbor should sometimes be
   Made a little tipsy; my wife was quite happy,
   We had plenty of wine and since it was sublime,
   It went down very well and we had a good time.
15 The feast lasted till dawn, I woke up at noon hour,
   My head as heavy as lead, I retched, and felt sour.
   My wife suggested tea, but it's a queasy brew.
   I happened to pass by a medicine chest in view,
   I smelled aniseed, a touch could not hurt my mood,
20 So I took a sip, perhaps it would do some good:
   After all, I was sick. One more, I felt better,
   Then came two companions from yesterday's dinner.
   How not to offer drink a guest in your dwelling?
   How to offer but not drink? This isn't becoming.
25 So back to vodka, by chance I tippled somewhat;
   Omne trinum perfectum,[1] for the drink that's hot
   Is good for the stomach. Indeed, without delay
   My nausea was over, my headache went away.
   Fit and gay I come out with my companions. Then
30 We find dinner ready. We sit down again.
   Sir Jędrzej praises abstinence, and so do we,
   Temperance above all, condemn insobriety,
   Meanwhile on the table the bottle stands untouched,
   Sir Wojciech who fears indigestion very much,
35 Suggests a little wine with the ham we'd eaten:
   One glass or two won't hurt the health of any man.
   And especially if the wine is dry and pure.
   We accept these truths, as not in the least obscure,
   We carry on discourses as the statesmen would
40 About the love of homeland and the public good,
   About splendid plans, manly determination,
   In Olkusz for silver and gold excavation,[2]
   We recapture Livonia and the Multan states,[3]
   We count those sums of Neapolitan rebates,[4]
45 We reform the republic, we fight a new war,
   Defeat some by one blow, with others peace restore,
   And the bottle gradually somehow runs dry.
   A second comes; and when enthusiasm becomes high,
   Very pleased that all our opponents have perished,
50 The third, fourth, and fifth we have not even noticed.
   Then the sixth and seventh, afterwards number ten,

Thereupon, when love for homeland seized us again,
Sir Jędrzej, recalling Żurawno disaster,[5]
Sheds tears over King Jan. "King Jan was a victor"--
55 Shouts Wojciech. "Not so!" and Sir Jędrzej is crying.
I try to reconcile them, do some explaining
But Wojciech rebuked me: "Listen, sirrah"--he says.
"Sirrah, indeed! Fellow, I will teach you some sense."
He came at me, I at him, at each other we tore,
60 Jędrzej held us back, men rushed in at the uproar,
I do not know how they ended our big squabble,
But I know and feel I got hit with a bottle.
   May it be taken to hell, this vile drunkenness!
What is in it? Only poor health, brawls, and grossness.
65 Here's the profit: nausea and bruises and plasters."
"You speak well, it's the fun of the rabble-rousers,
The man of integrity loathes this shameful thing.
From it grow quarrels and indecent backbiting,
It weakens the memory and the brain's performance,
70 It damages the health and shortens existence.
Look at the man who's seized by the power of drink,
A man but in appearance, he deserves to sink
Among the animals, when he drowns his good sense
And against Nature assumes a beast's existence.
75 If heaven by chance gave wine for man's benefit
So that he could raise his spirits by drinking it,
The use of God's gifts should be in moderation.
The senseless beast makes the drunk feel humiliation,
The animals reprimand our intemperance,
80 When they quench their thirst according to requirements,
They don't take more, man who looks at them with loathing,
Is worse when he acts so, even more disgusting.
Never mind bumps, plasters, it's pay for debasement,
Those who drink deserve greater disgrace, punishment,
85 Who in unrestrained blindness, wicked and vicious,
Dare to blunt or lose, for reasons that are various,
The mind which distinguishes man from animal.
What profit can repay such great damage at all?
What benefit will reward such a profound blow?
90 It's wicked joy, my friend, that's followed by sorrow.
See how those who don't go in for such indulgence
Gather up great benefits from their temperance:
Robust in health, their minds are of good cheer and free,

Strength and rare alertness, for work capacity,
95 Property in good order, estate well managed,
Reasonable expenses suitably covered.
These are rewards of temperance, goals that pull us up."
"Fare you well." "Where are you going?" "To drain a cup."

Notes

1. *Omne trinum perfectum*--'Every trinity is perfection'.
2. The silver and lead mines in Olkusz were ruined during Swedish wars. Some unsuccessful attempts were made to reopen them.
3. Livonia on the Baltic coast was divided after 1660 between Sweden and Poland. The Multan states Moldavia and Wallachia in the south east, given to Poland in homage in the fifteenth century, were gradually taken over by Turkey.
4. Queen Bona loaned to Philip II, king of Spain and Naples, 430,000 ducats, never recovered.
5. According to the treaty of Żurawno, signed by King Jan Sobieski in 1676, Turkey retained a large part of the Ukraine.

8. The Fashionable Wife

"Since you've received what for you a high price carried,
I congratulate you, Sir Peter, on getting married."
"Much obliged." "What does this mean? You thank with coolness
Or are you not yet aware of your happiness?
5 Are you already sick of matrimonial bonds?"
"Not completely, albeit it usually befalls
That the first days are sweet." "Are you bitter perchance?"
"I sure am!" "Friend, keep what you have gained in your hands!
Modestly, patiently, be silent like the rest,
10 Who of their wives have been the servants most modest,
Seemingly well-matched, in name master and mistress,
While at home woman is the ruler and empress.
Would yours be like that?" "Her gifts are extraordinary.
She brought me four villages, all hereditary.
15 Beautiful, well-bred, wise." "So much the better." "Worse.
It all turned out badly and will ruin me first;

Beauty, talent--great virtues in a woman's crown.
And yet what of that if she was brought up in town?"
"Does the town demoralize?" "Who can dispute it?
20 O for the country wife!" "Not from town?" "God forbid!
When I saw her first time some doubts came to the fore,
But what I perceived I explained in her favor,
Once involved, not wishing to disgrace the lady,
I sighed, a rustic Tirsis for my Philida.[1]
25 Her ways were unusual, her charms were truly grand,
And before the wedding and giving me her hand,
We followed the romances, but whether I smiled
Or complained or kept silent or spoke up or sighed,
I saw I was poorly playing the actor's part,
30 Fashionable Philis scorned the homebody's heart.
And I would have scorned her, but the point of honor,
And what I'd most regret, the allure of favor,
Those hereditary villages, next to mine,
They beguiled me and tied me in these bonds sublime,
35 It came to the marriage articles. First point read:
She'll live in town, by a fine French maid attended,
Who can, because she is French, care for her better,
Whenever some sickness she happens to suffer.
Point two: when in good health she stays in the country,
40 She'll visit each winter the capital city.
Point three: she will retain a carriage of her own.
Point four: we shall rent a large, pleasant house of stone,
With sumptuous chambers for visitors that come,
One in the rear for the man, in front for Madam.
45 Point five: God forbid! I was frightened. What's in store?
'It happens--said the kin--that by common accord
Either the bond breaks or it is separated.'
'What bond?' 'Conjugal.' 'That ends with death'--I stated.
Those present laughed at my rustic simplicity.
50 Thus paying for flawed courtship with my liberty,
After the usual rites preceding these matters,
I joined the fraternity of mourning brothers.
We set off for home. Madam displays her chagrins,
'What are we riding in?' 'A carriage.' 'Not on springs?'[2]
55 I search for the springs. By chance a young castellan,
Who brought an English carriage from a foreign land,
Lost a lot at cards. I bought it. Time to get in.
Madam feels weak. We have to postpone travelling.

When she gets better, up drives the English carriage.
60 In gets Madam, beside her the favorite bitch.
They put in boxes, small cases, bags, and packets,
Some are just for perfumes, others for snuff caskets,
Add a box of bonnets, a basket of trinkets,
In one cage a canary, singing canzonets,
65 A magpie in the next, bird food in a goblet,
Then a cat with kittens, a mouse on a chainlet.
I want to sit, no room, so as not to delay,
Cage under my arm, dog in my lap I display.
We drive off happily, but Madam sits sadly,
70 I keep mute, only the magpie screeches gamely.
Madam broke my train of thought: 'Do you have a cook?'
'Yes, my heart.' 'Fie, a joke from the almanac book.[3]
Dear heart, indeed! Pray unlearn such vulgar matter!'
I fell silent. Hard to talk or even mutter.
75 I say nothing. She asks about the cook again.
'I have one, Madam.' 'Do you a coachman retain?'
'He is driving us.' 'That is a carter. For show
We must have another. You can let the cook go
To some neighbor.' 'He is good.' 'Where's he from?' 'A serf.'
80 'For this reason he must certainly be superb--
He must make pancakes well, noodles like a master,
Suits the taste of judge's wife and steward's daughter,[4]
Let him go. They will take this Matthew[5] over there,
Maybe the vicar can use him for the church fair.
85 What about a pastry cook?' 'He could make pies too.'
'Believe me, sir, if we ever wish to pursue
A respectable life, hire suitable servants,
Fashionable pastrycooks, chefs from foreign lands,
We need a confectioner, too. Do you maintain
90 A mirrored dinner set, fine figures from porcelain?'[6]
'No.' 'How is that possible? But I understand,
And although of rustic ways I don't have command,
I can surmise. At dessert, extra boards they squeeze,[7]
In pretty pyramids put sliced and cottage cheese,
95 Also sweet rush, Chinese ginger in honey jell,
While for greater enjoyment and pleasure as well,
Candied caraway in twists of colored paper,
And a gilded Toruń gingerbread much higher
Needless to say, it's pretty, superb, and proper,
100 But please forgive me, sir, if I beg to differ.

I'm unworthy of these splendors, this luxury.'
I remained silent, allowing this drollery.
We're driving through the gate, from the carriage
   glancing,
She said: 'Fie, sir, a fence, and why not a railing?'
105 She got out, followed by the dog and cat and mouse;
She pushed back old Francis, dispenser in the house,
Tears came into his eyes, I just sighed, she entered.
'Our parish priest!' 'Greetings.' The good father glowered.
'Where's the dining room?' 'We eat here.' 'How can it be?
110 A small room, you couldn't seat forty for company.'
When my wife said these words, Francis shuddered outright,
While the housekeeper at once ran off in a fright.
I remained. We go farther. 'This is the bedroom.'
'And where's the parlor?' 'The same as the dining room.'
115 'That cannot be! And where is the study?' 'Elsewhere.
This will be for you, and we will sleep over there.'
'Over there? Dear sir, please go to your own chambers,
I must have separate ones for sleeping, for vestures,
For my books, for music, my private amusements,
120 Also for chamber maids, and for hired servants.
And the garden?' 'Boxwood and privet in cluster.'
'Throw them out! No need for additional luster.
That's the German fashion. I'll have groves of cypress,
Here and there small streams murmuring over pebbles,
125 A kiosk here, a little mosque there, and a Dutch bath,[8]
A hermit's hut, to Diana's temple a path.
Everything as if at random, as if for sport,
A little belvedere, for caged birds a small court,
A nightingale lovingly murmurs in your ear,
130 A turtledove laments and a pigeon coos near,
While I am meditating under cypress trees,
On the mishaps of Pamela and Heloise...'[9]
I took to my heels when Madam began to rail,
I couldn't listen any more to this fairy tale.
135 I fled. Madam rules the roost. The house in uproar,
Three couriers in a week were dispatched to Warsaw,
In two weeks I couldn't recognize my dwelling,
Full of ideas, in deeds overpowering,
She threw away the old beams from the dining hall,
140 Had Venus's offer on the ceiling install.[10]
There is a gilded alcove in the bedchamber,

A cabinet for dressing marbled with plaster,
All jars are gone from the pantry, preserves are gone,
A new work of art and architecture is on:
145 Mahogany shelf cases with countless books stored,
All of them in French; a globe on a little board,
The boudoir gleams with gold, china is everywhere,
Little tables of marble, mirrored walls elsewhere,
My small house has just surpassed Warsaw palaces,
150 While I in a corner, poor soul, cry over this.
Never mind that, but when guests drive up in a throng,
Elegant gentlemen and ladies of fashion,
A ball, masks, trumpets, drums, and a big orchestra,
The Chamberlain calls all Madam's health to muster,
155 The Adjutant is drinking up my good old wine,
Aside, Madam and the Subprefect's wife design,
And while I bustle around just like a servant,
She laughs and winks, again glances at me aslant.
   After supper, fireworks. The guests watch from the hall;
160 A squib fell in the stackyard, the barn's a fireball.
I rush out, put it out, rescue it, and whimper,
While the trumpets play 'Long live' even louder,
I come back exhausted from the burned up ruins,
More jokes, more allusions, and more derisive hints.
165 The visitors sit down, more and more of them come,
I mention excessive cost, hotheaded Madam
Speaks of these four villages of hers haughtily.
'Eight will not be sufficient'--I submit humbly.
'So let us go back to town.' I agree, we go,
170 We've been dallying here several weeks or so,
By now... But it serves me right, though I feel distress,
What to do? Harm done, they say, crying is useless."

Notes

1. Tirsis, Philidia (Philis)--names of a shepherd and a shepherdess, heroes of Greek and Roman eclogue.

2. Old fashioned carriage boxes rested on belts. The new ones, brought from abroad, were set high on iron springs.

3. Eighteenth century calendars and almanacs were criticized for their language, popular astrological horoscopes, and predictions of natural disasters.

4. Judge of peace and public order during war time was a minor office. Judge's wife and steward's daughter stand here for a provincial way of life.

5. A popular comic name, Matthew was also used to refer to any simpleton.

6. For special occasions, dinner tables were set with mirror panels and plate glass, then decorated with china figures and crystal pendants, reflecting the candlelight.

7. In less prosperous households, where the tables were narrow, extra shelves were put up to serve sweets.

8. A Dutch bath was a luxury room covered with Dutch tiles in the garden pavilion of the Czartoryski family in Powązki. The narrator's wife describes fashionable garden architecture, popular in some noblemen's residences, especially in Warsaw, featuring shrubs in the shape of bathtubs, elegant bowers, small temples dedicated to Diana, mosques, belvederes, and hermitages.

9. Pamela and Heloise were heroines of the popular romances by Samuel Richardson and Jean Jacques Rousseau.

10. A picture of Venus with her offering of two doves.

The Monitor
37, May 7, 1776

[About Two Types of Bad Readers]

Non ego ventosae plebis suffragia venor[1]

I went to town recently with Sir Ochotnicki[2] to assist him in making some purchases. When we returned home and were looking at the purchased items, they brought in among other things tobacco wrapped in *The Monitor*. At once my colleague became very upset at this profanation and I could barely dissuade him from chopping the merchant into pieces for such a careless treatment of our work. The patriotic zeal of Sir Ochotnicki did not stop there. He began to despair about the fate of the whole homeland, he cursed the ungrateful nation, and developed such hatred towards tobacco that I believe he will quit using it. Looking at this amusing scene, I was fortified on the one hand by my companion's kindness of heart and on the other hand, the fate of our work gave rise to various observations.

Every book, when it comes to the world, acquires all types of masters and judges. As it falls under various judgments, it often receives varied evidence of contempt or respect. There is no book so abominable that it would not find a reader and at that a reader who likes it. An unrefined mind or fundamental ignorance or an insignificant agreement between one's own feelings and the author's way of thinking, and a sensible reader will be imperceptibly forced to offer a less impartial judgment.

On the contrary, envy, prejudice, desire for eccentricity, lack of understanding of ideas that are beyond the reader's reach will sharpen his judgment so much that although he will grasp the quality of the work, he will act against his own conviction, and if he does not understand it, he is ready to revile the book and its author, as if they were the cause of his mind's dullness. There is also a third type of those people who pass judgment on books, and they are similar to the tobacconist, who unwillingly suggested this discourse to me. All common people, and especially those in our country, who even in the cities are barely able to read, judge books by their physical features, and depending on the thickness or thinness of paper either use them for wrapping or put them under cakes in the oven. Contempt for the best books should be ascribed to this type of judges, for otherwise we would have to despair every time we happened to see the constitution on pepper funnels or the lives of saints on curlpaper.

Each author who puts his book to press loses by this very act his claim to it. Therefore all critical comments not based on the book but on the person who wrote it are unjust. And again, any blame which a reader assigns to a poorly written work, as it refers only to the text, should not harm the author's standing, morals or even his excellence in another type of his writing or craft.

If therefore the author cannot bring blame upon the book and the book cannot bring blame upon the author on account of different origins of criticism, those people who wreak their rage at the text are unjust, because they hate the writer or, despising the book, take lightly the author, who is perhaps quite worthy in other circumstances.

There are so many circumstances surrounding the author's craft, the work is so hard and the duty so heavy, in addition the pain caused by poor results is so unbearable that we should show some pity in our sometimes too harsh judgments. In vain an author humiliates himself before a stern reader in an elaborate foreword and asks on his knees for forgiveness; not only will he fail to soften him, but also by his humiliation he will bring upon himself new contempt and ridicule. If he at least could win the type of readers that Horace talks about:

> *Vir bonus et prudens versus reprehendet inertes,*
> *Culpabit duros, incomtis allinet atrum* [3]

--the fate of an author's work would be more bearable, for having criticized what was wrong, they would praise good things. But the age of Horace passed long ago and it is very difficult nowadays to find such a reader. A present custom, keeping too close to the axiom: *malum ex quocunque defectu,*[4] insults and disgraces the whole work. What is worse, it is said as if referring to books: *filii portabunt iniquitatem patris,*[5] and many times they have to answer and suffer for their authors.

It is true that often less attentive authors digress from their goal of entertaining and educating. Some bore you *in folio,* others put you to sleep *in quarto,* perhaps our text *in octavo*[6] might not be to someone's liking. If this is so, Sir Ochotnicki has nothing to be angry about; and if we suffer unjustly, each of us should arm himself with these words of Horace I quoted at the beginning:

> *Non ego ventosae plebis suffragia venor.*

Notes

1. "I coax no fickle rabble for their votes" (Horace, *Epistles*, I, 19, 37) in *The Complete Works of Horace.* Ed. by Casper J. Kraemer, Jr. New York: Random House, The Modern Library, 1936.
2. Ochotnicki was a pseudonym of Franciszek Bohomolec, one of the editors of *The Monitor.*
3. "A kind and sensible critic will censure verses when they are weak, condemn them when they are rough; ugly lines he will score in black" (Horace, *The Art of Poetry*, 445-446).
4. 'Completely bad on account of any defect.'
5. 'Children will carry the iniquity of parents' (paraphrase of Exodus 20:5).
6. The sizes of a piece of paper. *The Monitor* was published in octavo format.

Mister Pantler[1]
(selection)

When I was once travelling during harvest time, I happened to pass through a populous and well-settled village. As I noticed a spotless inn, I stopped there for the night, even though it was long before sunset, and when I asked the innkeeper who the owner of the village was, he responded: "Mister Pantler." "Who built this inn?" "Mister Pantler." "Who built such a good dike?" "Mister Pantler." "Who built a brick bridge on the river?" "Mister Pantler." Indeed, the church, manor-house, grange, granary, brewery, even cottages--all of these were the work of one man, that is Mister Pantler. I became quite interested in getting to know him; I was anxious not to be an intruder, but the innkeeper assured me that Mister Pantler was glad to see anyone in his house. It was already after sunset, a beautiful evening, when taking a walk on the dike, I noticed a man walking towards me, dressed in a white jubah[2]; he wore a leather belt, a large straw hat on his head, and held a straight stick in his hand. As he approached, and I noticed a serious face, ruddy cheeks, gray mustache, I guessed that he must have been Mister Pantler. We approached each other and after first greetings, I said: "This chance, I presume, meeting with the lord of the village is a welcome occasion for me, for I cannot conceal from you, Sir--I continued--my admiration for everything I see here; and my admiration grew when I found out that everything came from your ingenuity and work." He thanked me for my good opinion, accepted the praise without false aversion, and since we were close to the gate, invited me to his house.

A vast courtyard was enclosed by a fence made of big posts, surrounded by tall willows, in the middle stood four spreading lindens, turf seats under each, a stone table in the middle. On the right hand side was a solid kitchen outbuilding, with rooms for farm hands, I thought; on the left, stables, coach-houses, on one side a brick lumber-room with iron gratings and shutters, opposite a granary. The manor-house was made of wood on a solid, quite high brick foundation. We entered a room; in the middle was a table covered with a Turkish rug, a cupboard was by the door, ornate with trays, goblets, silver and gold pitchers opposite the door hung a portrait of King Jan.[3] In the second room, equally elegant, we encountered the lady of the house sitting at the hand-loom; she was embroidering, as I learned later, a table-cloth for the church. She stood up immediately and greeted me, then she turned to her husband and taking him by the hand with a graceful smile which fashion cannot teach, she said that the children were coming home from school that night. Soon it was announced that they had arrived; they entered the room with a teacher; the older could be no more than sixteen years old, the other a year younger. The evening meal was served promptly; the host and hostess sat down, also their children, teacher and I, a housemaid, also a matron advanced in years, and two Reformati.[4] During the meal the discussion was general, as is usually the case when people meet for the first time. When we stood up, the host told me that he kept an old custom of praying with his servants after supper, so we went to the chapel and when we finished our litanies, we returned to enjoy conversation until ten o'clock, at which time the host took me to my lodgings. I found two rooms that were small but elegant and clean; I did not find anything lacking. Before leaving, Mister Pantler asked me (if I had no pressing engagement) to rest and settle down in his house, leaving up to me how long I wished to stay. The business which took me away from home was not urgent, the house just what I had always wished for, so I easily allowed myself to be persuaded and promised to stay for several days.

Notes

1. Pantler, originally a servant in charge of the bread and the pantry, was an honorific title.
2. Jubah, a long robe of Arabic origin, was a Polish nobleman's national costume.
3. King Jan Sobieski, conqueror of the Turks at Vienna in 1683.
4. Members of the Order of Reformati (Order Fratrum Minorum).

Texts: Krasicki, Ignacy. *Dzieła wybrane.* 2 vols. Ed. by
Zbigniew Goliński. Warszawa: PIW, 1989, I, 85-87, 104-105,
107, 109-111, 317-318, 326-327, 466, 469, 472, 473, 477, 480,
481, 484, 485, 488, 490, 491, 492-494, 499-500, 516, 527-528,
539; II, 28-30, 35-40.

Monitor 1765-1785. Wybór. Ed. by Elżbieta Aleksandrowska.
Wrocław: Ossolineum, 1976, 95-99.

Chrzanowski, *Historia literatury,* 594-596.

STANISŁAW TREMBECKI (ca. 1739-1812)

Born to a nobleman's family of modest means in Jastrzębniki near Sandomierz, Trembecki went to school in Nowe Miasto Korczyn and Cracow (1753-1757). He quickly squandered his share of family fortune on cards and women in Poland and abroad, mostly in France, and engaged in numerous duels. He also became acquainted with intellectual and artistic ideas of the French Enlightenment. After returning to Poland, he attached himself to the King and other magnates, looking constantly for rich protectors and means of support.

A gifted poet who cared little about his talent, Trembecki published many poems anonymously, as some of them were libertine or obscene, others malicious, still others panegyrical. He is best known for his rich and sensual language as well as for his poetic craftsmanship. Trembecki authored many occasional odes, epigrams, and epistles, and gained recognition for his fables and a long descriptive poem *Sofijówka,* in which he combined long passages depicting scenes from nature with philosophical and historical observations. He was also an excellent translator of Voltaire.

To Madame Kossowska When Dancing

What is this nature's delightful display
Which with a graceful step sets out to dance?
Who is this goddess that began to play
And charm the world with her fine appearance?

5   People draw around, all of them wide-eyed,
Seeing the wonders of beauty and charm,
While Cupid,[1] sighing silently aside,
Tightens his strings, unable to do harm.

Of beautiful figure, quick as a doe,
10   Her eyes like the dawn, lips of ruby red,
She is running along the swift wind's flow,
She captures each heart that passes ahead.

XXVIII. Ball Room in the Łazienki Royal Palace in Warsaw

From here her fine legs can barely be spied
And only at times they're touching the ground,
15 All her limbs at play in harmony glide
And Zephyr frolics with soft robes around.

Zephyr who himself is deserving spite,
For all his desires met with full success,
Can see the places hidden out of sight,
20 Kissing her lips in a gentle caress.

When during a turn to some small extent
Her light apron or skirt will get askew,
The greedy eye will suffer a torment
In its attempt to spy at least a shoe.

25 Your glory, Graces,[2] is truly in vain,
When you amaze Olympus with your dance,
For our Kossowska can well entertain
Mortals of this world in their existence.

To paint with skill the picture truly grand
30 Of beauty and charm of her countenance,
I pass the pen into Krasicki's hand,
Leave the brush for Smuglewicz's[3] talents.

But in doing so, I feel a great fear;
Before this work is brought to conclusion,
35 I have to give an early warning here:
Beware the destiny of Pygmalion.[4]

Notes

1. Cupid was a god of love, represented usually as a naked boy holding a bow and arrow.
2. Graces were three sister goddesses in Greek mythology who were the givers of charm and beauty. They lived on Olympus, a mountain in Thessaly, the abode of the gods, usually attending Venus.
3. Franciszek Smuglewicz (1745-1807), a painter of historical and religious pictures as well as of portraits, was one of the first representatives of classicism in Poland.

4. Pygmalion was a legendary king of Cyprus who made a female figure of ivory and fell in love with her. She was brought to life for him by Aphrodite.

Epithalamion for Dorant and Clymene
or United Love

Away all troubles, worries, and labors!
A new day shines, more happy than others,
Dorant is counting its hours with keenness,
For nightfall promised him still more sweetness,
5   And when the daylight died out in the sea,
Dawn gave the lovers a sign to be free.
Now a desire for a novel thing reigns,
Now a panic fear chills fires in her veins.
Rest disappeared, she tries to sleep in vain,
10 Her ears are on guard, her heart throbs again.
But what most disturbs her mind in this plight
Is waging a bloody, uncertain fight:
Without a second, no shield and no arms,
What will protect her from a blow that harms?!
15 Prepare, maiden, for a loving torment:
Love is bringing in Dorant by his hand,
Now the door creaked, where she rested below;
The brash boy is running like an arrow,
With one stroke drawing aside on the wing
20 Silk, satin, cotton, sheets from the bedding.
He devours all charms with his greedy eyes:
Her rosy knees, her alabaster thighs.
He kissed the beautiful lips of his bride,
Six times close to death, six times he revived.
25 Clymene, pierced with Cupid's dart of love,
Lifts her fainting eyes to heavens above.
The shout of her excited pretty face
Shows the door to desire is a tight place.
O happy pair, enjoy constant pleasure,
30 Let your nights seem to be brief forever!
No one will surpass you in sincere love,
In lovesome cooing not even the dove.
The ivy does not wind around the tree,
As Dorant hugs the neck of Clymene,

35 Nor is an oyster ever closed so tight,
    As your legs are linked together tonight.
    Give thanks to heavens for such happiness:
    Angels do not know an equal caress.

To Miss Tekla

Who will be able truly to convey
Wealth of your worthy attributes?
Yet I am ready on this page today
To list just some of your strong suits.

5   In spite of boredom of daily meetings,
    You make sweet all our merriments;
    Most attractive seem those night gatherings,
    When you put in an appearance.

    Will words be able to show your actions?
10 What is not virtuous in you?
    Always judicious your conversations,
    Your deeds are very noble too.

    Your forehead shows that cheerful thoughts you nurse,
    And child-like is your complexion,
15 Eyes are expressive, while all your manners
    Are decent, sweet, pure perfection.

    We all love you, the younger and older,
    Those bent under burden of years.
    When I say I love, ladies just snicker,
20 They think I have seen better days.

    Bald as the ice, also white as the snow,
    While inside Mount Hekla[1] aflame
    Is the only true equal that I know;
    I hope Tekla believes the same.

Notes

1. Mount Hekla, an active volcano in the south of Iceland, erupted more than twenty times since 1104.

In the Album of Marcjanna K.

When I'm drawing words, Marcjanna, in your volume,
I express only what I feel, what I presume.
I noticed that to make your life much more pleasant,
Nature lavishly gave you many a present:

5   A vivid wit, spirit's swiftness,
           In every movement graciousness,
           In deeds polite, looks that entice,
           Able to warm up the old ice.

Happy is he, who close to your beautiful face
10 Would ever deserve, obtain, or steal an embrace!
If not for that gray snare that time had trapped me in,
I would still like to commit this last little sin.

Some Fables from Aesop
Translated when possible in the style of de La Fontaine

A Deer Looking at Himself

Once upon a time, close to clear water,
   A deer looked at himself with great pleasure,
Wondering at the beauty of his branching antlers,
But seeing that his legs were as thin as dry stalks,
5   He blamed the gods with bitterness:
"Where are proportions? Such a head! Legs that one mocks?
My antlers make me as tall as the high bushes,
   But these gaunt legs look quite dreadful."

And while he right then anguishes,
10 He looks around, a hound comes at him like a bull;
Not far behind, a whole pack follows him enraged.

Fear takes him deep into the wood,
But his great swiftness is somewhat delayed,
For his antlers catch against dense wildwood.
15   He ran away, and yet he found
Holes in his pants made by the hound.

He who loves beauty and treats useful things with shame
Will often be ruined by these pretty elements,
Like the deer that looks at his legs with great disdain,
20   But admires harmful ornaments.

Texts: Borowy, Wacław. *Od Kochanowskiego do Staffa. Antologia liryki polskiej.* 4th ed. Warszawa: PIW, 1981, 58-59. Trembecki, Stanisław. *Wiersze wybrane.* Ed. by Juliusz W. Gomulicki. Warszawa: PIW, 1965, 48-49, 145-146, 162, 78.

KONSTANCJA BENISŁAWSKA (1747-1806)

Konstancja Benisławska came from a family of modest means in Livonia. She married into a well-off family and became an efficient administrator of a large estate. Family tradition had it that she gave birth to twenty-two children, of whom eight survived into adulthood. Even though Benisławska spent her life far from major literary centers, she was keenly interested in books and poetry. In 1776, encouraged by her brother-in-law, she published a collection of religious *Songs Sung for Myself*. The first two books of the *Songs* were inspired by the Lord's Prayer and Hail Mary, the third one by the Old Polish religious poetry and Spanish mystics, all of them united by a dominating motif of God's love.

Calling on All Creatures to Praise God

O You that turn the stars and the eye of heaven,
Pure Spirits and bodies by mud never smitten,
Divine Chamberlains, celestial inhabitants,
Praise our Lord, praise Him forever with reverence!

5   And you, subcelestial spheres, chariots of the sun,
Light silver moon that comes when the dark night is done,
And you, stars, many thousands spread over the skies:
Hum a sweet rhyme for the Maker, let a song rise!

Waters that are aloft over the earthly star,
10   Clouds, rainfall, hail, hoar-frost, with snow drifts stretching far,
Dew, mist and sweltering heat, frost and ice aground:
Sing together to the Lord, let sweet odes resound!

Lightning that roams in the clouds, forest-breaking winds,
Thunder with triple tongues, also the air that spins,
15   Storms and whistling gales, freezing Acquilo[1] current:
With joyful hymns praise the Lord most magnificent!

Seas, rivers, lakes, and you, clean and translucent spring,
Waters of the earth, streams gratefully murmuring,
And you, that inhabit the crystalline lagoon,
20   Raise your voices to heaven and play a new tune!

Grain bearing hillocks, jungles where tall trees amass,
Bald mountains, and valleys overgrown with high grass,
Golden harvests, berries of the forest, ripe fruit:
Give the highest Monarch your reverent salute!

25   Four-footed beasts of the field, birds in a gay choir,
Elements of the air, earth, underground empire,
All livestock and inhabitants of the forest:
Carry thankful songs to your Lord in the Highest!

Whimpering infants and laughter-loving young men,
30   Gray-haired elders, virtuous maidens, and women,
Hasten here all together, come quickly nearby!
Send abundance of praises high up to the sky!

All-powerful Ruler of the earth and heaven!
Let the east, west, south, and north praise You once again!
35   Let savage Americans know Your holy name,
Let them bow humbly, with others the faith proclaim!

Let descant, alto, tenor, bass praise You in turn,
Let organ-pipes worship You too for Your concern!
Violin, oboe, trombones, French horns, recorder,
40   Together with harps, lutes, trumpets, drums, dulcimer!

Notes

1. Acquilo was the north wind.

Midday Prayer

Now the joyous fire of the golden sun
That splits in half the vast empyrean,
From its lofty peak sets the earth ablaze
    With its sweltering rays.

5   And You, O Maker, our righteous Maker,
    And also Father, merciful Father,
    Deign to melt the ice that makes my heart dire
        With Your redeeming fire.

    O yes, forthsooth, let Your holy fire burn,
10 The fire of Your love, let it sear all men:
    So they would deem that each thing on this earth,
        Except You, has no worth.

    Let no might on earth make this fire weaker,
    But day after day attain more power,
15 So that it binds us to You, living King,
        With an eternal link.

    From the depth of our souls we send these prayers,
    From our very souls to Your holy ears,
    Highest Ruler in Heaven and this vale
20   Among all who travail.

    Let our pleas sent out with humility
    Become answered through Your authority,
    For Your, timeless Lord Commendatory,
        Always present glory.

Text: Benisławska, Konstancja. *Pieśni sobie śpiewane.* Ed. by Tadeusz Brajerski and Jerzy Starnawski. Lublin: Towarzystwo Naukowe KUL, 1958, 146-147, 165-166.

FRANCISZEK KARPIŃSKI (1741-1825)

Karpiński, born to a family of an impoverished gentry in Galicia, in south eastern part of Poland, was educated in the Jesuit College in Stanisławów (1750-1758) and at the Jesuit Academy of Lwów (most likely between 1758 and 1762), where he studied theology and philosophy. After working for some time as a lawyer in Lwów, Konarski began in 1776 to serve, often as a tutor, at the courts of magnates. In 1770 he went to Vienna, where he spent a year and a half attending University lectures and studying in the Emperor's Library. His first collection of poems, *Playthings in Verse and Exempla,* was published in Lwów in 1780. In the same year Karpiński moved to Warsaw, where he worked as a librarian of Prince Adam Czartoryski and became friendly with Julian Niemcewicz and Franciszek Kniaźnin, taking part occasionally in the Thursday dinners at the Royal Castle.

During his stay in Warsaw Karpiński published three new volumes of poetry, prose, and translations (1782-1783). In 1783 or at the beginning of 1784, Karpiński left Warsaw and returned to his village of Dobrowody in Galicia. He travelled, farmed, published three more volumes of works (1786-1787), returned to Warsaw for a period of time, and became involved in political events during the Four-Year Sejm (1788-1792).

After the final partition of Poland, the embittered Karpiński, now a Russian subject, wrote a moving poem *The Lament of a Sarmatian at the Grave of Zygmunt August* (1796). In the last years of his life, he wrote a moralistic book for children and worked on his diaries, entitled the *History of My Age And People With Whom I Lived,* finished in 1822 and published posthumously in 1844.

Karpiński is best known as a representative of sentimentalism in poetry, a poet of simple people and intimate emotions, described best in his eclogues. His *Religious Songbook* (1792), based on native folklore, contains several hymns and a carol *God Is Born* that have been sung in Poland to this day.

XXIX. Franciszek Karpiński

To Justina. Longing in Spring

So many times the sun has reached its height
And graced the day with its splendor,
But what has ever happened to my light?
It doesn't shine for me as before.

5   By now the grain has risen very high,
Before long it will yield an ear;
The entire field has turned to green nearby,
But no one can see my wheat here!

The orchard nightingale began its rounds,
10   The grove echoes its melody;
The forest birds fill the air with their sounds:
But my bird does not sing for me!

The earth has brought forth so many flowers,
After the flood two days ago;
15   The meadow dressed up in different colors:
But my little flower won't grow!

O Spring, how long will I be begging you,
The master so deeply distressed?
I washed the soil enough with tearful dew:
20   Bring back to me my dear harvest!

Recollection of Past Love
A pastoral song

A brook flows in the valley,
Maples grow over the brook.
There, Justina, we'd dally,
And of sweet evenings partook.

5   The night seemed so short and sweet,
We parted in the morning;

Love carried away our sleep:
Love lives when it's not sleeping.

When dawn made the world brighter,
10 Each maple was clearly marked,
Where we both sat together,
Our names remained deeply carved.

None saw us, none mocked nearby,
The sky our only witness!
15 I wasn't ashamed of the sky,
Our love was truly guiltless.

My eyes looked into your eyes,
My hand was squeezing your hand,
Our lips united likewise,
20 Our souls communed without end.

Once a big cloud had gathered,
Thunder crushed the oak thicket,
You embraced me and trembled,
"I won't die alone!"--you said.

25 Just on the edge of this brook,
Just close to this apple tree,
How many times I partook
Of water her hand gave me?

Now, when adverse destiny
30 Put us in anger apart,
A shepherd, quite heedlessly,
Scratched out the letters we carved.

No traces will now appear!
The woods with brush overgrown;
35 The brooks and trees are still here,
But you, Justina, are gone!

*The Lament of a Sarmatian at the Tomb of Zygmunt
August, the Last Polish King of the Jagiellonian Dynasty*

    You are asleep, Zygmunt, while your neighbors
    Arrived here as guests[1] in your residence!
    You sleep, while your men toil to open doors
    To those who honored you, pledged obedience!
5   Bitter remembrance when sunshine is gone,
    Why won't this memory perish anon?

    You left no son in the seat of power,
    Perhaps the Lord became angry with us;
    Today his grandson along the border
10 Would spread mortal fear and respectfulness!
    The crown that you once wore became vended,
    The throne abased and the counsel blunted.[2]

    O my fatherland, you fell at the end!
    One time so rich in glory and power!
15 From sea to sea you did one time extend,
    Not a small plot left for your sepulcher!
    How much we are now moved by this great corpse!
    The soul of millions was this body's force!

    Just look! A mother's child is lying there!
20 A deep wound appearing in his proud breast
    His noble life escaped through it elsewhere!
    He didn't flee, struck from the front in his chest!
    His face still showing that he craves vengeance!
    He seems indignant, why this despondence?

25 There--good faith, church, chastity assaulted;
    The whole settlements are consumed by flame!
    Into a charred house the squire pushed ahead,
    First they plundered his warehouse when they came.
    Everywhere fierceness breeds flames, death slashes,
30 Wherever you look--grief, corpses, ashes.

    After this loss, some of them, most wary,
    Scattered everywhere under foreign skies,[3]
    Others oppressed by extreme misery

In homes once their own beg for bread with cries!
35 Others, under the Russians and Germans,
Weep on fathers' land--now they are aliens.

You, that cried over the country's defeats,
Went to save the ungrateful nation then!
Your victorious arms in so many feats
40 Showed to the world the skill of Polish men!
What have you brought back to your home regions?
Poverty, scars, hopes without illusions!

This beautiful soil is stained with blood now,
It feeds the horse and the savage rider,
45 And mother must teach hungry children how
To speak in the language of the ruler!
This is as some hard sentence dictated:
Some were inscribed, Poland eradicated![4]

Vistula! A stranger drinks your water,
50 Even the Pole's footsteps are now rubbed out,
Today he's hiding his name much deeper,
Which once gained fame from great ancestors' clout!
The world won't bow as it used in past days
To the White Eagle and its friendly Chase![5]

55   King Zygmunt, by your shrine,
    If winds aren't prosperous,
    I'll put down at this time
    Sword, mirth, hope now useless

    And this humble lute!
60   This is all I see!
    Only tears acute
    Are left now for me!

Notes

1. This is a sarcastic reference to the partitioning powers.
2. The crown was traded at the free election, the royal power was limited, the Senate's role diminished.
3. During the time of partitions, Polish soldiers fought in many foreign countries.

4. The name of Poland was erased from the map of Europe, while the names of the partitioning powers were put down in its place.
5. The White Eagle represented Poland, the Chase Lithuania.

Mazurka

Good night, my Jacenta,
And the lips most modest,
The eyes that are dainty
And twin orbs of your breast.

5   I'm ready not to sleep
Whole night for good measure:
For who can stay asleep
So close to this treasure?

The magic of your eyes
10   Took my sound sleep away;
I won't flirt with these eyes
In a daring display.

To the church I will go
When the morning light flares,
15   And against your charmed glow
I will ask for some prayers.

I will buy a taper,
Spend my sovereign apace,
So I won't yearn after
20   The fair Jacenta's face.

At least I'll say a prayer,
If she is impudent,
That what I have to bear
Will be, too, her torment.

Morning Song

When the morning lights are rising
Soon the earth and sea are singing,
The whole creation sings to You,
Be praised, Great God, be praised anew!

5   Also man who beyond measure
Has been showered with Your treasure,
Whom You created and saved too,
Why would he not be praising You?

I will barely open my eyes,
10   When I send to the Lord my cries,
To my Lord who is in heaven
And I look for him near me then.

Many who went last night to bed
Fell into sleep of death instead,
15   And yet we still woke up today,
So that to You, Lord, we could pray.

Night Song

All our daily cares that we bring,
Receive with mercy, righteous King,
When sleep takes us in its embrace,
Let our dreams sing also Your praise.

5   Your eyes that see all from the height
Keep looking at us day and night,
Where man in utmost feebleness
Is looking to You for redress!

Turn back the mishaps of the night,
10   Protect us from all harmful plight,
Keep us forever in Your mind,
The Guardian and Judge of mankind.

Song on the Birth of Our Lord

    God is born, the power trembles,
    Lord of heaven is stripped clotheless;
    Fire freezes, brightness darkens,
    He has limits--the limitless.
5   Despised--yet in glory arrayed,
    Mortal--the King since long ago!
    And the Word into Flesh was made
    And dwelt among us here below![1]

    What have you, heaven, more than men?
10 God abandoned your happiness,
    He came among his dear flock then,
    Sharing with them toil and distress!
    He suffered, was deeply dismayed,
    For we were most guilty and low,
15 And the Word into Flesh was made
    And dwelt among us here below.

    He was born in a wretched shed
    And His cradle was a manger!
    Who is He? By what surrounded?
20 Cattle, shepherds, and hay nearer.
    Poor folk! Before the rich you paid
    Respects to Him by bowing low!
    And the Word into Flesh was made
    And dwelt among us here below.

25 Afterwards the kings could be seen
    Crowded in the communal fold,
    They brought gifts to the Nazarene
    Of myrrh and frankincense and gold.
    The Son of God had them all laid
30 Where peasants' offerings would go!
    And the word into Flesh was made
    And dwelt among us here below.

    Raise Your hand, Infant All-loving,
    And bless our cherished motherland.
35 With good counsels, in good living--
    Support its strength with Your strong hand,

Also our home, our whole estate,
Your hamlets and towns that we know!
And the Word into Flesh was made
40   And dwelt among us here below.

Notes

1. "And the Word became flesh and lived among us." (John 1:14)

Text: Karpiński, Franciszek. *Wybór poezji.* Ed. by Juliusz Kijas. Kraków: Wydawnictwo M. Kot, 1949, 3, 4-5, 38-40, 45, 53, 54, 55-56.

FRANCISZEK KNIAŹNIN (1750-1807)

Born in Witebsk, Kniaźnin attended the Jesuit schools in Witebsk, Połock and Nieświerz, where he entered the Order and continued his studies. In 1770 he was transferred to teach in the Warsaw Jesuit College. After the dissolution of the Order, Kniaźnin worked as a secretary of the Czartoryski family and as a librarian in the Załuski Library (1781-1783). His health gradually declining, he spent the remaining years of his life mostly at the court of the Czartoryskis in Puławy.

Kniaźnin debuted as a translator and co-authored the publication of the complete edition of Horace's odes (1773-1774). In 1776 he published *Fables*, in 1779 two volumes of *Love Poems*, and in 1783 a collection of *Poems*. Three volumes of *Poetry*, a valuable document pertaining to the artistic milieu of Puławy, appeared in 1787-1788.

To the Stars

Stars of golden night, O host shining bright,
Minute brothers, lofty inhabitants!
Who under the sky, casting flickery light
Silently turn in an unerring dance.

5   Silvery circles soar then in the air
Sporting with the heavens in their sweet play;
When mankind and living things everywhere
Are gently embraced in sleep's dusky veil.

O how pleasing it was to look at you,
10   My gold pageant of eternal lightness;
When, as it happened, your eyes would pursue
My lady's fair charms and sweet caresses.

So why do you now from the vast skies glow,
Where nothing can make blazing fires abate,
15   And send your light into narrow window
Of that sunken house? You will not see Kate!

XXX. Franciszek Dionizy Kniaźnin

The Looms
In a pastoral genre

Mother, you're setting up the looms in vain:
    Another thought I hold more dear.
Let me instead look through the windowpane,
    To see if my Philon rides here.

5   When we looked at each other tenderly,
    He just said two words and no more.
Now without him the time weighs heavily:
    He is a half of my soul's core.

What is keeping him there such a long time?
10   It is not a very long way.
He does not yet know well this heart of mine,
    That for him is pining away.

By that little grove my beloved will ride;
    When will his face at last appear?
15 Just this instant birds from there fly outside:
    No doubt he is galloping here.

The magpie screeches to him from the fence:[1]
    What now? He is still not in sight.
My Philon! When I see your eyes' radiance,
20   I shall clap my hands in delight.

Now I can see him--my dear guest rides on,
    He still holds my heart in favor!
Love's guiding his gaze in this direction,
    His gray horse in playful canter.

25 I'll sit by the loom for a precious wink,
    So as to disguise my delight;
Let Philon who has just come in not think
    That I was yearning for his sight.

Notes

1. It was generally believed that the shrieks of a magpie announced the arrival of guests.

To Whiskers

Adornment of the face, twirly whiskers!
An effeminate crowd turns against you.
They poke fun at you, those dreadful daughters,
Polish women's fame they don't keep in view.

5   When the sword ruled over foreign frontiers
And the martial gaze over hearts held sway,
The god of love[1] settled on the whiskers,
Making the eyes of women look his way.

When once our knights appeared in a parade,
10   And each splendid face displayed manliness,
One girl looked and whispered to the next maid:
"I'd give up my life for those black whiskers!"

When our Czarniecki[2] made the sword famous
And sacrificed his blood for his homeland,
15   All Polish women praised him in chorus,
While he would twirl his whiskers with his hand.

When Vienna sang the praise of John the Third[3]
One could hear then German women converse:
"This is the Polish king who saved our world,
20   How attractive he looks with his whiskers!"

Now changes in the land are spelling doom:
Nice[4] finds loathsome the knightly features,
And for her sake Dorant, soaked with perfume,
Treats with disdain both courage and whiskers.

25   Let them hold in contempt their own nation,
Be ashamed of mothers, fathers, brothers,

But I, proud of our native expression,
And still a true Pole, will twirl my whiskers.

Notes

1. Cupid was the god of love.
2. Stefan Czarniecki was a famous military leader who defeated the Swedes in the war in the seventeenth century.
3. Jan III Sobieski was the king of Poland (1674-1696) and conqueror of the Turks at Vienna in 1683.
4 Nice, Dorant--fashionable French names.

Two Linden Trees

Two verdant lindens in summer
Bow to each other from their banks:
One bending towards the other,
The branches are touching their flanks.

5   Why did they become divided
By cruel depths of the river?
Desire still nearby resided,
But they are apart forever.

So spoke Coril roaming astray,
10   When he thought of faithful Ismen,
And he breathed a sigh of dismay
From the wound in his heart hidden.

To Love

O Love, Love that is pitiless!
You served a cup of bitterness,
I drink it, poisoning my days.
These swarms of longings and dismays
5   Overshadow all in my mind,
I see this world is most unkind.
So this is your lavish sweetness,
O cruel, deceitful goddess?
Ah, who I accuse of rancor?...

10 Clymene, in joyless ardor
    I utter curses and blame this
    That allows me to feel your bliss,
    And that stirs with your resemblance
    My heart and my fancies at once.

To God

   You have ruled over us, impartial Lord!
   Power and glory are bound with Your name;
   It cannot be by the whole world ignored,
   An arrow struck us, Your hand took the aim;
5 You wished to find out if we still loved You,
   You did; we accept, we trust in You, too.

   A vile slander and cursed sly maneuvers
   Oppress virtue in this horrible hour,
   Caught in the snare and in shameful fetters,
10 Only our blood flows free from base power.
   What does this flock say, kneeling before You?
   "Father, let Your hand come to our rescue!"

   For You have pushed us from above down low,
   So that Your arm could be seen much clearer,
15 Lifting us from the humble vale below,
   It strikes our pride and makes its horns shatter,
   When pride's in ruin the world will know then
   That You are the Lord, and we Your children.

   Where is this might which in a heedless race
20 Thinks little of You, cruel and possessed?
   Whose bold steps are marked by blood in each place
   And which feeds with tears the snakes at its breast,
   Which curses You and barks with great disdain
   At Your emblem and at Your shield's domain.

25 Thunder, o Lord! The world will listen hard.
   But what shall we do? Where to go in need?
   Lighten and command! For we lose our heart
   Deprived of Your fire and without Your lead;

Behind Your arm extends the open field,
30 Virtue is armed with wonders that won't yield.

Give us endurance, give us faith thereon!
It touches graves and moves over mountains,
It will bring back fathers' days that are gone,
It'll bring lush crops to their fields and gardens;
35 And Your white birds that are roaming today
To nests on the home rock will make their way.

Where on the rock that'll last forever hence,
Your Providence's temple will stand strong,
A distant offspring to give evidence
40 Will every year renew a joyful song;
There on the altar, the flock blest by You,
Will place the book, with it the just sword too.

On Eliza

Eliza looked most displeased yesterday:
    Maybe I caused her ill temper.
Tossed with her white hand the chaplet away,
    Bit her lip five times in anger.

5 There was no way her anger to dispel,
    I didn't dare beg her in her spite,
I walked off sad, with myself to quarrel,
    And I could not sleep the whole night.

Today she greeted me with her dear voice,
10   She's given her heart back to me!
Hope in sweet destiny makes me rejoice,
    Yet I face next day with worry.

Text: Kniaźnin, Franciszek Dionizy. *Wybór poezji.* Ed. by Wacław Borowy. Wrocław: Ossolineum, Biblioteka Narodowa I 129, 1948, 81-82, 106-107, 109-111, 119, 143-144, 180-181. Kniaźnin, Franciszek Dionizy. *Wiersze wybrane.* Ed. by Andrzej K. Guzek. Wraszawa: PIW, 1981, 63.

KAJETAN WĘGIERSKI (1756-1787)

Kajetan Węgierski was born in Śliwno, in the region of Podlasie. In 1764 he entered the Collegium Nobilium in Warsaw and gained a reputation as a promising poet. He was a student of Adam Naruszewicz, to whom he dedicated an ode on *Little Respect for Learned Men*. After spending several years at the court of the Branickis, Węgierski returned to Warsaw and obtained a position in the Justice Department. His poems and translations gained him recognition and opened the doors to the Royal Palace. But his malicious satires on some members of aristocratic families, e.g., *Portraits of Five Elizabeths* (1776), and on a nobleman who raided his father's estate brought him into conflict with powerful men. Węgierski was jailed for a week and lost his office. He turned to gambling and kept winning large sums of money, but instead of settling down in the country, as he had planned earlier, he left Poland in 1779.

Węgierski spent the last years of his short life wandering from city to city, country to country. He went to Germany, Austria, Italy, and France, where in 1781 he wrote his last poem. He spent two years in Paris, travelled to America, and back to Ireland, England, and the Netherlands, gambling and engaging in love affairs. His health deteriorating, he spent the last two years in southern France; he died in Marseille and was buried at Sainte Marie-Majeure cemetery.

An admirer of Voltaire, Węgierski attacked religion, church, and clergy in his mock-heroic poem *Church Organs* (1776). A poet of great promise, he went through life, in his own words, "without any system, without any plan, submitting to my passions."

A Complaint of a Canon Against a Smith

A smith awfully bitter towards a canon,
Disregarding his state and holy condition,
Pinched the cleric from the back with his red-hot tongs,
Who stood innocently behind the smithy doors.
5   This horrible crime that shocked all the villagers
Was judged in Osiek[1] and their decision was terse:
"The smith sinned, but we need the smith around here yet;
The tongs hurt the priest, so let's hang the tongs instead!"

Notes

1. Osiek, a little town, most likely near Sandomierz, was mentioned in many proverbs as a place notorious for its injustice. It was said that in Osiek a tailor was hanged instead of a smith, as there were two tailors, but only one smith.

Every Man to His Taste

    Let a drunk hold on to his glass in play,
    A shark spend at cards best part of his day,
    A rider gallop on his horse around,
    A soldier slay others on the battle ground,
5   A courtier scurry in the palace maze,
    A usurer keep Fridays, Saturdays,
    A jurist talk when he is at the bar,
    A priest skin others, even a lazar,
    Let a monk lose his sandals in great haste,
10 Because it's best--every man to his taste.

A Philosopher

    With lots of gold, without it too,
    I am always keen and joyous;
    The good man is graced with virtue,
    He's not ashamed when penniless.

5   I have no wife, I want no wife,
    Because I know what marriage is;
    I'm not stroked by vain pride in life--
    Why would I want to have riches?

    When things are going well for me,
10 I offer thanks for Fortune's call;
    When her good will isn't given free,
    I'm not distressed by it at all.

    Even if Fortune would chase me,
    Threatening a most severe blow,
15 She'll never make me so needy,
    So as my virtue to forego.

My needs are truly limited
To cover my small expenses:
I can exist without white bread
20 And without costly meat dishes.

I do not need any treasure
To show the world what I achieved,
I do not dress beyond measure
In order to be well received.

25 I don't make a compact with those,
Whose friendship may carry a price,
This reason I hereby disclose:
To buy friends with money isn't wise.

Friendship that ends when one is poor,
30 That has no traits of quality,
That just in money sees allure,
Cannot be called virtue by me.

So residing in my own home,
I feel I am quite prosperous,
35 When I do not have any loan,
I am content with my status.

A Letter to Rhymesters

Scribimus indocti doctique poemata passim.
(We, the learned and unlearned, write poems everywhere.)
Horace, *Letters,* II, 1, 118.

My most respected brothers and most noble lords,
For at times lord's fantasy in empty heads boards,
Poets of different estates, age, and learning,
Bastards or rather Apollo's lawful offspring,
5 Listen--for to listen can never be unwise,
If any of your friends offers you sound advice.
I'm an unworthy apprentice of your order:
I wrote and I did not escape praise and laughter,
I still write and will keep writing until the day,
10 When with the just on Parnassus I'll make my stay.

There're some who graced with laurels still in their life spans,
Deal with us as if they were dealing with infants,
And after soaring very high in their swift rise,
At our trifling output will barely cast their eyes;
15 I will not be begging them in their uncurbed pride
With flattering incense, for this act I deride,
And no one will be able to put blame on me
That I would debase the bard's gifts with flattery.
Bishops, canons, lay men, and Piarist brothers,
20 In a word all those who happen to write in verse,
Do what I do: scribble, print whatever you like,
But don't praise them as if all of them were alike.
Wherever I turn, in whatever direction,
I'm buried under a boring rhyme collection:
25 One calls a man without conscience an honest man,
One praises to the sky a traitor of homeland,
One, who sees that someone has just bought his office,
Cheers and wants to put him with the meritorious.
They write poems because someone has his nameday;
30 Poems again because someone has his birthday;
Still more poems, as someone bored at home alone,
Made vows at the altar, for whom it is unknown!
Presses are groaning, while poor printers work in sweat,
And those stupid noddles turn upside down upset.
35 They promise the homeland improvement of its fate;
Why? Because some pantler[1] gets married on this date!
All country mishaps will be scared away sooner
By some cupbearer who weds a judge's daughter!
Let a husband in bed with praiseworthy vigor
40 Make his respectable better half a junior
And she will bear it, after a nine month sickness,
Owing to a doctor's or midwife's helpfulness,
Parnassus gets noisy! Empty heads do not rest,
All flatterers are ready for a rhyming test.
45 If a son, it will surely be Alexander,
They cry wistfully that he was not born earlier;
He would have no doubt by his deeds and his bold stand
Defended what foreign power took from Poland,
But they conceived of definite hopes anyway
50 That with his help happiness will shine forth next day.
If a girl, it'll be Lucretia,[2] that's evident,
It's already quite obvious from her deportment.

Each foretells these things, but not a single poet
Has up to this day managed to guess it right yet.
55 Our hope is fortified by your rhymes every day,
This land will be merry, we'll find a better way;
Each day people are born, each day join together,
Yet our fate by no means changes for the better.
Leave it then alone, since nothing ever comes true,
60 What's more these prophecies bring no profit to you.

Notes

1. Pantler was a servant or officer in charge of the bread and the pantry in a great family.
2. Lucretia, known for her beauty, was the wife of Tarquinius Collatinus. When she was violated by Sextus Tarquinius, she took her own life (cf. Shakespeare, *The Rape of Lucrece*).

Text: Węgierski, Kajetan. *Wiersze wybrane.* Ed. by Juliusz Gomulicki. Warszawa: PIW, 1974, 78, 88, 89-90, 103-105.

ANONYMOUS

This popular song of the Confederates of Bar (1768-1772), filled with religious and patriotic zeal, was characteristic of many anonymous poems written by soldiers defending their country against Russia.

A Brave Pole on the Field of Mars

      I enter the field on the Lord's command,
      For life in heaven, I forgo my rank.
      I die for freedom, my faith won't abandon,
            This is my venture.

5   The cross is my shield, salvation my gain,
      I will march on; although I'll fall down slain,
      No matter, I seek in homeland battle
            True peace for my soul.

      Blood from His wounds spilled for my redemption
10   Confirms my desire, soothes my passion,
      To the faith most true, my heart is pierced through,
            A Catholic man.

      Savior's death--the password for reveille,
      So that evil deeds are put out promptly,
15   Freedom's abuse and holy faith's misuse
            Are brought to a halt.

      I won't fulfill the will of Providence,
      At least let me with my life recompense,
      So that faith is not down, but in renown
20   All over the world.

      I'm not afraid of my foes' betrayal,
      I know You'll give me Your saving counsel,
      So that things will turn, so Your laws return,
            As to a recruit.

25	I trust gracious Mother will join our stand,
	She will bless me with Her courageous hand,
	When I am her son, my fight will be won,
	Defender of faith.
	It's nothing new for Mary with Her shield
30	To safeguard Poland, fight with knights afield,
	To come in person and help you along,
	My dear fatherland!
	Not vain are hopes in Polish patron saints,
	The zealous men's hearts should not feel constraints,
35	The saints will report and swords for support
	Provide to the Poles.
	By wordly allures let's not be made blind,
	The Lord's holy faith let us stand behind,
	And for our labor, we'll live forever
40	With God in heaven.

Text: Maciejewski, Janusz (ed.). *Literatura barska (Antologia)*. 2nd ed. Wrocław: Ossolineum, Biblioteka Narodowa I 108, 1976, 316-318.

JÓZEF WYBICKI (1747-1822)

Józef Wybicki was born in Będomin near Kościerzyna in Pomerania and educated by the Jesuits near Gdańsk (1755-1763). He practiced law in Poznań, was a deputy to the Sejm, and took part in the Bar Confederacy. In 1771 and 1772 Wybicki studied law in Leyda. He worked for the Commission for National Education and took part in political debates (*Patriotic Letters*, 1777-1778). He also wrote occasional poems and comedy. After the fall of the Insurrection, Wybicki went to Paris and together with General Jan Dąbrowski organized the Polish legions, for whom he wrote in 1797 *The Song of the Polish Legions in Italy*, now the Polish national anthem. In the last years of his life, Wybicki wrote didactic works, edited his diaries, and occupied high positions in the judicial system of the Kingdom of Poland.

[*If One Could in a Few Days*]

If one could in a few days bring bliss to this land,
The Pole would be able to save his fatherland.
Keen in urgent need, active at the beginnings,
He makes sacrifices of life and belongings,
5   But where a true manly spirit has to bestir,
Above fate's favor and above a disaster,
Where we must withstand storms in order and concord,
Let's admit, these traits weren't given us by the Lord.

The Song of the Polish Legions in Italy[1]

Poland has not lost her life yet,[2]
Inasmuch as we live,
What foreign power had wrested,
With swords we shall retrieve.

5   March on, march on Dąbrowski,
To Poland from Italy,
When we follow your command,
We shall see our kinsmen's land.

Just like Czarniecki[3] to Poznań
10 Returned across the sea,
In order to save his homeland,
When Swedes sacked the country.

March on, march on ...

We'll cross the Vistula, Warta,[4]
15 We'll be the Poles once more,
We were shown by Bonaparte
How to triumph in the war.

March on, march on ...

German, Muscovite won't defy,
20 When with the sword in hand,
Concord will be our password cry
As well as fatherland.

March on, march on ...

Then father says to his Helen,
25 And to crying succumbs:
"Just listen, these must be our men,
Who are beating the drums."

March on, march on ...

With one voice they cried to the skies:
30 "Enough of enslavement!
We still have Racławice scythes,[5]
God will Kościuszko send."

March on, march on ...

Notes

1. The Polish Legions were organized in 1797 as an auxiliary corps attached to the army of the newly established Lombard Republic. Commanded by General Jan Henryk Dąbrowski (1755-1818), a hero of the Kościuszko Insurrection, the Polish units consisted of two regiments of infantry (about

7,000 men), one regiment of cavalry, and one artillery unit. Dąbrowski participated in the campaigns of 1806-1807, 1809, and 1812. In 1813, he was nominated Commander-in-Chief of the Polish army by Napoleon.

With several changes, the song became Poland's national anthem.

2. It was wrongly reported that when Kościuszko fell from his horse at the Battle of Maciejowice (1794), he uttered the words 'finis Poloniae' (the end of Poland). Wybicki's opening line is a bold expression of faith and hope for the rebirth of the republic.

3. Stefan Czarniecki (1599-1655), Hetman of the Crown since 1655, distinguished himself by his courage during the Ukrainian and Swedish wars.

4. It was planned that the Legions would defeat Austria, enter Little Poland, end after defeating the Prussians free Great Poland.

5. During the victorious Battle of Racławice (1794), Kościuszko's peasant troops were armed with the scythes set erect.

Text: Wybicki, Józef. *Poezje wybrane.* Ed. by Andrzej K. Guzek. Warszawa: Ludowa Spółdzielnia Wydawnicza, 1982, 21, 91-92.

WOJCIECH BOGUSŁAWSKI (1757-1829)

Born in Glinna near Poznań, Bogusławski was educated by the Piarists in Warsaw and then spent some time at the court of Bishop Sołtyk in Cracow. In 1775 he joined the National Guard, but left after three years and spent the rest of his life working as an actor and theatre director. In the course of his long career, Bogusławski organized and directed theatres in Warsaw, Lwów, Grodno, Wilno and staged plays in Łowicz, Poznań, Kalisz and other cities.

Bogusławski laid the foundation of the national theatre, organized its professional life, and trained several generations of actors. He supported literary efforts of Polish playwrights, giving them a forum to present their ideas. He also translated librettos and wrote an original, popular national opera *A Supposed Miracle or Cracovians and Mountaineers* (1794), which featured peasants and their folklore, as well as several comedies, e.g., *Henry VI on a Hunt.*

A Supposed Miracle or Cracovians and Mountaineers

Act I

Scene VI

A wedding song

Girls

Ah, Sophie, good bye, you must go,
You'll be a woman tomorrow,
Your color will not be so red,
And you will lose your dear chaplet.

Boys

5   It's not so, dear Sophie, better a zestful beau,
Than a flower in the bare field, lying fallow,
Your chaplet will be worthless when withered away,
You girls that cry would be glad to lose it today.

Girls

          You've already lost your mother,
10   And among strangers found shelter,
          You won't see your native bower,
          Where you spent many a sweet hour.

Boys

          A skylark under a stone, a swan near water,
          A nightingale in a cool grove enjoys leisure,
15   So a girl in her man's home will find well-being,
          Because it's so ordered by Nature's wise teaching.

Girls

          You didn't know worries till today,
          Now you will feel lots of dismay,
          You won't be able to dance more,
20   To work for bread will be your chore.

Boys

          Yet each soul that lives is created to labor,
          And the one who eats our bread is a true idler,
          You girls in maidenhood have often lots of woe,
          But in marriage there are pleasures that you don't know.

Girls

25   Yet each mother's worries abound,
          When many children are around,
          Then you will soon break down and cry,
          That to stay single you didn't try.

Boys

          Hops spread out, an apple tree bears fruit, and birds nest,
30   If all things didn't multiply, the world wouldn't be blest,
          Miserable are those girls that roam high and low,
          They keep wandering alone, no husbands they know.

Scene 7
Aria III
[A Song of Bardos]

    This world is cruel, quite athwart,
    And all things keep going amiss,
    A worthless man is a big lord,
    While a good man is penniless.
5   Yet reason will win the contest,
    This notion makes my life quite sweet;
    One day I will feather my nest,
    Though now I've no shoes on my feet.

    Not clever he who on his way
10 Is losing his courage for fear,
    The harder all thorny dismay,
    Then victory is much more dear.
    Fame lives on somewhere in the sky,
    Good fortune in a loftier realm...
15 But if one's resolve does not die,
    He will get close to both of them.

    The more we are harassed by fate,
    The more manly should be our stance,
    The one who meanly falls prostrate,
20 In vain calls heavens' assistance.
    Although I am gnawed by hunger,
    My soul is not wounded at all,
    With songs my troubles I smother,
    For gaiety makes worries seem small.

Text: Bogusławski, Wojciech. *Cud mniemany czyli Krakowiacy i Górale.* Ed. by Stanisław Pietraszko. Wrocław: Ossolineum, 1954, 59-61, 64-65.

FRANCISZEK ZABŁOCKI (1752-1821)

Little is known about Zabłocki's childhood and youth. He was probably born in Volhynia and attended school in Międzyrzec Korecki. In 1773 he came to Warsaw, in 1774 obtained a position in the Commission for National Education, and became associated with the court of the Czartoryskis. Influenced by Krasicki, he wrote occasional poems, translated, and then began to write for the theatre, publishing several comedies in 1780. During the next ten years Zabłocki wrote about forty plays, among them *The Fop Suitor* (1781), edited three textbooks, and authored many political odes. In 1778 he became the secretary of the Society for Elementary Books.

He took part in the defense of Praga and when the Insurrection was suppressed, he escaped to Rome, where he studied and was ordained a priest. After returning to Poland, Zabłocki settled in a parish in Końskowola, near Puławy, where he spent the last twenty years of his life, taking care of his mentally ill friend Franciszek Kniaźnin.

On a Decree Authorizing an Army of One Hundred Thousand [1]

    One hundred thousand men took the field. Praise the Lord!
    Now all over Europe will thunder Poland's sword!
    One hundred thousand men took the field. They muster.
    Praise the Lord! Where are they? Where indeed? On paper.
5 Let's give for the army everything, half or more!
    Praise the Lord, there's pay for a hundred thousand corps!
    Some are crying, others are laughing excited;
    There are millions ... Where? Still in everyone's pocket.
    No one will doubt our government, our bravery,
10 Our magnificence, and in truth, our perjury.
    From now on we won't fear those guests[2] we remember.
    There's refuge! In whom? Surely God's our Preserver...
    Braggarts! Let not Providence beguile you!
    Let it not be shown "God's with the merry-andrew."

XXXI. Franciszek Zabłocki

Notes

1. A unanimous resolution to establish a standing army of one hundred thousand men was passed by the Sejm on October 20, 1788, and met with great enthusiasm. A discussion how to obtain contributions for this purpose went on for several months, but the goal of fielding one hundred thousand soldiers was not reached.
2. Zabłocki refers here to the partitioning powers.

To the Assembled Estates

Let every sinner beat his breast in penitence!
Throughout Warsaw there appear most dreadful omens:
A maiden with a duck's nose was seen in the lane;
This night at twelve o'clock a brass weathercock vane
5   Crowed with a shrill voice on the Holy Cross tower;
At masked balls frenzied youth don't show up in power;
The sun often won't shine from the south this winter;
In Solec[1] a new well doesn't want to give water;
In an Ujazdów barn grain sheaves are in blossom;
10   A castellan in the Sejm spoke with great reason.
I don't want to fathom the Lord's hidden judgments,
But these are omens and warnings of dire events.
We miss the prophetic spirit of Father Mark;[2]
My opinion, though it is true, no one will hark.
15   Though the spirit of holy seers doesn't possess me,
I'll say, however, what plain logic would decree.
I do not know if Saturn is close to the sun,
If a comet with a fiery tail will make its run,
I do not know what the beak-nosed woman will bring
20   Or why in a Polish city the brass would sing,
But if on similar impossible matters
Everyone agrees with me and no one differs,
If reason has now arrived at castellans' gates,
Make good use of these wonders, assembled estates!
25   For up to now, as at the tower of Babel,
You wished to put freedom at the throne's high level,[3]
But since the Creator kindled the hopeful ray,
Gave to some courage, enlightened others this day,
Since for Poland's good luck to each neighbor nation

30 He threw a hard bone of the longed for contention,[4]
    If with this clear favor of Providence's way,
    You won't give help to the fallen freedom today,
    Your virtue's mask will fail to fool your descendants:
    They'll trust it as much as you in my strange events.

Notes

1. Solec and Ujazdów were villages near Warsaw.
2. Marek Jandołowicz, a carmelite, was a prophet of the Bar Confederacy.
3. These were adverse positions that could not be reconciled.
4. Prussia, Russia, and Austria were involved in many international conflicts, giving Poland a hope for independence.

The Fop Suitor
(selections)

Act I, Scene V

Aryst
(in his night robe)

A guest, dear guest! Welcome in my house, my good sir!

Fop
(embracing him hard)

Well, how are you, my good-hearted tiller!

Aryst
(trying to free himself screaming)

                              Ouch, it hurts!
Let go! God, what are you doing! Young man, my side!

(freeing himself)

Ah, I see you could strangle dragons, my good knight!

Fop

5   For us in Warsaw this is a friendly token.

Aryst

Well, hang you, something in my neck has been broken!

Fop

You shouldn't coddle yourself. Under the country sky
You are more healthy, wealthy, but we are more spry.

Aryst

And what's new in Warsaw?

Fop

                    Very bad, pestilence.

Aryst
(jumps back frightened)

10   For people?

Fop

Much worse.

Aryst

By God!

Fop

                           For my affluence.
I lost everything--not a penny in my purse!
Those card players are meaner than the worst robbers.
When they caught me yesterday, they wouldn't let me quit,
Until they had robbed me clean of my last ducat.
15   In six games the three, that darling of the bank,

Was most friendly, but for me it just drew a blank,
And when it was over I lost twenty four times...

Aryst

That cannot be or you fell for the sharks' designs.

Fop

So deeply that in just one hour I lost all told
20 One thousand ducats in highly valued Dutch gold--
And whatever I could not pay from my coffer,
With a note for the Twelfth-day I had to cover,
For the Lwów fair.[1] But then I will be in Dubno,
They'll have no chance to catch me or touch what I owe.
25 But I am so worried... I lost a lot somehow...

Aryst

Well, maybe a guardian should take care of you now...
Should a young man of such a decent heritage,
Beautiful traits, kind heart, sizable appanage
Be drawn into a habit which is so fatal,
30 The more pitiful since it is unnatural?
Doesn't man have enough of inborn wickedness:
Senses fighting spirit, virtue against excess,
Suffering, longing, worries, disquiet, disease,
To seek new ones by using some odd recipes?

Fop

35 My dear philosopher, my most astute cynic![2]
Syllogisms good at school, at the table won't stick.
Go away with your morals, I didn't ask for them.
Help me, for I am exhausted, give me your hand;
I have nothing but a constant desire to play.
40 Don't you know a widow I could engage today?
No matter if she's old, young, or a hunch-backed witch,
Upright or lame or blind, so long as she is rich.

Aryst
(making fun of him)

Maybe we'll find you one... Only choose a goodwife.
We have here a blind hag, just about sixty five;
45   That's the one you'd need?

Fop

Has she a big endowment?

Aryst

For some years now she is a church home resident.
A good and sure endowment, it is from Firlej[3]--
Vicar handles villages, while old women pray.

Fop

Go to the devil, do not tell me such nonsense!
50   I want a rich old dame, a blind one he commends!
Hard times nowadays! My heart is truly aching,
When people could live well--they don't have a farthing.
Hard times in Poland, misery. The Olkusz mines
Are flooded, while salt pits now in Austrian confines,[4]
55   Grain cheap, customs high; while father is a miser,
As old as hills, gives nothing, but won't die either.
That would truly be a choice morsel of the cake:
A year I could sow my wild oats and play the rake,
In time I would get married to some warm woman,
60   *Notandum*[5] to an old and quite sickly matron.
But what? Tons of old ladies! They are plentiful!
Some are rich, so what? Each as healthy as a bull!
Damn it, some of those stiffs could live longer than I!
Many a green shoot in the ancient trunk gets dry...
65   But why I worry my head in vain, I don't know,
I recall: I know one most beautiful widow.
It would be good to take care of her perquisites.
My good friend, lend me about two hundred ducats!
(..)

Act II
Scene V

Fop, Pantler's Widow Podstolina
(her head covered, elegantly dressed, but in mourning)

Fop

O, my Podstolina! The change is marvelous!
70 Just look at that! Attired in such a tasteful dress:
Those flowers, those costly trifles, those pendants there!
Let me be allowed to ask: for whom is this snare?

Podstolina
(with an indifferent look)

Surely not for you, Sir.

Fop

                        Grant me not to believe.
Why do the world and death in union interweave:
75 This mourning in agreement with the bright colors?
This hairdo for the victory dressed up in curls?
Those eyes, given by nature to set hearts afire,
Concealed by a deep cloud, filled with pretended ire,
In which, in spite of constraints, through a veiled recess,
80 One can see a kind heart, not the mind's fretfulness?
What's this blend of modesty and desolation,
Kindness and cruelty, courage and prostration?
All of these make you a thousand times more charming,
But you will gain much more, when you aren't in
   mourning.

Podstolina
(pretending to be angry)

85 How much more of this joking and this wantonness?
I do not see the point or wit in your address.
This kind of revelry with our sex, my good sir,
Will not win you affection, regard, or honor.
Instead of being humble, docile, and tongue-tied

90 In search of affection, you forge ahead with pride.
    Forsake this amour propre, this insolent chatter,
    This bold cajolery hurtful to our gender.
    Serve, pay court, and fear, and tremble in hopefulness:
    These are the roads to the heart, that is love's progress.
95 Ten years are not enough, let alone one moment ...

Fop
(interrupting her very quickly)

True, I read it myself in the Old Testament.
I'll say even more: ten years won't be a long spell,
When Jacob had served fourteen years to win Rachel.[6]
But it's, my Podstolina, from the old times date,
100 The customs were different, and different the world's state.
People used to live then three hundred years and more,
How can we follow now this example of yore?
And yet, and yet, à propos, you yourself told me
That I bore you, that my presence doesn't bring you glee,
105 How will this agree with your wish of ten years?
Yet still I want to comply with your desires,
But to make it more pleasant, voice of wisdom speaks:
Let us reduce ten years to just several weeks,
Or even, to calculate in more exact ways,
110 Why wait ten long years, let us do it in two days!
For if, as in my case, love does not bring success,
Different flow of days, different time's progress:
Moments change to months, hours to days, days to years,
That's how unhappy lovers complain of time's curse!

(Podstolina is smiling)

115 What's this look in your eyes that are inclined to smile?

Podstolina

How can one not laugh hearing nonsense of this style!
Whatever I tell you, I tell it seriously:
While your answers are always given jokingly.
My young subprefect, these are not traits of love's fire,
120 A true lover doesn't treat this way his heart's desire!
He who loves attempts not to part from his idol,

Franciszek Zabłocki

Wants to be like her, to hold her as his model,
To think alike and to feel in the same manner--
Almost to unite two persons in one nature.
125 But please do not assume that these words of advice
Could apply to me, my good sir, at any price!

Notes

1. Fop signed a promissory note to be paid during the annual Lwów fair held in January (thus the day of January 6, the day of Epiphany). After 1774, there was another fair in Dubno in the district of Lublin, which Fop was planning to attend.
2. A proponent of the school of philosophy, founded at Athens by Antisthenes (c. 440 B.C.), who was interested principally in the practical side of morality.
3. The magnate family of Firlej was well-known for its grants and charitable donations. The church shelter mentioned here must have been founded by a Firlej.
4. The Olkusz silver mines which prospered in the sixteenth century were ruined during the Swedish wars and were never restored. The famous salt mines of Wieliczka were administered by the Austrians after the partition of Poland
5. *Notandum*--'one should note.'
6. Jacob served fourteen years to receive Laban's daughter Rachel for his wife. After their marriage, he served in Laban's house for seven years more. (Genesis 29:30).

Text: Kostkiewiczowa and Goliński, *Świat poprawiać,* 304, 305.
Zabłocki, Franciszek. *Fircyk w zalotach.* 3rd ed. Ed. by Janina Pawłowiczowa. Wrocław: Ossolineum, 1965, 48-52, 78-80.

HUGO KOŁŁĄTAJ (1750-1812)

Born in Dederkały in Volhynia, Kołłątaj grew up in Nieciesławice, a village near Sandomierz, which his father took as security and later inherited. He attended school in Pińczów and in 1761 moved to Cracow. He studied philosophy at the Cracow Academy, from 1771 to 1774 read law in Vienna and then theology, especially moral sciences, mostly in Rome. After his return to Cracow, he was ordained a priest in 1775. In 1776, Kołłątaj began to work for the Society for Elementary Books and then was given the task of reforming the Cracow Academy, serving as its chancellor from 1783 to 1786. In 1786 Kołłątaj settled in Warsaw, associated himself with the patriotic group, and became involved in political reforms of the country.

At the time of the Four-Year Sejm, he founded a group of politicians and publicists, called by its opponents Kołłątaj's Forge, that formulated a reform program. In his *Several Letters by the Anonym* (1788-1789) and *Political Law of the Polish Nation* (1789), Kołłątaj presented a radical program of reorganizing social, educational, and state institutions. In the memorial *To the Illustrious Deputation* (1789), addressed to the Sejm and the King, Kołłątaj advocated new political and economic laws for the burghers and plebeians. He was a co-author of the Constitution of May 3, 1791 and rallied Warsaw burghers in its support. Decorated with the Order of the White Eagle and holding the office of Vice Chancellor of the Crown, Kołłątaj coordinated the task of reforming the state. When King Stanisław August joined the Confederacy of Targowica, Kołłątaj, who supported the King's decision, left Poland, returned in 1794, and took part as minister of the treasury in the Kościuszko Insurrection. Arrested by the Austrians, he spent from 1794 to 1802 in jail, from where he wrote to Kościuszko: "I live as if I were to die tomorrow, I think as if I were to live yet a whole century." After his release, he continued to write, but was not allowed to participate in political activities.

To Stanisław Małachowski, Crown Referendary, Speaker of the Sejm and of the General Confederation, Several Letters by the Anonym

Ninth Letter, November 28, 1788
(selections)

(...)
There is still a lot left to be improved in the Commission for Education.[1] Honored by the Republic with highest executive power, composed of bishops and laymen, the Commission should have the highest and sole authority over all types of education in the country. It should know how to educate a priest or a monk, it should provide him with appropriate rules, it should take the School of Cadets under its supervision so that the young men polishing their skills to become good soldiers remembered to keep close bonds with the citizens, and even if a variety of denominations or rites divided people in their opinions, the Commission should try its best so that public education united them in one civic spirit, in one allegiance to the Homeland. Whatever the denomination and rite of a person educated in the public schools, he should be under the supervision of the Commission for Education, and the Commission should prescribe the same rules for all types of education.

What to say about the enlightenment of the common people, for whom the parish school is the beginning of education and an enlightened rector the most dependable guide to lead them out of darkness?[2] If only today's legislators recognized the importance of this great good for mankind and Homeland! There is no way in which our country could ever grow in conduct, wealth, power, and character, if the common people in towns and villages were not enlightened by good shepherds according to human needs and the national law. The Commission for Education undertakes efforts which are not indifferent towards parish schools, but what can be accomplished in these frequent governmental quarrels? Stronger decrees of law are needed for it, it is required that in all its educational directives our clergy be in agreement with the Commission. Sacredness of religion and the prerogative of the clerical estate will not be infringed upon at all, when bishops sit in this magistracy. If one wants to do good for the common people, it is necessary that he is listened to, and that

XXXII. Stanisław Małachowski

all his commands are executed. The Commission for Education, which not only had bishops,[3] but also used the clergy for instruction, mainly in the Elementary Society[4] as well as throughout the teaching profession, would have for sure brought more visible results, if it had not had to struggle with different opinions, if it had found more power in the law and more compliance by the clergy.[5]

An enlightened legislator who takes to heart these important needs of national education can easily notice what relationship should exist between the Commission for Education and our clergy. I mentioned above that I will speak separately about matters concerning the clergy. I will make only a brief remark here that for a good government a close agreement between the Commission for Education and the clergy is essential, for if there are any benefits that the government could put to a double use, they can be seen best in the clerical and educational functions. The clergy's goal is to enlighten people, so that their conduct is directed to the revealed religion, and they put this conduct into practice. The goal of the Commission for Education established in the Republic's territories is to enlighten a person so that he becomes a good citizen. He who is not a good citizen is not a pupil of Christ's school; he who drowned out in himself the voice of conscience, who takes for nothing the sacred rules of religion is not a good citizen. That is why the Commission should use as many clerical people as possible for public education; but it does not mean that it should use them without any selection. The clergy are divided into two groups, that is lay and monastic. The lay clergy, employed in parishes or administration of parishes, divided into dioceses, and used to serve citizens, are fully bound to the national law, and if we find any fault with them, it is caused in general by the neglect of education, carelessness of superiors or unskillful discharge of duties in such important offices. The monastic clergy, quite different from the lay clergy in their discipline and monastic vows as well as in their independence from the national authorities,[6] even though not antagonistic to the government, are still harmful in education, because they owe allegiance to their superiors in foreign countries and in matters of opinion become obedient to the will of their superiors to such a degree that to disobey a guardian, abbot, provincial, let alone general, is a bigger sin for a monk than to disobey a bishop or local authorities. Humility and outward appearance[7] bring the highest glory to the monastic order. One would be mistaken, however, if one assumed that a humble monk would not proudly spurn the commands of local authorities, when they were not in agreement with those of his superiors. (...)

What to say about the education of the female sex?[8] One half of the human community is completely forgotten in education. Through cheap imitation, girls' boarding schools proliferated in the capital city. The new trend endangered morals, good form dictated that noblemen's daughters were to be actresses, elegant dancers, and to put it briefly, by sending these innocent victims to the capital for education, we want to destroy the old morals of the nation. We occupy ourselves with the education of the female sex so that they entertain us or flirt, not thinking at all they should looked after our character and morals, that they strengthen our manliness, and give support to a good government. Whoever thought so, apparently did not reflect on the steadfastness of the weak sex, which not being what the laws prescribed, was able anyway to prove that men become what women want them to become. It would be useless to discuss at length all the reasons for this. It is just enough to reflect on the needs of the human community to come across this important truth that the mothers of the Republic, mothers of the estate of knights, mothers of landowners and noblemen, should be excellently educated, should be of untainted morals, should be above all filled with love of civil liberties, for otherwise their descendants will not become what the law of the free government wants them to be. In this aspect, public education would derive great gains from the clergy. How many things could be achieved with so many endowments for the girls' convents! Having reached an agreement with the appropriate authorities, one could vest these endowments very well, and even relieve the distress of these poor victims, who did not know the inconstancy of their own hearts.

Notes

1. Kołłątaj is writing about the Commission for National Education.
2. Parish schools educated peasants' children.
3. Two bishops were original members of the Commission, two more joined it later.

4. The Society for Elementary Education was established by the Commission in 1775 for the purpose of systematic preparation of textbooks for the new progressive school programs.

5. In the Commission schools the majority of teachers were the clergymen, in general opposed to the new teaching methods and the spirit of nonreligious philosophy.

6. Some monastic orders were independent of Polish bishops, as they owed allegiance to Rome. Their generals lived in Rome and took orders only from the pope.

7. Monks were expected to observe strict rules of their holy orders.

8. Schools for girls were established in Poland in 1745. The issue of women's education was discussed at length by the Commission. In 1775, Adam Czartoryski published a set of rules for private boarding schools. One of them, the Congregation of Canonesses (Zgromadzenie kanoniczek), a school for girls from noblemen's families, required that young women lived in a community under a rule, but was lay in character.

To the Illustrious Deputation Appointed by the Sejm to Prepare the Draft Constitution of the Polish Government [1]
(selections)

(...)
The measure of enlightenment was the measure of good or bad legislation in all ages, but the way law was passed on to common people was always different in all nations and ages. Some employed hypocrisy for that purpose, a tool which is the source of vileness and subjugation of human beings, while others walked openly carrying the truth in their hands. Hypocrisy was always attempting to deceive people and if not successful in muffling the truth, it took the sword in its hands and spilling human blood tried first to make man a slave, before he brought himself to obey its law. These are the sources of despotism under which dejected mankind groans, these are the common causes of misery and oppression. Throughout countless ages the hypocrite was capable of subjecting people to his cruel and unrighteous will, while the lawgiver of the truth never found it necessary to arm himself against a man for whose happiness he wrote laws; on the contrary, he exposed himself, not the common people whom he wanted to make happy, to oppression and thousands of blows.

Rising above himself, despising the tyrant's cruelty and hypocrisy, he was able to make the people and their descendants happy. But he was unable to accomplish such a sacred and almost godly work in any other way but by sacrificing himself. That was the road taken in Europe by Socrates,[2] the teacher of human conduct, in Asia by Jesus Christ, the lawgiver and Redeemer of the whole world. (...)

Elected statesmen! This is a model for you, this is the road along which your names are to be carried to immortality. Do you have enough courage? Are you brave enough to be worthy to deliver the truth to the Polish nation? Do not concern yourselves with your contemporaries, it is not this corrupt age that is to bless your names. You indeed are to give battle to prejudice and hypocrisy, you are to restore justice, you are to resolve general chaos, and therefore you should fully prepare yourselves against calumny, hatred and vengeance, which will be brought to bear upon you by private interests, corruption of human hearts, and depraved audacity. Yet do not fear that your laws will be spurned or rejected. The truth will have its adherents, they will spread throughout the nation, they will carry it under the thatched roof of the oppressed and despised man, time will do the rest. It is up to you not to abandon the truth nor think in what way this sacred deity will rule universally over the nation. Therefore I trust that in ordinance of your laws there will be no room either for artful hypocrisy or for base fear and still less for injustice associated with private gains. Man and his security, a citizen and his happiness, the homeland and its integrity will be the only principle in your labors.

But prudence, the most noble attribute of the human reason, will probably make you inclined to think, on account of vast knowledge and long experience, that the time has not yet come to disclose the truth in all its fullness to the Polish nation. Yet the same prudence never permits to entertain such despondent thoughts, as its service in legislation is necessary only to find the means of telling the truth to the people, and not for the purpose of concealing it from them for a time or for breaking the laws of justice and humanity on account of prejudice. There is no time or consideration of a time in which it would be appropriate to violate the rights of man or not to restore them if they were already violated. That nation cannot call itself free where man is unhappy, that country cannot be free where man is enslaved. Therefore no legislation should pass over the rights of man in silence, no society may sacrifice some people for other people. Such prudence would be called either injustice or fear. For to say that the unenlightened people cannot have their rights restored to them in their entirety, is to speak against the rules of rightness and prudence, for there is no case, excepting infirmity of years and senses, in which man could lose his rights. Even a minor or madman is under a protection of human beneficence, and only a criminal may be a slave of the society. The destiny which happens to come to man is a matter of chance, while the feeling of his heart results from his natural rights. Whoever tries to put the yoke of slavery upon an unenlightened man, may he turn to his own heart, may he ask himself whether he would consent to be deprived of his natural rights, to be deprived of his personal security and of his property, if chance placed him among the common people? Can we really say that the gentry, to whom Polish laws guarantee not only freedom, but also equality in governing, is universally enlightened? What are these splendid names whose descendants must seek food on a piece of useless land or from a magnate's annuity? Their poverty is the evidence of unenlightenment and their freedom to influence the government of the nation is and always was a game played by the leading magnates. Such prudence then which does not want to restore the rights of man to an individual only because he is not enlightened would be just as hard and unjust as that prudence which for the very same reasons would rob the impoverished nobleman of his civil rights.

True, not only Poland commits such injustice. The Muscovite state, Bohemia, some French and Spanish provinces, have maintained the same cruelty towards the common people. The French isles, Dutch and English colonies treat much more cruelly the Negroes, these unfortunate inhabitants of two worlds, whose tear-besprinkled products serve to enrich the elegant Europeans' cuisine and comfort. But can one justify the violation of the law of nature by injustice in other countries and by inveterate prejudice? Is it possible to suppress the pangs of conscience while human nature is so clearly wronged? Is it not enough for the common people in their poverty that they are exposed to the greediness of lords and cruelty of lawlessness? Is it still necessary to make them objects of sophisms and victims of injustice? I cannot understand how Mr. Linguet[3] dared to take under consideration such a major matter and support the legal enslavement of the common people, equaling them with purchased cattle, whose welfare is assured by the owner's great care. Philosophers! You that persecute bigotry, that write against numerous cruelties caused by false and fleeting zeal, why do you write so little against the legal enslavement of people who are equal to you? Why do you not rise against such great wrongs which man does to man with the help of law?

What does it mean to be the subject of someone's landed estate? How is he to be regarded in the natural order of things, in which Providence wanted everyone to be equal? Whether he is a white or black slave, whether he is groaning under the oppression of unjust laws or in chains--he is a human being in no way different from us. Whether in Europe or in any other part of the world, he is an equal citizen of the earth and can boldly address everybody with these words of Terence: "Homo sum, humani nihil a me alienum puto."[4] You that desire to have me for your slave, take a look at me and at yourself, examine if Nature intended me to be in any way different from you! *Homo sum.* You that insist on freedom, take into consideration your feelings and mine, take measure of yourself and feel shame in your heart that in this land, under the government, under which you secure freedom for yourself, you want me to be your slave. *Humani nihil a me alienum puto.* If the work, which bound me closer to the soil, and my poor nourishment provided for your luxuries and splendors, you owe me gratitude and justice for them; and if you pay me back with enslavement, it is not me but you who are not a human being. You are a monstrosity of human nature, you drown out in yourself the voice of reason and feeling, and having torn away freedom from a being equal to yourself, you will be a slave of your own or a tyrant's passions.

The misery of human beings grows in proportion to their enslavement. A republic does not allow for the rule of individuals, in a monarchy there is only one ruler, but in a feudal aristocracy almost every peasant has a different despot. What kind of government do we desire in our country? Do we want a true republic or the rule of magnates? Do we want to restore freedom to Poland or only to some families ruling over the rest of the slaves? Let us do whatever we want; nature itself will take vengeance on us for such an evident injustice. The common people will then be, as they have been until now, the property of the squires, but the gentry will without fail become the common people and the same sophisms which we use today, contrary to our own hearts in order to drown out the voice of truth, will serve our greedy neighbors to make slaves of us. They will say: "Poles are a barbarian nation, they cannot agree among themselves, they cannot obey the law, they cannot institute for themselves a good national law, they desire freedom, but do not know much about it, they are despots over common people, but do not wish to tolerate any rule over themselves. Drunkenness, bribery, meanness, vengeance, recklessness rule over their deliberations, therefore they are not worthy of the freedom they possess. They have already shown that in the partitioned provinces they can be slaves, so it is necessary to make them into the creatures they are capable of being, for this land feeds millions of people, and only a handful remains as a meretricious aristocracy."[5] Is it possible that this monarch or his ministers could be right, making such malicious and scornful accusations? Wouldn't it sting our feelings to the quick ? Who could bear such humiliating shame? And yet the wrong done to the Polish nation in this way would not differ at all from the wrong we do to other people.

A free man sharpens his intellect, eagerly takes care of his needs; enslavement deprives him of the gift of understanding, of thinking about himself and other people. "When Jove--says Homer--brings enslavement to man, he at once takes away from him half of his mind"[6]--and indeed, dullness and debilitation are much more useful in enduring poverty. Heaven lends them to the slave as a gift needed in his state. How can we reprove the subjugated common people when all these charges are, I say, a natural result of their poverty and enslavement? Can't we compare them to the existence and capability of the free men that we can find in many provinces in spite of the national law? Can't we compare them to ourselves after all? They are people just as we are and they will be what we are, if they are free.

(...)

But would it not be better first to educate the common people in order to prepare them prudently for the acceptance of the sacred gift of freedom? It would not, I answer. Truly he would be the most cruel lawgiver who would expect people to be educated in order to grant them freedom. There is nothing more terrible in human nature than an enlightened slave; then he feels then the entire oppressive weight of injustice and thinking only of regaining his natural rights, he turns all his thoughts to revenging himself upon the one who until then unjustly held his inheritance, setting his heart on fire so that it could dare to carry out the harshest acts of vengeance. Let no one be surprised by the cruelty of the people about which we may have happened to hear or read, for the fruit whose father is oppression and mother is enslavement must surpass in venom and cruelty anything rapacious and deadly that we can imagine. Let us hasten to restore to the people what nature provided for them. The enlightened people will claim what is theirs, but the unenlightened will be a tool of the hypocrite and the despot who strip us of our liberties. The less we are ready to remedy the situation during today's changes, the more certain we may be that either we or our descendants will become the victims of the people's despair and vengeance. (...)

I will say boldly that it is no longer possible to rely on temporary and limited reform. We know too well the results of these feeble changes which so many times permitted the country to be ruined and destroyed, but never brought it happiness. This is already the fifth time during this reign[7] that we undertake to reform the government and for the fifth time we will be deceiving ourselves, if we do not do it thoroughly, if we are not bold enough to surrender to the rule of the truth. This is the most excellent time to use your authority with the nation, this is an opportunity to bring to test the bravery of your mind and will, now is the time, if you desire the true welfare of your Homeland or if you want to bring about fruitful results. Fear and base reliance on the future to fulfill what you are feeling today will only bring about a new fall for the entire nation. Despair will settle in, despair most cruel in its consequences, and if the legitimate power will not choose to arrange these matters rightly and justly, blind vengeance, without order, without consideration for the entire political system, may run its full course. Blind Samson,[8] pulling down the whole building, killed himself, this is true, but the rubble falling on his head buried the whole community.

Notes

1. The deputation, more exactly a Sejm commission to improve the organization of the government, was appointed on September 7, 1789. It was headed by Bishop Adam Krasiński.

2. Socrates (470-399 B.C.) was considered in the eighteenth century not only a great philosopher, but also a most decent human being.

3. Simon Linguet (1736-1794) was a French political writer.

4. A quote from *Heauton Timorumenos* by Publius Terentius (Terence, ca. 190-150 B.C.): "I am a human being and I think nothing human is alien to me."

5. Kołłątaj's footnote points to the *Oeuvres posthumes* (1788-89) by Frederick II, King of Prussia, as the source of these negative opinions.

6. *The Odyssey,* XVII, 322-323. More accurately: "And broad-seeing Zeus takes away half the excellence of a man, from the time the day of slavery comes upon him." (Tr. and ed. by Albert Cook. New York: W.W. Norton & Co., 1974.)

7. The author refers to various reforms of 1764-66, 1768, 1773-75, and 1776.

8. Samson was a Hebrew hero who wreaked havoc among Philistines by using his great strength (Judges 13:24-16:31)

Political Law of the Polish Nation
(selection)

Book I

containing the fundamentals of legislation and government or otherwise cardinal laws, *materias status*,[1] as well as the general laws of the people born in the territories of the Republic, residents and newcomers.

Chapter I

CARDINAL LAWS BASED ON THE LAW OF NATURE

1

Every man born in the territories of the Republic, resident or newcomer, is free. He is allowed according to God's laws and the laws of this country to use his powers and his possessions as he considers best for himself. No man can seize another man by himself or in collusion with others, nor help someone else to do it, nor all the more to harm his fellow man's in possessions, person or life.

2

Every man may seize a malfeasor in the very act, that is: a murderer, a violator, an assailant, a thief, the one who would set something on fire, a rebel against the national government, and should immediately turn in such malefactors to the courts.

3

All agreements concluded among people, whether they are born in the territories of the Republic, residents or newcomers, so long as these agreements are not against God's laws and the laws of this country, should be preserved.

4

Neither parents for their offspring nor guardians for the minors are allowed to make any agreements or promises concerning anything that pertains to the freedom of their persons and damage done to their movable or real property.

5

Every man who owns land property is its legal and single master as far as the boundaries of his estate reach. On this land, he is allowed to make use of all means of production to increase his income and comfort, so long as it is done without any harm to his neighbor; he is allowed to make agreements with the people who have settled on his land or intend to settle there, and when he comes to terms with them, he should keep these agreements.

6

Every man born in the territories of the Republic, resident or newcomer, who does not have any plot of ground on the squire's own land, whether he has settled or intends to settle, when he agrees with the squire as to duties, labor or rent, should fulfill faithfully all obligations he has taken upon himself in the agreement, and not avoid under the guise of personal freedom what he has taken on himself.

7

All people born in the territories of the Republic, residents or newcomers, are only subject to the law of this country and are not allowed to recognize any other rule above themselves, but the rule of the law and the protection of the Republic.

8

The entire land, which constitutes the land of the Republic, is a land of free people.

9

Don't do unto others what is not agreeable to you, and what you want to be done to you, do unto others.

Notes

1. Cardinal laws are the foundation of the entire legislation, while *materias status* are the foundation of the entire government.

Text: Kołłątaj, Hugo. *Listy Anonima i Prawo polityczne narodu polskiego.* Vol. II. Ed. by Bogusław Leśnodorski and Helena Wereszycka. Warszawa: PWN, 1954, 88-94, 163-190, 215-217.

STANISŁAW STASZIC (1755-1826)

A son of the mayor of Piła in Great Poland, Staszic was educated in a seminary in Poznań, became a priest, but never performed any religious duties. He considered religion to be a means of oppression and was critical of the Church and the clergy. Unable to aspire to high offices on account of his plebeian origin, Staszic devoted himself to science. He studied in Leipzig and Göttingen, then at the Collège de France in Paris, where he came under the influence of the naturalist Buffon, whose *Epochs of Nature* he translated into Polish (1786), and of Jean Jacques Rousseau. After his return to Poland, he found employment as a tutor of the children of Andrzej Zamoyski, a former Chancellor.

In his two major works, *Remarks on the Life of Jan Zamoyski* (1787) and *Warnings for Poland* (1790), Staszic critically evaluated the condition of the country and formulated a program of radical reforms. He called for the union of small gentry and burghers against aristocracy and for improvement of the peasants' lot. In 1801 he settled in Warsaw, where he founded the Society of the Friends of Learning, which later became the Polish Academy of Sciences, and the Agricultural Society, whose main goals included increased production, improved cultivation of soil, and development of agricultural markets. He carried out pioneering research on the geology of the Carpathian Mountains and described the flora and fauna of the Tatras. He also translated Homer and Voltaire, and wrote a historico-philosophical poem *The Human Race* (1819-1820), in which he described the principal stages in the development of human societies.

XXXIII. The Senators' Hall in the Royal Castle of Warsaw during the proclamation of the Third of May Constitution, 1791

Remarks on the Life of Jan Zamoyski,[1] Chancellor and Grand Hetman of the Crown, adapted to the current situation in the Polish Republic
(selections)

Education

(...)
And since a man is most likely to harm another man, therefore according to the natural order of things the citizen's education should allow him first to get to know these people with whom he has to live. I call this *moral* knowledge.

And I say it once and for all that human nature warns *that throughout education theory should be combined with practice.* It is useless to torment children by teaching them what they are incapable of doing. Therefore all those theories which cannot be used in practice should be left out from *general teaching* and be seized upon only by more outstanding minds.

A guarantee of moral education is provided by teaching a *history of the country.* Each citizen should learn it first. A child that opens his eyes for the first time should see nothing except his Homeland, for which alone it will be his duty to close them one day. The first book he takes in his hand should be a history of those people with whom he has to live. (...)

National history should be taught first. A citizen, whose first and most vivid images pertain to his Homeland, will think about it more often--in this way he will love it more. Then one should teach history of neighboring states, that is those which are next to our own. Only at the end--and not necessarily everyone-- should read the history of remote times and states.

But just as the first place in education is occupied by moral teaching, so in moral teaching the basic principle should be constituted by *religion.* It teaches man of his relation to God. It alone threatens everyone, even the one who is above human truths, that when he intends to harm other people, he resists God's will and eternal order, for which he will be punished.

While learning to know about people with whom man must live, it is necessary to learn at the same time about the land which will feed him, its crops, and its animals. So *moral teaching* should go with *national geography, national history, natural history of one's district, arithmetic, and practical geometry.*

This type of information is absolutely necessary for each citizen and those subjects should be taught in the best and most common schools of the country.

Because man does not now depend directly on the crops of the land for clothing and food, the citizen's further education should teach him how to increase his country's bounty, improve its fruits, adapt them to his needs and comforts, and protect them from an attack by a neighboring nation. Therefore in the second type of schools in the country one should teach *history of the neighboring states, national laws, elocution, and financial topics*, through which a young mind will not only get used to comparing expenditures with income, but will also get to know the origin of all resources, will learn of a relationship and need for all conditions--*nation's natural history, chemistry*--applying them mostly to crops and country's needs--*experimental physics, surgery, mathematics*--not purely theoretical, but with applications to *military architecture or civil architecture, to mechanics*.[2]

To this type of school would belong, if the Republic could afford it, the School of Crafts and Trades.[3]

In the third and last type of schools one could offer those subjects which require imagination and intelligence in order to understand, perform, and perfect them. These subjects should be given in their generality, with full theory. One should, if possible, combine it with applications and avoid like pestilence the spirit of taxonomy. *General history, common law, politics in its general aspect, versification, astronomy, natural history, chemistry, physics, and medical science* will be taught in the last, excellent Main School.[4]

Notes

1. Jan Zamoyski (1542-1605), Chancellor and enlightened reformer, was the patron of arts and letters, and founder of Zamość.

2. Staszic is talking here about descriptive geometry, advocated in the program of the Commission for National Education.

3. The aim of this school was to prepare a well trained labor force for newly created manufacturing companies.

4. Main Schools were universities reformed by the Commission for National Education.

Warnings for Poland

To the Lords
(selections)

(...)
I will speak out on who does harm to my Homeland.

The perdition of Poland is caused by the big lords alone! They destroyed all respect for law. They, unwilling to suffer the rule of law, deprived it of executive power. They destroyed completely the idea of justice in the minds of the Poles. They turned law into an empty formality, valid only when it served their pride, greediness, and wrath.

In a country where the law is a tool of wrongdoing, the republic of citizens changes into the republic of plunderers, traitors, perjurers, mercenaries. The result is that from the smallest official up to the Throne, the one who dares to commit the greatest offenses sits in the highest place.

Who teaches the citizens treason, deceit, vileness, and cruelty at the dietines? The lords. Who cheats, bribes, and turns into drunkards the innocent gentry, who most decently and most sincerely wish the best for their Homeland? The lords. Who, for a century, made the legislative power inactive and broke the Sejm sessions? The lords. Who turned the courts of law into a market of justice or a place of drunkenness, bribery, and violence? The lords. Who has been selling the crown? The lords. Who has been buying the crown? The lords.

Who brought foreign armies into the country? The lords.

Who by their unwise and unbridled self-interest and pride tore away the tribe of valiant Cossacks from Poland and forced them to become her enemies?[1] The lords.

Who for a period of time, pretending to make the Sejm active again, changed the will of the Nation into the will of the Moscow Court?[2] The lords. Who was selling the Poles? The lords. Who during the partition was taking foreign payments?[3] The lords. Who during this Sejm prevented reforms of the army planned by the Military Commission? The lords.

Yes, indeed: the lords brought our beloved Homeland to this degree of decline, weakness, and contempt, from which today the petty gentry alone are trying to lift it up with great effort, in spite of the obstacles put in their way by the very same lords.

Immoral, reckless, greedy and wasteful, proud and despicable, all their passions unbridled, the lords in Poland destroyed the power of laws. One marriage, one rich widow, one office, bishopric, starost[4] title not awarded according to their intentions, quite often an opinion held against them, a word not according to their desire, sent them into frenzy against a nobleman or another lord. Just to satisfy their pride, just to have their revenge, they were even ready to bring the Republic to ruin. First, looking for popular topics, although most harmful to the nation, they gained followers among the gentry by treacherous flattery; soon from one country they made two nations. Immediately, the dietines turned into an armed mob under two ringleaders. The servants of two lords, not the representatives of the nation, went to the Sejm, Tribunals[5] did not mete out justice, but demonstrated who was stronger that year.

The family[6] that led a majority of the gentry, having the most people at each assembly, held in their hands all elections, legislative power, and all courts of law. Not that was taken into consideration which was most conducive to the public good, but that which hurt an adversary or satisfied a particular need. Not he who possessed merits, virtue, and required knowledge took office, but he who most tarnished his life and conscience. Not he who presented law to the judge was assured justice, but he who gave him the lord's letters. Indeed, without the will of the more popular family one was prevented from becoming not only an official, but could not even be a parson, canon, dean, provincial,[7] reader, prior or monastery superior. God forbid if any nobleman had dared to uphold the law, the common good--indeed, if he opposed any of those braggarts, he would be lucky if he were not cut to pieces on the spot, and surely from that time on his life would not be safe either on the road or at home. Soon he would receive summons and documents that he owned a village that belonged to someone else. Therefore everything would grovel before towering pride. He who wanted to maintain peace, possessions, and justice, submitted to the lord's power.

Parents made even innocent children become used to baseness. They taught them to be mean, destroyed their will and pride so necessary for a free man. Every day they demonstrated the wicked methods by which they dishonestly acquired their fortunes in the lords' service. The clergy in their teaching, preachers from the pulpit, teachers in schools exerted themselves at every public occasion in praise of the virtue, citizenship, and justice of those who committed the worst sins, abuses, and crimes. A nobleman brought up in this way had no will of his own. He did not feel his own soul.

The Pole had lost completely the idea of justice and law. All people repeated: "Tribunals, County and Castle Courts, Dietines and Diets" and because they were allowed to repeat these words, and based their freedom on them, they did not know at all the substance of these decrees. Seeing that all originates with power, they were not offended by anything which was achieved by treason or violence. In this way, a bigger part of the gentry, accustomed to the lawlessness of vices and wrath, lost their shame and even the feeling of being a tool of their lords' vices.

And the family[8] which was less popular among the gentry, unable to destroy an adversary, transformed its anger into the hatred of its own Nation. They began to mock everything that existed in Poland, scorned local manners, scoffed at the national custom, and called the nobleman's simplicity and sincerity plain 'Sarmatism.' They abandoned the Polish costume, filled their houses with foreigners. They infused their children's upbringing with a hatred of the Poles, took them around to foreign countries, tried to persuade them into believing that Polish attire and language were the attire and language of nonsense. I myself, always with a justified contempt for such Poles, looked at those ignoble parents' sons, now advanced in years, who received everything from Poland, but could not speak Polish.

But it would be less harmful if those malicious families had left the dislike of their Homeland only to their children. They filled all who were attached to their houses with hate towards the country, prepared young and old minds for foreign influence. In this way, they changed another group of Poles into enemies of Poles. Without substance, light, and virtue--such a tainted nobleman was neither warm nor cold, neither a German nor a Frenchman nor an Italian nor an Englishman-- he had in himself a bit from all nations. He was in Poland, but had no Homeland. He called himself a citizen, but was an enemy of the Republic.

The infamous pride of that mighty house was not appeased by this transformation of Poles into enemies of Poland. In order to wreak vengeance, in order to oppress their adversaries, paying no regard that they were ruining the country, they called in a foreign army on one occasion.[9] They came to all public sessions with that army, made promises and threatened everyone with a

Moscow footlogger, gave out money, promised offices, guaranteed property or its loss. They recruited under their sign of violence the majority of gentry and again instilled a new infamy in their minds. Those who could not be deceived or did not fear threats, they took under guard; they expelled others from the country, they aimed their cannons at still others and killed them, they destroyed by fire the possessions of all who defended the law and killed them. When the majority was already under Russian guard, they surrendered Tribunals, Dietines, and Diets to the foreign soldier.

The foreigner went further. He took and partitioned the country. (...)

Notes

1. An allusion to the abuses of some Polish magnates in the Ukraine and to the Polish-Cossack wars in the seventeenth century.
2. The adherents of Russia among Polish aristocracy, e.g., some members of the Czartoryski family.
3. During the first partition of Poland by Russia, Prussia, and Austria in 1772, many magnates, including Adam Poniński and King Stanisław Poniatowski, were accused of accepting bribes.
4. A starost was the head official in a district.
5. Tribunals were courts of appeal.
6. This is a reference to the activities of the Potocki family during the Saxon period.
7. A provincial was the head of monasteries in a province.
8. The author refers here to the Czartoryski family.
9. This is another allusion to the Czartoryskis during the interregnum in 1764.

Peasants' Lands or an Industrious Peasant

I have five classes[1] of the Polish nation before my eyes. I see millions of beings, some walking half naked, others covered with skins or coats of coarse cloth, all dried up, emaciated, hairy, covered with soot.[2] Their eyes are sunk deep. They breathe rapidly with asthmatic lungs. Gloomy, benumbed, and dull, they feel little and think little: that is their greatest fortune.

One can barely see a rational soul in them. At first sight their outward appearance resembles an animal more than a human being. 'Peasant'--this very name is most contemptuous. Their food is bread of coarse flour and during a quarter of a year consists of weeds,[3] their drink is water or the inside-burning vodka. Their lodging is dungeons or cabins barely raised above the ground; the sun's rays gain no entrance there. They are filled with stench and that benign smoke which deprives them of light so that they would look less at their poverty, so that they would suffer less, as it suffocates them day and night, shortening their miserable lives--and kills most in infancy. In this dark place of stench and smoke, the goodman, exhausted by his daily chores, sleeps on a rotten pallet. Next to him sleep his little, naked children, in the same place where the cow stands with its calf and the sow lies with its piglets ...

My good Poles! These are the pleasures of this group of people on whose shoulders rests the fate of your Republic! This is the man who feeds you! That is the condition of the farmer in Poland!

Notes

1. These classes were: peasants, burghers, clergymen, noblemen, and magnates.
2. Many a peasant cottage was just a chimneyless cabin with a hole in the roof for the smoke.
3. In the last weeks before the new harvest when grain was gone, some peasants used pigweed and moss in their diet.

Testament
(written in Warsaw on September 20, 1824)

Being strongly convinced that man's destiny on this earth is to do good, to attempt by the deeds of his whole life to improve the fate of his brothers, the fate of other people, and to even try by the results of his beneficent deeds to bring happiness to future generations, I have endeavored to fulfill this goal throughout my entire life. With this single intention, with constant thrift and economy, I have been accumulating the possessions which by this last will, as the laws permit me, I dispose as follows:

My hereditary estate of the town of Rubieszów and all villages that belong to it, inns, mills, ponds, forests, manorial farms, indeed everything which comprises the Rubieszów property and is my legal possession, I assign to the inhabitants of this community in order to make them happy, freeing them from all duties, tributes, and servitude, granting them land as inheritance, under the condition that they form an Agricultural Society to sustain each other in misfortunes, according to the statute, assigned to the said Society by me and accepted by the general consent of all inhabitants of this community and confirmed kindly by the Most Gracious Majesty.[1]

Notes

1. The statute of the Agricultural Society of Rubieszów was formulated in 1816 and confirmed by Alexander I in 1822.

Texts: Staszic, Stanisław. *Wybór pism.* Ed. by Celina Bobińska. Warszawa: Książka, 1948, 3-6, 130-131.
Staszic, Stanisław. *Przestrogi dla Polski.* Ed. by Stefan Czarnowski. Kraków: Krakowska Spółka Wydawnicza, Biblioteka Narodowa I 98, 1926, 76-81, 163-164.

JAKUB JASIŃSKI (1761-1794)

Jakub Jasiński was born in Węglew near Pyzdry in Great Poland. He received an excellent education at school, entered the Corps of Cadets at the age of twelve, and graduated in 1783. Promoted to the rank of colonel, he took part in the military campaign of 1792. In 1793 Jasiński joined the conspiracy movement in Wilno, led the Insurrection in Lithuania, and fell on the ramparts of Praga on November 4, 1794.

Jasiński's poetry ranged from sentimental lyrics to revolutionary poems, in which he called on the nation to fight for social justice. His 1794 poem *To the Nation*, written on the eve of the Kościuszko Insurrection, appealed to citizens' republican virtues and patriotic feelings. Only two of Jasiński's poems were published in his lifetime; the remaining ones were circulated in handwritten copies. His collected works were published in Cracow in 1869.

My Song

I am always calm, I am always gay,
I don't care about sorrow, toils, dismay,
Things go right or wrong, I am not ranting,
When happy I dance, when unhappy--sing.

5   Let my fate turn this or the other way,
Heartache or joy, rest or hard work all day,
Hunger or plague, peacetime or enmity,
Content in good times, calm in poverty.

Let misery hurt me, let hunger maul,
10 A moment of peace will reward it all,
When I hold in my fist what I wished for,
I will not cast back my eyes any more.

From a penniless peasant to a king,
All men in the world have worries that sting,
15 He who is free, joyful, also honest,
If he has good brains--will always be blest.

To the Nation

Nation once great, today in doleful circumstance,
Deprived of its strength, riches, fame, and confidence,
That once with its sword's might and learning distinction
Was for others a wonder, scourge, and paragon!
5 Under a yoke of shame, defeats, bondage today,
A plaything of the proud to wantonness fell prey.
You, that could subdue foreign nations with your sword,
Look at the outcome of your domestic discord!
After long sorrow, with an enlightened spirit,
10 You began to rebuild your famed house with best grit
And your unworthy neighbor could then see with fright
What the Poles could be, when in freedom they unite.
Alas! How you fell short of your profound desire:
You flashed like a star, died out like a spark of fire!
15 For you were condemned to suffer many a sling,
Betrayed by a friend, brother, and your beloved king.
Why did not fate save you at least from the torment
And bring death by alien's sword, not by your own hand.
Nation! It's time not to trust any assurance,
20 You yourself hold seeds of fall or deliverance!
Don't mind you are now in heavy chains of serfdom,
Where men said: "We'll be free"--they always gained freedom!
Keep firmly in your mind the lessons from the West,
Tyrants are strong, yet people's power is greatest.
25 Arise and try your hand, if it still has the might
To wield the sword once used to carry on a fight,
You'll learn what you tried not to learn: in your defense
There are arms, there are hearts, and counsels of prudence!
But learn well that before fate tells you to progress,
30 A lot of concord is needed, more hopelessness.
He, who controls the fate of nations and all men,
Will once more create a ray of light for you then,
If you one more time will lose this moment of chance,
You won't be worthy of favor, of resurgence.
35 Here are two nations,[1] souls worthy of each other,
That join their brothers' hearts in a bond forever,
Soon they will show to the world by their brave actions
What the truth's light can do, what ire and distortions.
But you at this time under an alien power
40 Are waiting, till they stretch out a hand by favor,

And still able to use the remnants of your grit,
You would take out of mercy what you could merit!
Motherland! My dear country! Aren't there for you then
Happiness on this earth and pity in heaven?
45 Under a dangerous ax, downcast forever,
Isn't a Pole able as well to die with honor?
By God, is this a pleasant dream or by day's light
Do I see arms in Polish hands for a great fight?
Go on, valiant young men, full of sacred virtue,
50 To avenge our oppression and our disgrace, too.
Go on, for motherland demands that your sword's blade
Polished off the raider and the one who betrayed!
In vain your sly soul threatens you with feebleness,
Only one thing can ruin you--your soft-heartedness.
55 Just know, virtue alone when not at the right time,
Can bring disgrace to your honor just as a crime.
You, father of great truth, father of your children,
When will your great day shine for us first time, pray when?
It is now time for the clenched fingers of your hand,
60 To pull us from shame, the nation from the deep strand.
Let your holy voice echoing through earth and sky
Tell us what we are and what we can do hereby,
And you, who wait for us, our worried motherland,
Know that you'll have no children or be a free land.

Notes

1. The author refers here to the United States and the revolutionary France.

Text: Kostkiewiczowa and Goliński, *Świat poprawiać*, 328, 336-338.

JULIAN NIEMCEWICZ (1758-1841)

Julian Niemcewicz's life spanned the last years of Poland's independence, the periods of three partitions, Kościuszko Insurrection, the Duchy of Warsaw, the Kingdom of Poland, and the November Insurrection of 1830. He participated actively in the major events of his times and recorded them in his writings.

Niemcewicz came from a nobleman's family in Skoki near Brześć in Lithuania. He was educated at the Military Academy in Warsaw (1770-1777), and served as adjutant of Prince Adam Kazimierz Czartoryski. In this function he travelled to Austria, Italy, France, and England as well as throughout Poland. In 1788 he became a deputy at the Four-Year Sejm, spoke eloquently in support of reforms and wrote plays (e.g., *Władysław at Varna*, 1787-1788, *Kazimierz the Great*, 1787-1788, *The Return of the Deputy*, 1791) and fables, which popularized the Sejm's programs. He also edited *The National and Foreign Gazette* (1791-1792), the first political periodical in Poland, whose goal was to popularize the program of the patriotic party. He wrote pamphlets against the Confederacy of Targowica, went to Italy, but returned to Poland and took part in the Insurrection as Kościuszko's secretary and aide-de-camp. Wounded at the battle of Maciejowice, he was imprisoned together with Kościuszko in the Petropavlosk fortress for two years. He was freed by Tsar Paul II in 1796 and travelled with Kościuszko to America, where he married and lived for many years (*Diaries of Travels Through America 1797-1807*). In 1807 Niemcewicz returned to Poland, served as Secretary of the Senate, and held important educational offices. He wrote *Historical Songs* (1816), in which he described the great men of Poland's illustrious past, and a three-volume *History of the Rule of Zygmunt III* (1818-1819), a continuation of Adam Naruszewicz's *History of the Polish Nation*. He also authored *The Two Gentlemen Sieciech* (1815), a novel in the form of two memoirs from different periods, *Lejbe and Siore* (1821), the first novel in Polish about Jewish life, written in the form of letters by star-crossed lovers, and *Jan of Tęczyn* (1825), a historical novel after the manner of Walter Scott.

Niemcewicz's patriotism and integrity earned him the title of "the moral dictator of Warsaw." During the November Insurrection, the seventy-two year old poet went to England on an unsuccessful mission to win Western powers' support for the Polish cause. In 1833 he settled in Paris, where he continued his political and cultural activities, and edited the *Diaries of My Days* (1848). He died there in exile.

Yearnings in Solitude

Happy is he who fond of his sanctuary
Divides his time as those who are most discerning,
Between sweet hope and affectionate memory,
    Between restful hours and learning.

5   Happy is he who falls asleep free from heart-sore
And does not fret dreaming what next day will offer,
Who is not put to sleep by an oppressive bore
    Or wakened by an intruder.

The Return of the Deputy

The protagonists of this popular political comedy, set in a country manor, are Valery, a patriotic deputy to the Four-Year Sejm, and Mr. Charming, a fashionable dandy, rivals for the hand of Teresa. The author mocks Teresa's step-father, Mr. Chatterbox, for his ignorance and pretense, his wife for her slavish imitation of foreign fashion and penchant for sentimental literature, and Mr. Charming for his shallowness and greed to acquire Teresa's dowry. In the end, Mr. Charming's real motive is exposed, and Valery is able to marry Teresa.

Act II, scene IV

Valery and Mr. Charming

Mr. Charming
his hair coiffed, with a large foulard and in an elegant dress coat, he throws himself at Valery and kisses him

Allow me, my good friend, to take you in my arms,
To kiss you and recall the sacred brotherhood,

Conceived fondly at the boarding school in boyhood.
It must be ages since we parted company,
During this time magnates changed Poland thoroughly,
When I came from abroad, I couldn't recognize her,
But how's that? I've been in this town the whole summer:
I did not see you?

Valery

I was quite disappointed;
Perhaps the parties, houses, where I attended
Were just not those places to which you would retreat.

Mr. Charming

At that time at Kolson's[1] I'd occupy a seat,
In Ujazdów Street. And during this hard work there
You did not go out to fish at least once somewhere?

Valery

Yes, it is true I really feel great dismay;
But my loss is repaired when I see you today.
And how long did you spend on your foreign travels?

Mr. Charming

Just a year, but I've adopted all their manners.
To tell the truth I couldn't stay here any longer:
First, father told me to toil on business matter,
Have cases heard at court, that's great pastime for you!
I'd rather lose property than see the case through.
In a year he had me in king's secretariat,
I left: I do not know how to keep a secret.
Then, testing my will for soldier's accomplishment,
Bought me a unit in infantry regiment;
That became boring as well. And yet Providence
Chose to take father to eternal residence.
When I saw I owned quite a sizable treasure,
At first I didn't know what to do in my pleasure ...

Adjusting his foulard and assuming a graceful position

30 It is true, God created man quite pleasantly,
But to shape this little figure accurately,
I wanted to visit Paris, so first I saw
That my estate was leased, and then left dear Warsaw.

Valery

So you found yourself in Paris during the days
35 Of the revolution,[2] when fire began to blaze?

Mr. Charming

This very commotion chased me from France away.

Valery

Just then in that country you should have tried to stay,
To look at the valiant nation, oppressed for years,
Which learned to know itself and tore off its fetters,
40 On ruins of tyranny raised a free government:
That was a view worthy of a sensible man.
I'm sure you tried to see and be in every place,
Pondered their decrees and even erroneous ways?

Mr. Charming

I'll confess to you: I don't know what happened then,
45 To me all of their deeds were of little concern.
Thank you for this famous freedom and those labors:
You won't believe the boredom that in Paris reigns.
Nothing in the world will make up for this grievance;
You will not see any girls, theatres, gardens,
50 Boulevards and amusement parks are one emptiness;
One has nothing to do, spends days in tediousness.
Once, I remember, I went to buy some buttons
For my crimson dress coat; merchants and artisans,
As if they were on purpose deprived of reason
55 Were standing guard[3] in town to keep order thereon;
It just made me so angry that as if on command,
I stirred about and went through Calais to England.

Valery

At least that famous country, so sensibly free,
Was able to attract your attention clearly?
60   Their government, factories, numerous decrees,
Did they keep you much longer?

Mr. Charming

                       Only three Sundays
I spent in England: the air is unhealthy, Sir,
I bought two pairs of buckles and a steel rapier;
I went to the Parliament: as here, shouting reigns,
65   On the other hand what stores, buttons, little chains,
Horse races! That's the world's best legal document!
Ah! My friend, what good fortune, what entertainment;
Which a foreigner should not miss whatsoever.
What a show it is! You rack your brains in order
70   To comprehend how some riders chase other men
On those horses, they just look like little children.
I remember well, one day I laughed in contempt,
An Englishman, in a small wig, quite corpulent,
Lost a massive bet; in an outburst of anger
75   Wanted to shoot the horse, luckily I enter
Give him a hundred pounds: and so I save this way
A poor thing from death, poor mare, a white legged bay.
Then, after buying many trifles for presents,
I returned at last to our homeland settlements.
80   When I was playing like that, you, covered with fame,
Constantly took care of the Republic's good name;
You toiled for a long time for civic works progress:
I congratulate laws, don't envy tediousness.

Valery

The friendship, about which you kindly informed me,
85   If it allows me to tell you the truth freely,
I'll say: this travelling which does not make much sense
Perhaps can be excused by age, inexperience.
From now on you should strive for a different goal:
Remember that you are a citizen, a Pole,
90   That first to the homeland your services belong.

Mr. Charming

Again to work for merit? This route is too long!
High offices, honors, in one word all desires,
Are easy to reach, when someone money acquires;
They will bow to me, although I will not labor.

Valery

95 They will bow to you, but won't respect you ever;
Only he is sure of respectful public place,
Who works honestly and who helps the human race:
But he won't reach it just idling his time away.

Mr. Charming

You want me to be a Sejm deputy today?
100 Get even more bored than all of you deputies?
Ah, my good Sir! I prefer health above all this.
Last summer, when you were at your convocations,
When all day long you toiled, uttered exclamations,
I, hair combed with powder and sweet-scented pomade,
105 Would get in my cariole[4] or on horse promenade
All over Mokotów, Wola, Królikarnia,
Łazienki, Powązki, at times Bażantarnia;[5]
In the evening I'd change, with cool breeze blowing in,
And with others scold the Sejm in Saxon Garden;[6]
110 I drank some punch with my friends out of big goblets,
I ate peaches, apricots for a few ducats,
Then about ten o'clock, ending the pleasant day,
Those amusements were through as darkness came to stay.

Valery

If all wished to live like that, what would Poland be?

Mr. Charming

115 I don't know what would come, but she would be merry!
Your opinions, Sir, are always too rigorous,
If your could just give me half of your steadiness!
But I hear you think of changing your condition,

That you're madly in love, soon will pop the question
120 To a beautiful, dowered, well-bred, honest dame.

Valery

I have just heard about you exactly the same.

Mr. Charming

By God, no, but my annoying family lot
Will not leave me in peace, want me to tie the knot.
What trouble it has been, what constant misery:
125 Here parents pull, there a young maid in love with me--
Nearly ready to force me; and what can I do!
Prepare to be a husband to solve the issue,
Let these countless pleas and sighs make me dutiful:
True, it's a misfortune to be born beautiful.

Valery

130 This grumbling designates a man of modesty;
Happy is he who complains just of his beauty.
You should be congratulated cordially then,
It seems you are the happiest out of all young men,
For without smallest efforts, as if by mere chance,
135 You can arouse in women sweet flames of romance.

Mr. Charming

Happiness has attached itself to my person,
But I have my methods, it ought to be let on:
And whoever wants to follow my rules elsewhere,
No woman will be able to elude his snare.
140 To prove that I do not count my praises in vain,
I will show you at once all I managed to gain,
Letters, portraits, locks of hair, signet rings, and bands:
From unmarried women, widows, someone's wife's hands.

3

    Young Bolesław, imbued with joyful zest,
        Soon reached for laurels with his hand,
    He devoted himself to armed contest,
        While serving, he learned to command.
    When trumpets call to battle, he's eager,
        He runs to the front of the ranks,
    He lies in ambush, bears cold and hunger,
        And in hardships he gains his strength.

4

    He counted with victories his young years,
        He subdued Rus', Pomerania,
    When he held the scepter of his father's,
        Henry, who then ruled Germania,
    Certain that with bands of hired partisans,
        He'll frighten the brave Polonians,
    Not knowing how this insult would offend,
        Demanded homage from Poland.

5

    "I to pay homage?--Bolesław's answer--
        I to suffer such dishonor!
    The Pole will not bow before a stranger,
        So long as he has arms, valor!
    Hundred times in bloody occupation
        I'll lose my crown and existence,
    Rather than bear disgrace of the nation
        And pay the odious allegiance."

6

    A bloody battle near Wrocław breaks out,[2]
        And in the air trumpets resound,
    The prince attacks, Germans suffer a rout;
        Piles of their knights lie on the ground;
    Howling terribly, packs of dogs of prey,
        Tear apart the bloody remnants,
    And all people call the place to this day,
        The Dogs' Field, for stern remembrance.

Notes

1. Madame Kolson was the owner of a fashionable restaurant in Warsaw.
2. Valery is speaking with approval about the French Revolution which began on May 5, 1789.
3. Mr. Charming makes a reference to the National Guard, citizens' militia in Paris.
4. Cariole was a light, two-wheeled, one-horse carriage.
5. These were suburban sites for outings, known for magnates' mansions and gardens.
6. The Saxon Garden is a park in the center of Warsaw.
7. Mr. Charming is calling his servant.

Historical Songs

Bolesław the Wrymouth
(born 1085, 1102-1138)

Historical Song

1

When Bolesław was still just a youngster,
    He strongly wished to reach for fame,
For when the king, to stop Czech intruder,
    Sent Sieciech[1] Moravia to claim,
5   The young prince, upon seeing the armed corps,
    Turned to his father and implored:
"Please let me also--he said--go to war,
    Let me learn how to use the sword."

2

Father, moved by Bolesław's eagerness,
10   Placed a helmet on his son's head,
Gave him sword, shield, golden armor with crest;
    "To defend your country--he said--
Use only these devices of the knight,
    Let them serve glory, not proud quest,
15   People will entrust the scepter outright,
    To him who will use the arms best."

3

Young Bolesław, imbued with joyful zest,
    Soon reached for laurels with his hand,
He devoted himself to armed contest,
    While serving, he learned to command.
When trumpets call to battle, he's eager,
    He runs to the front of the ranks,
He lies in ambush, bears cold and hunger,
    And in hardships he gains his strength.

4

He counted with victories his young years,
    He subdued Rus', Pomerania,
When he held the scepter of his father's,
    Henry, who then ruled Germania,
Certain that with bands of hired partisans,
    He'll frighten the brave Polonians,
Not knowing how this insult would offend,
    Demanded homage from Poland.

5

"I to pay homage?--Bolesław's answer--
    I to suffer such dishonor!
The Pole will not bow before a stranger,
    So long as he has arms, valor!
Hundred times in bloody occupation
    I'll lose my crown and existence,
Rather than bear disgrace of the nation
    And pay the odious allegiance."

6

A bloody battle near Wrocław breaks out,[2]
    And in the air trumpets resound,
The prince attacks, Germans suffer a rout;
    Piles of their knights lie on the ground;
Howling terribly, packs of dogs of prey,
    Tear apart the bloody remnants,
And all people call the place to this day,
    The Dogs' Field, for stern remembrance.

Notes

1. In 1092 or 1093, King Władysław Herman (1079-1102), father of Bolesław, sent Sieciech, the palace *comes* or *voivode*, from the family of Starża-Toporczyk, to Moravia. According to Gallus Anonymous, Sieciech and Bolesław "devastated a large part of Moravia, brought abundant booty and captives back from there, and returned with no accident on the battlefield or on the journey." (Mikoś, Michael, *Medieval Literature of Poland*. New York and London: Garland, 1992, p. 11).

2. In 1109, Bolesław won a victory over the German King Henry V and the Duke of Bohemia.

Funeral of Prince Józef Poniatowski[1]
(1763-1813)

Funeral Song

1

Back from battlefields and from fiery hail,
Faithful to the cause, under their banners,
A group of Poles walked slowly on the trail
    To their native shelters.

2

5   When people saw the white and red pennons
Fluttering in the wind as they passed by,
The whole town cried out in joyful response
    "Our men return thereby!"

3

Short lived their joy, each asking urgently:
10   "Where is our brave chief commendatory,
Who for a long time led us happily
    On the field of glory?"

XXXIV. Prince Józef Poniatowski

4

He can't be seen at the head of his corps
Of which he once was soul and paragon,
15 Black mourning covers eagles and armor
    Of marching echelon.

5

He can't be seen with his brave regiment,
Where is he ... Can you hear their deep despair?
Look, laid upon a bier for interment
20   The knight's body rests there.

6

This bier, this carriage, rest after labor,
Grateful people's bitter tears of distress,
Faithful comrades are pulling him hither,
    With ropes upon their chests.

7

25 His valiant horse walks behind the casket
With a bent head, carrying black armor,
Steed, walk sadly, your master knows no threat,
    His days gone forever.

8

O plaintive trumpets and you tearful flutes,
30 And you silver sounds of swaying eagles,
Be still! My sore heart is cut to its roots
    By these sorrowful wails.

9

Look: just by the church in the dying out light
Young men lift up the burden they adore
35 And bear it, while guns thunder with great might,
    Through the eternal door.

10

Prayers of churchmen, cries of your brothers
Soar to eternal God in His manor.
Ah! Do acknowledge their final farewells,
        Most valiant commander.

11

You shared with us most grave predicaments,
Great sacrifices, work without payment,
Instead of sweet hopes of accomplishments,
        Bitter disappointment.

12

Let our tears dry, your joy is now restored!
He who fought for the homeland, bravely died,
Received a garland from the righteous Lord
        Forever glorified.

13

Grateful compatriots laud your life and end,
They will not let the time your feats erase,
They'll build a grand grave, at the top suspend
        A garland of laurels.

14

They'll engrave how in the final danger
Choosing your death rather than a lost dream,
You threw yourself with your horse and saber
        Into the rapid stream.

15

Large crowds will surround your monument here,
Hard stones will preserve the words that profess:
"Just here lies the knight who fought without fear
        And whose life was spotless."

16

A soldier of a chivalrous nature
Will sharpen his sword on edge of your shield,
Assured that now he acquired your virtue
    To face legions afield.

Notes

1. Prince Józef Poniatowski (1763-1813), king's nephew, Commander-in-Chief of the Polish army and Marshal of France, perished in the River Elster covering the retreat of the French army after its defeat in the Battle of Leipzig on October 19, 1813. His body was brought back to Poland and buried with honors in a solemn national ceremony.

Diaries of Travels Through America 1797-1807

Travel of Julian Ursyn Niemcewicz from Petersburg to Sweden on His Way to America in the Year 1796

We left Petersburg on December 10, 1796.[1] Mostowski, Wawrzecki and several other friends[2] visited us one more time before our departure. Friendship, strengthened by the bond of misfortune and long suffering, the thought of separating, perhaps forever, made our leave taking most painful. Doctor Rogerson, to whom my friend General Kościuszko owed his life, came when we were getting into our coach, embraced his patient, gave him some final instructions, and also a packet for the trip with medicines, drops, powders, etc. After we left the splendid district of the Admiralty, we crossed the Neva and found ourselves in the opposite part of the city, in which wooden houses that resembled huts looked quite different in comparison with those magnificent buildings which we admired on the other shore. When we passed the tollhouse, Sir Nelidov, the Emperor's adjutant, whom the monarch sent over to take the general out of the city, bade us farewell. Kościuszko asked him to be so kind as to convey to His Majesty his utmost gratitude for all acts of kindness and all signs of nobleness and grace with which were showered upon him. Just at that moment we noticed that the general's Chinese robe was missing.

For the first time in twenty six months, that is since the ill-fated day in which we were deprived of our freedom, we found ourselves without witnesses. After looking around to make sure no one eavesdropped on us from behind or next to the vehicle, we began to talk to each other openly about the enslavement of our homeland, about our personal sufferings, and about all that pertained to it. Kościuszko divulged to me two secrets which I will record here. During the battle of Maciejowice, when everything was lost and when the Cossacks were just about to capture him, he put the pistol in his mouth, pulled the trigger, but it did not fire. And life became so abhorrent to him at the beginning of his imprisonment in the Petersburg fortress that he wanted to starve himself. For a certain period of time he would eat nothing but several spoons of soup. As a result, his stomach would shrink and he became so weak that he was expected to die at any moment. It was then that the kind Rogerson, court physician, was sent to look in on him. He saved Kościuszko's life using the greatest skills of his art, but was not able to bring his stomach back to normal, and to this day two cups of coffee and an ounce of paltry meat constitute his whole meal.

The road that leads to Finland passes through an empty, barren region, the saddest of all that surround the capital. You will not see there any country houses or gardens, you will not see on the road any coaches or wagons, so numerous in the vicinity of big cities; the eye of the traveller rests only on stunted pine trees or on rock fragments. Fifteen versts[3] away we met a regiment of the Vyborg infantry, which received the order to relocate to Moscow quarters. These men will be cold. I am talking about the soldiers, because as for officers, it is known how well they travel. What a multitude of vehicles, coaches, coachmen, kibitkas[4] follow each unit of the Russian army in the time of war as well as of peace. There is a lot of snow here, our home, that is our coach, is comfortable but very heavy, we barely travelled one station the first day. When we stopped there, a quarrel broke out between our guardian angels and the postmaster, they say that it even came to blows. Reconciliation was reached without bloodshed. While we were waiting for the evening meal, Libiszewski[5] sang for us and played the guitar. Finally, we sat down to dinner or supper, whatever one prefers to call it. At night I was awakened three or four times by a visit of several rabbits. A mother with five or six little rabbits took a fancy to walking over my body; I got rid of her with difficulty. I woke up at four, happy, for I was not in jail any more.

Although we were only one station away from Petersburg, we did not see Muscovites anywhere, we virtually did not hear their language. Our host was German, our hostess was German, all servants, just like the population, were Finnish. Is it not quite peculiar that the capital of the largest country in the world is surrounded by foreign provinces? Finland and Livonia have as much similarity in speech, in faith, in customs to the Russians as to the French. What is this state? How sudden the growth of its powers, of its domination in Europe, what was it in the last century? Does it not remind one of an illusion and of the passing splendor of a theatre spectacle? Perhaps it will only last as long as that spectacle!

On the twentieth we started very early. A lot of snow, extremely cold. A shaft broke at the first station. Finnish postillions have neither the skill nor experience of the Russian ones. Let anything happen to a coach or travellers, they are not even moved and, ugly as Egyptian idols, they will not even bend to repair the damage which they themselves caused. That day we barely travelled two stations. On the twenty first the same snow, the same cold, and the same slowness. At our night's lodging we met thirty Poles to whom the kind Emperor gave back freedom. They were in exile together with six hundred companions on a deserted and unhealthy island called Kotka. They were given only several kopecks a day and they were assigned the most unpleasant and most sordid jobs, which filled all hours of their unhappy lives. So when the magnanimous and pious Catherine, whose graciousness was proclaimed by so-called philosophers, whose magnanimity was praised especially by newspapers, whose charming smile brought delight and inspired admiration in all those who surrounded her, when--I say--Catherine played in her Hermitage the role of a kind-hearted and good-natured woman, thousands upon thousands of the unfortunate people who did not surrender to her scepter populated the icy Siberian steppes, filled jails, and deprived of any consolation cried over the annihilation of their homeland and sank under the burden of their misery. The general assisted those unfortunate former companions in arms with monetary gifts and supplies of food.

It is truly dreadful to travel in the month of December at the latitude of 61^0. You get up at four in the morning, you put on a coat over a coat, a fur over a fur, you become a huge, heavy and shapeless log, you give orders to be packed into the coach, and you barely breathe when your freezing breath makes the fur stick to your face. You covered a half of a verst and the coach comes to a halt. What for? Why? The road is covered with eight feet of snow, you cannot go any further. All people get out of the coach, they sink up to their bellies in snow, neither loud "gee-up! gee-up! gee-up! gee-up!" nor whipping the poor horses helps at all. We lose an hour or two like this, finally about nine, it dawns, they send for peasant horses and when they come, they pull us up from the precipice. This is the course of our daily swift travelling by post; and also on that day we lost four hours in the snow-drift, before we dragged ourselves to Vyborg. (...)

December 26. (...) On that day we travelled faster than in previous days, we approached the border still before dawn; in spite of the nigh darkness we saw strong redoubts, which Russia built near the border in order to protect itself against Swedish attacks. One cannot be surprised at these precautionary measures, but it is admirable that Catherine reserved for herself in secret the condition allowing her to strengthen the border, when it was stipulated that Sweden could not build the smallest fortress from its side. In plain language it means: you are not permitted the audacity of attacking my territory, but I, Her Majesty of All-the-Russias, am allowed to conquer your country at any time. A river called Kymene, I think, separates Russian Finland from the Swedish one. With what emotion we found ourselves on Swedish soil: even though our bonds were already torn off, yet we were still dragging behind pieces of the chain; now it seemed to us that we left its last link on the other bank of the river. We embraced one another with tears in our eyes. It was the same country, the same season of the year, and yet everything appeared to us in a different light. The landscape seemed happier to us, houses more attractive, people looked at us boldly and talked with us as if with their neighbors.

So I tore myself free from your clutches, Russia, the perpetrator of all misfortunes of my homeland, the country where for twenty-six months I suffered in the most terrible jail, from which I would never have come out, if death had not snatched the scepter away from the hands of Catherine to pass it to the benevolent hands of Paul I!

Notes

1. According to the new calendar, Kościuszko left Petersburg on the nineteenth of December.
2. Tadeusz Mostowski and Tomasz Wawrzecki, who were jailed with Kościuszko and Niemcewicz in Petersburg, were also released by Tsar Paul I and helped prepare the long trip to America.
3. A verst is a Russian unit of distance equal to 0.66 miles.
4. A kibitka is a Russian covered vehicle on wheels or runners.
5. A Polish officer Libiszewski, a big and strong man, accompanied Kościuszko in his travels and carried him when necessary. As a result of his wounds, Kościuszko suffered a partial paralysis of his legs.

Texts: Kostkiewiczowa and Goliński, *Świat poprawiać*, 318-319.
Niemcewicz, Julian. *Powrót posła*. 9th ed. Ed. by Zdzisław Skwarczyński. Wrocław: Ossolineum, Biblioteka Narodowa I 4, 1981, 46-53.
Niemcewicz, Julian Ursyn. *Śpiewy historyczne.* Warszawa: KAW, 1986, 28-30, 169-173.
Niemcewicz, Julian Ursyn. *Podróże po Ameryce 1797-1807.* Ed. by Antonina Wellman-Zalewska. Wrocław: Ossolineum, 1959, 3-7, 10-11.

CYPRIAN GODEBSKI (1765-1809)

Cyprian Godebski came from a family of modest means in the region of Polesie and was educated in the Piarist school in Dąbrowica. He early became involved in conspiratorial activities against the Russian and Prussian authorities and had to leave the country. He helped organize the Polish Legion in Rome and fought in the battles of Legnano and Magnano, where he distinguished himself by his courage. From 1799 to 1801 Godebski took part in various military campaigns. In 1802 he returned to Warsaw and coedited the journal *Pleasant and Useful Amusements* (1804-1806), for which he wrote his own poems and translated, mostly from the French literature. In 1805 he wrote his major work *A Poem to the Polish Legions*, in which he extolled the deeds of the Polish army fighting for "your freedom and ours" and a year later a novel on the same subject *The Grenadier Philosopher*. In 1806 he joined Jan Dąbrowski and Józef Wybicki in organizing the army for an uprising. He died a hero's death at the Battle of Raszyn in April of 1809.

A Poem to the Polish Legions
(epilogue)

Alas! What thanks for it were given to your band?
My blood is running cold, the pen drops from my hand,
Sorrow is stifling my words, now I am tongue-tied!
But why should I add to the horror of this sight?
5   You answered brothers' call, but o, what cruel fate!
One in the grave, without a limb returns his mate,
Far away from his brothers, family, homeland,
Many drink bitterness on the sweet cane island,[1]
Others, crossing over terrible wilderness,
10   Sated someone's want or died of hungriness.
O shame! O blindness beyond imagination!
Those who became free used chains for subjugation!
They used them, but didn't escape a just punishment:
Beyond the sea they found death, at home enslavement.
15   O ungrateful nation! So this is your reward,
By sending friends far off to perish by the sword,
By turning mothers' hopes into despair and fear.

This is the road you showed us to our homeland dear?
A witness of your courage, partner in grief too,
20 My companions and friends, will I ever see you?
We shall be sharing stories of our experience,
In strong inner belief looking for recompense?
Ah! Why the ungracious Fates for the Pole proclaim
No relief for his brothers, though he shares their fame?
25 He roams like a boat tossed by storms on a vast sea,
Like a small leaf that fell in Autumn from a tree,
So each of you far away from your native land,
Wanders without knowing what fate had for him planned,
Or struggling on the briny waters against death,
30 He sighs for his mother country with his last breath.
O you dear remnants of the enormous nation,
Not enough to die? With no commemoration?
No one will announce your great deeds the world over
Nor will throw down on your grave a native flower?
35 Are you to drink bitterness, scattered everywhere,
Or to perish and, more, perish forgotten there?
No, sweet thoughts console me that memory's daughter[2]
From the native pen's fruit prepares us an offer
And that from your ashes (my feelings tell me so)
40 Will rise the Polish Maro with Jasiński's soul[3];
He'll write your deeds for eternal evocations
And blotting out my rhymes, will cite good intentions.

Notes

1. Some 6,000 Polish soldiers, who joined the legions to fight for Poland's freedom, were sent by Napoleon to San Domingo (present day Haiti) to put down the uprisings of Negro slaves. Most of them died from swamp fever, the remnants surrendered to the British.

2. A muse; the Muses were daughters of Zeus and Mnemosyne, the goddess of memory.

3. Publius Vergilius Maro's *Aeneid,* describing the wanderings of Aeneas after the fall of Troy, was a popular reading among the Legions' soldiers. Godebski suggests that the Polish Virgil who will write the history of the Legions must be a heroic soldier ready, like Jakub Jasiński and later Godebski himself, to sacrifice his life for his country.

Initials on the Sycamore Tree

Places, adornments which were once charming,
Why do you now bear the stamp of mourning?
Where is this sweet pleasure that I once knew,
When with my dear Filon here we withdrew?

5   Ah, a cruel fate from my lover's hand!
Today all these charms my heart cannot stand:
The nightingale's voice, murmur of the stream,
Everything changes with the heart's esteem ...

But I don't wish to add to my distress
10   Nor blame for your dealings with him express;
This lovely turf, this pleasurable breeze,
Assisted him in breaking his promise.

Sycamore tree! Witness of tender blaze!
Behold all these streams of my tears these days!
15   I wish they washed off the betrayal mark,
Of which his hand left traces on your bark.

Easier from the tree to scratch out letters,
Than from the heart remove the love embers.

Texts: Godebski, Cyprian. *Wybór wierszy*. Ed. by Zbigniew Kubikowski. Wrocław: Ossolineum, Biblioteka Narodowa I 161, 31-32.
Kostkiewiczowa and Goliński, *Świat poprawiać*, 417.

ALOJZY FELIŃSKI (1771-1820)

A son of a judge from Volhynia, Feliński was born in Łuck. He attended a Piarist school in Dąbrowica and then moved to Lublin, where he studied law. In 1789 he went to Warsaw, worked for Tadeusz Czacki, a historian and influential administrator, and wrote some political pamphlets and poems. During the Insurrection, Feliński joined Kościuszko and served as his secretary. In 1795 he returned to Volhynia, read the classics, and translated Delille's popular poem *L'homme des champs*. In 1809 he began to work on his tragedy in verse *Barbara Radziwiłł*. It was finished in 1811 and staged in the National Theatre in Warsaw in 1817. The play was received enthusiastically. In 1818 Feliński accepted the position of curator and principal of the Lyceum in Krzemieniec. He died suddenly in 1820.

Hymn on the Anniversary of the Proclamation
of the Kingdom of Poland

Ordered to be sung by the Polish Army by its Commander-in-Chief[1]

      Lord who through ages protected Poland,
      Veiling her in power and glory's light,
      And guarded her with the shield in Your hand
      From all the mishaps threatening her outside:
5   To Your high altars we bring humble pleas,
         Save our King, o Lord, we beg on our knees!

      You that sustained her, touched by her distress,
      When she fell fighting for the holiest aim,
      Wishing the world to see her fearlessness,
10   Among misfortunes You enhanced her fame:
          To Your high altars we bring humble pleas,
         Save our King, o Lord, we beg on our knees!

      You that revived her by new miracles,
      And joined two brothers' lands by Your decrees,
15   Famed for mutual defeats in battles,

Under one scepter of angel of peace:
   To Your high altars we bring humble pleas,
   Save our King, o Lord, we beg on our knees!

Give to new Poland her ancient splendor,
20 Make her live under him in happiness;
Let two friendly nations thrive forever
And let for his reign their blessings express:
   To Your high altars we bring humble pleas,
   Save our King, o Lord, we beg on our knees.

Notes

1. The poem was written in 1816. The King of the Kingdom of Poland was Russian Tsar Alexander I. Great Prince Konstantin, Commander-in-Chief of the Polish Army, was Alexander's brother. With music by Kaszewski and the words "Homeland, freedom..." in place of "King" in the last verse of the refrain, the song gained popularity and was sung in Polish churches as a patriotic prayer.

Barbara Radziwiłł
(selections)

This tragedy, written between 1809 and 1811, was based on a historical fact. In 1547, the young king Zygmunt August, son of Zygmunt I the Old and the Milanese princess Bona Sforza, married clandestinely Barbara Radziwiłł, daughter of Jerzy Radziwiłł, a Lithuanian hetman. After the death of Zygmunt I, when Zygmunt August was ready to assume power, a group of powerful senators opposed the king, as his wife was not of royal blood, demanding his divorce or abdication. Zygmunt August overcame the opposition and obtained the Sejm's permission to have his wife crowned, but the young queen died soon after.

The play shows the inner conflicts of the king, who is challenged to choose between his wife and the crown, and of Barbara, whose feelings of love clash with her fears of causing her husband to renounce the throne. In his Sejm speech, Piotr Boratyński, urges the king to divorce Barbara for reasons of state, while two powerful senators, Jan Tarnowski, Grand Hetman of the Crown, and Piotr Kmita, Grand Marshal of the Crown, representing two antagonistic factions, advance their arguments supporting and opposing the king.

The play concludes with Bona, the vicious queen mother, poisoning her daughter-in-law.

Act II, scene III
August, Barbara

Barbara

My restless feelings chase you everywhere, my Lord!
Since with a trembling foot I passed through this gateway,
Everything fills me with terror and deep dismay.
I feel safer for a while, when I look at you,
5   No sooner away, I wish to see you anew.
Even if you look at me full of tenderness,
Black premonitions poison your wife's happiness:
Everything augurs my fate will change instanter,
Everything that I'll part from August forever.
10   What for did I ever leave that most beloved place,
Where for the first time, dear August, I saw your face![1]
Where our hearts and beings formed a unity,
And where both you and I lived in felicity?
Here, wherever I look, wherever I advance,
15 The most frightening sights overwhelm me at once:
I see pale sorrow on new faces everywhere,
I run into conspiring factions here and there.
My family fears for me, crowds of agents spy,
Tarnowski avoids me, Bona threatens nearby,
20 Even she[2] who doesn't wish to see my hopes upset,
Cautions me through her copious tears, shed in secret,
That she foresees for me many a dire event,
Which her keen friendship is unable to prevent.
O, you most loving husband! You, my dear lover!
25 Master of my fate! Object of fearful tremor!
Don't leave Barbara alone ... make my soul bold anew.
I am in fear of losing not my life, but you.
If I have to die, I will depart unshaken,
But please hold me in your arms, when I am taken.

August

30 What do you say? Let's live, let's live for each other!
I wouldn't defend you? I would outlive you ever?
Why do you renew the pangs of uncertainty?
I love you and reign--but you show anxiety!
Let the earth and hell plot against us together,
35 No might will be able to divide us ever.
This day of storm will be the day of happiness,
Triumph of your virtue, triumph of tenderness!
I'll adorn your lovely face with crown today,
Or give my life for you, which is yours anyway.
40 Today two nations[3] will behold your gloriousness,
Today whole world will learn of August's happiness.
And although Bona still dares to threaten your life,
Although foreign sovereigns don't recognize my wife,
Although the Sejm frightens you with stern solemnness:
45 Next day all will kneel before Polish Queen's greatness.

Act III, scene VIII

King, Boratyński, Deputies

Boratyński

O King! You see two strong nations in these senators,
Which, ruled for a long time by your brave ancestors,
Had united under them, gained glory, and grown.
Father's and forebears' virtues raised you to the throne,
50 Homeland owes them, you owe your homeland gratefulne
Now, August, is the moment to make a redress,
In her name we're bold enough to demand from you
A sacrifice, whose extent we truly value,
But a sacrifice for nation's prosperity
55 Was never painful for Jagiełło's dynasty.
    You took a wife, King, against Senate's intention,
You damaged the state, weakened your own position,
Your marriage insults our holy book of laws now,
A husband's vow infringes on a Monarch's vow.
60 You swore it earlier to Poland than to your spouse:
Witnessed before the altars, not in your own house.[4]

In the eyes of the world, all monarchs are brothers;
A bond with a subject will dim your throne's splendors;
Your forebears raised the throne, will you make it otiose?
65 We don't want to offend the princess that you chose,
She would be counted among queens; we respect her,
If home virtues were rewarded with a scepter.
Her virtues and her charms gained enough eminence,
When you judged she was worthy of your preference.
70 A crowd of women who shone and shine wearing crown,
In time sank into oblivion and will sink down;
They will always receive gratitude and glory,
Who knew true self-sacrifice for their own country.
Let Barbara enter this select group on her own!
75 Still higher than the Throne, not being on the Throne,
With the rulers' wives let her in virtue compete,
Since she cannot surpass, let her equal Hedwig,[5]
Who in love with Prince Wilhelm, and dear to his heart,
Through her love for Poland, let love for him depart.
(...)

August[6]

80 Deputies! Men of virtue and erudition,
Guardians of liberties, chosen by the nation:
Is it proper of you to request of my throne
To break faith I swore to my wife on my own,
And not faithfully keep with everyone my vows?
85 You advise I break most sacred bonds with my spouse,
Since I made them in castle, not under church dome?
Because the King may be released from them by Rome?
O, blindness! Let heavens' grace keep danger at bay,
So that the weapons you use against me today,
90 My successors would not some day turn upon you!
Without their full trust will your freedom continue?
    I know my obligations, I know my rights too:
No decree orders Polish Monarch to eschew
His own inclinations in choosing out a wife.
95 Would King of the free men live in bondage his life?
If I, despite the Senate, took wife from my land,
And so ancestors' old custom I abandoned,
Should I a small infraction correct with a crime,
And the dawn of my reign by breach of trust begrime?

100 By rejecting, disgracing, and betraying her,
    Should I for my fault doom the guiltless to torture?
    No! No court in the world, nor any lawgiver
    Would order that--and you are not able either.
    Titus[7] dismissed his lover, he's rightly honored;
105 He would stain his name if he renounced his consort.
    You yourselves pay homage to her virtues, most due,
    So why is she not able to rule over you?
    Do you not think it is a more distinct honor
    To deserve the king's hand, not to be his killer?
110 If her house was never with the crown glorified,
    She is the queen of Poles, she is Jagiełło's bride.
    When I asked your compatriot to ascend the Throne,
    I hoped for your gratitude, not accusing tone.
    Foreign kings' daughters, who shared this throne in old days,
115 Were they always faithful to their new homeland's ways?
    You have mentioned two, well known for good offices,
    But those known for people's tears are more numerous.
    (...)

Act IV, scene I

Tarnowski, Kmita

Kmita

The scale of our mishaps is by now weighing more:
Now August sets on fire the torch of civil war.
120 Firm in his goal to shame Jagiełło's ancestry,
    For Barbara he gives up his throne, fame, and country.
    He gathered the troops and his recent oath to spite,
    Threatens guardians of law with thunders of king's might.
    Tarnowski! Your independent soul, I infer,
125 Takes offense at this wrong that all of us suffer?
    Yet those who forgive the King for his misjudgment,
    Find you are the cause of present predicament.
    He, they say, who is the soul of August's council,
    Pours into him venom of blind, passionate will,
130 And he is working to extend the royal claim,
    So that he himself could then rule under his name.
    Yet the Sejm, not judging lightly a great leader,
    Expects you'll exculpate yourself from this matter.

Alojzy Feliński 373

It's your chance. Most deputies agree in discourse,
135 They deem August not worthy of his ancestors.
Before this honor, stained by the last Jagiellon,
Will be placed in more worthy hands by the nation,
Before the Great Council will announce a new king,
You'll have to carry the whole burden of reigning.
140 During peace, which for a moment people ignore,
We need experienced men in council and in war.
You were crowned with glory in either circumstance,
So we call for your courage and for your prudence;
Support us, but before that tell us openly,
145 If we can rely upon your support freely,
If freedom of Poland will spur your efforts then.
Speak up, are you King's follower or citizen?

Tarnowski

You would better answer who has encouraged you
To exclude loyalty from citizen's virtue?
150 Who gives you power to judge and condemn the King?

Kmita

Our laws, my high office, and the nation's bidding.

Tarnowski

The nation's? What do you dare to call the nation?
Some rebels, Bona and foreign agitation?
Handful of sold out deputies, bad citizens,
155 Licentious squanderers, odious rabble-rousers,
Who think of vile gains when people's losses have grown,
And want to build their might on ruins of the throne?
This is your nation! And you filled with them Cracow...

Kmita

Mind with whom you talk and respect Poles now!

                    Tarnowski

160 True Poles know how to hold in esteem their master.

                    Kmita

True Poles aren't able to suffer an oppressor.

                    Tarnowski

Whose tears, whose misery, whose blood freely streaming
Attest to August's crimes and people's suffering?

                    Kmita

The King wants to subdue the nation.

                    Tarnowski

                              No, protect.

                    Kmita

165 We defend our liberties.

                    Tarnowski

                       You want the state wrecked.

                    Notes

    1. Barbara met Zygmunt August in Wilno, capital of her native Lithuania.
    2. The whole sentence refers to Izabella, daughter of Bona and Zygmunt the Old.
    3. The king refers here to Poland and Lithuania united in one Commonwealth.
    4. The marriage ceremony took place in a castle.
    5. Hedwig (Jadwiga) was betrothed to Wilhelm von Habsburg, Prince of Austria, but she was compelled to make a sacrifice for Poland and the Church by marrying Jagiełło, founder of the dynasty.

6. August's response is based on the King's actual address to the Sejm on November 7, 1548.

7. Titus, Roman emperor (79-81 A.C.) fell in love with Berenice, daughter of the Jewish king Herod Agrippa I, but the Romans disapproved of this connection with a Jewess, and Titus dismissed her.

Texts: Kostkiewiczowa and Goliński, *Świat poprawiać*, 412.
Feliński, Alojzy, *Barbara Radziwiłłówna*. Ed. by Marian Szyjkowski. Kraków: Ossolineum, Biblioteka Narodowa I 9, 1924, 59-60, 83-84, 87-88, 90-92.

KAZIMIERZ BRODZIŃSKI (1791-1835)

Born in Królówka near Bochnia, Brodziński attended schools in Lipnica, Tarnów, and Cracow, becoming well acquainted with Polish and German literature. In 1809 he joined the Polish army and took part in Napoleon's campaigns of 1812 and 1813. Wounded at Leipzig and taken prisoner, Brodziński returned to Poland in 1813. He settled in Warsaw and devoted himself to teaching and writing. He published his poems, literary essays, and translations in Warsaw periodicals. From 1818 to 1822 he taught Polish literature at schools and from 1822 to 1831 at the University of Warsaw.

Brodziński's most important study was *On Classicism and Romanticism*, with an appendix *On the Spirit of Polish Poetry* (1818), in which he attempted to reconcile both literary movements and to identify the essential elements of Polish national poetry. He maintained that the idyll best expressed the Polish character, showed great interest in Slavic folklore, especially folk songs, and in his long eclogue *Wiesław* (1820) described the life of peasants in the region of Cracow.

To Hanna

The sun descended behind the beech trees,
The meadow puts on a silver chemise;
The day will return, though chased by the night,
But pleasure once gone, will not see the light.

5   The oaks turn yellow, the pear becomes red,
The fierce wind fills with leaves the forest bed;
Yet the branches will see the spring again,
While joyful youth will not return to reign.

Near a small church a sexton digs a pit,
10   An old peasant and spry boy sleep in it,
All will be asleep to the same moment,
As if life brought them the same contentment.

My dear Hanna! In this world's emptiness
The wind sweeps freely the fruit and flowers,

15   Its stingy hand sows pleasures on our track,
      Forbids the tardy to cast their eyes back.

A Shepherdess's Song

You are flying, little bird, across alder groves,
Why don't you sing for me now where my Johnny roves.

Take these little violets which I picked with care,
My crying eyes were looking for them everywhere.

5   Take them in your small beak wherever he will stay,
      Tell him I'm thinking only about him each day.

But the bird is flying across the pine forest,
Carrying in its beak a blade of grass to its nest.

You are flying now, little bird, to your lover,
10   You are not surprised at my tears and ardor.

The Raszyn Field[1]

Silent night--a fragrant breeze fans across the plain,
Hobbled horses neigh in meadows awash in rain,
Alder branches murmur woefully by a spring,
The stream runs away between throngs of reeds, crying.

5   A quiet field, only a horseherd at times
      Cracks his whip, loud noise goes through the forest of pines;
      The moon, which a little cloud passes as it plays,
      Reflects in the stream here and there its golden rays.

      O Moon! God's guardian in the celestial archway!
10   Your stream reflection was different in the past day;
      Smoke of war enveloped you, and gunfire's thunder
      Echoed through blackened groves into every quarter.

Peasants ran from their fathers' huts on fire around,
Children nestled to trembling mothers below ground,

15 Rattle of drums, rumble of guns, hoarse sound of horn,
    Hoof-beats, groans of the wounded were through these fields borne.

    Where the blood was showing red, now dew shines away;
    Fragrant grass has been cut by a scythe to make hay;
    These days only oxen leave footprints on the ridge,
20 When they bring haystacks to the barn in the village.

    Verdant graves arose above the fields over there,
    The wind whistling sadly shakes tall weeds everywhere;
    A cricket chased away from the cut down meadow
    Is singing of its exile in tones of deep woe.

25 Ah! What does sad remembrance allow me to see?
    Across the groves here the spirits of knights pass free,
    A shade is chasing a shade through the full-eared land,
    A corpse here, a sword gleams there in a wiry hand.

    And there, where from the spring, the edge of alder weald,
30 A trilling nightingale's voice reaches far afield,
    Whose shade is this? It's Godebski[2] on his sad route,
    Over piles of armor the winds blow in his lute.

    O shades of my brothers! How long will you still try
    To wander on this earth with wounds that are not dry?
35 Passing by mother's grave in your bloodstained vestures,
    For the fruits of your wounds you call on your brothers.

Notes

1. The Polish Army of the Duchy of Warsaw, with 12,000 men under the command of Prince Józef Poniatowski, mounted a successful defense against the Austrian army of 25,000 soldiers at Raszyn near Warsaw on April 19, 1809.

2. Colonel Cyprian Godebski, a poet, was killed at the Battle of Raszyn.

Kazimierz Brodziński

To the Muse

You made your strings sound like the clang of the sickle,
A whistle of ship ropes, and cry of the battle,
But it is hard to match them with the workshop din.
It's announced to the world a new, changed life sets in.
5   Poverty will disappear, despair, dream, and dread,
A golden age may come, but age of prose instead.

Text: Kostkiewiczowa and Goliński, *Świat poprawiać*, 439, 439-440, 443, 446.

KAJETAN KOŹMIAN (1771-1856)

Kajetan Koźmian came from a prosperous country squire's family. Born in Gałęzów near Lublin, he attended schools in Zamość and in Lublin, where he worked later as a lawyer. In 1810 he became a referendary in the State Council of the Duchy of Warsaw, then a senator. During his long career he held many other high administrative positions and was active in the Society of the Friends of Learning. After the failure of the November Uprising, Koźmian spent the last period of his life in his country estate in Piotrowice.

Throughout his life Koźmian remained faithful to the classical literary style. His major works included the political odes, written between 1800 and 1813, *Stefan Czarniecki* (1858), an epic poem in twelve songs, and *Polish Georgics* (1839) in four songs, modeled on Virgil and Delille, containing excellent descriptions of nature and glorification of life and work on the land. Koźmian's most durable work, however, is his *Memoirs*, a faithful document of the times.

To the Dancing Cracow[1]

When Fate, determined to break the country's power,
Draws near Poland's destiny in its final hour,
When from the last remnants of their native shelters
Brave Poles are pushed out and leave for foreign quarters,
5 When no one would protect us or wished to do so,
Many would ruin this land, few for its defense show;
What a happy occasion for feasts and prances,
Careless dwellers' wives and daughters join in dances,
Knights dance, so do the most important officials,
10 They dance in their homes and almost outside the halls.
Foreigners applaud us and tell us to go on,
The Pole always kept dancing to the piper's tone.
The ball in this land began with the waltz, quadrille,
It ends with the cossack,[2] this is a custom still.
15 And although it will not take long for the last prance,
Some can do well the first, others the second dance.
A coquettish Grace herself, if one is willing,
After a quadrille in cossack is excelling.
O thank you, Polish women's superb deportment!

20 Poland dies ... Let's dance, so long as time our servant,
    Let us dance, what will happen next not worrying,
    Let's end the scene with grand airs, our light heads spinning.
    There is not, fair sex, any reason for chagrin,
    Dance is with all nations held in highest esteem:
25 Whether a Muscovite or German takes this land,
    He'll destroy our language and laws, but he'll waltz grand;
    I can't contain my sighs, for among Polish women,
    When their mother dies, I see dancing children.

Notes

1. The poem, written in 1813 during a critical period caused by Napoleon's retreat from Moscow, refers to numerous balls and dances organized in Cracow by the refugees from the Duchy of Warsaw.
    2. The waltz, quadrille, and cossack, are all foreign dances.

To Sophie Przewłocka Copying "Czarniecki"[1]

    Sophie, to please your uncle you began
    To etch that old piece as if in copper,
    You will never save it from oblivion,
    Young people's eyes won't visit it ever.

5   Though so elegant your hand in writing,
    Just for these merits we'll be blamed much more,
    The faddish scribbling, of pen and thinking,
    Will rise against you and me with clamor.

    Hard times commenced for arts and for science,
10   Vile profit made good friends with a spoiled taste,
    They will like scribbling, if they like nonsense,
    No one will read it though he paid in haste.

    Youth tore away the reins of sanity,
    Conceit has carried minds to raging noise,

15   It dreams, it begets monsters, oddity,
       And like a wonder sings in peacock's voice.

       Protect my grandsons from dire pestilence,
       Turn away from nonsense, rot, temptations,
       There's no beauty without art in science,
20   There is no art without regulations.

       In vain this generation set its mind
       To deny this truth, and stubbornly errs,
       Their offspring will tell the truth when they find
       Your lettering more pretty than my verse.

25   Though deeply hated, the old school stands strong,
       The folly tries to destroy it in vain,
       Until it carries Omar's torch along,[2]
       It must crawl before it, it must feel shame.

       We will not misjudge what the ages tell,
30   The pen should search for challenge most sublime,
       Better foolish with Homer and Virgil,
       Than a great genius of the present time.

Notes

1. Sophie was Koźmian's niece. *Czarniecki* was an epic poem by Koźmian, written between 1832 and 1847, published in its entirety in 1858.

2. Caliph Omar (ca. 592-644) was famous for his religious zeal. After the conquest of Egypt, he was reported to have burnt the library of Alexandria for, as he argued, if any books in it were against the Koran, they had to be destroyed, while if they repeated the truths of the Koran, they were useless.

Text: Kostkiewiczowa and Goliński, *Świat poprawiać*, 483, 483-484.